THE DIG TREE

THE DIG TREE

The Extraordinary Story of the Ill-Fated
Burke and Wills Expedition

SARAH MURGATROYD

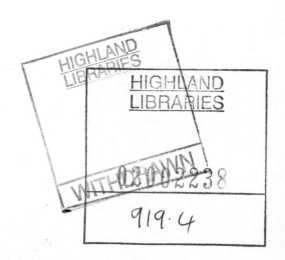
BLOOMSBURY

ILLUSTRATION SOURCES: Grateful acknowledgment is made to the following for permission to reproduce the illustrative material in the text: p. 5, p. 58, p. 74, p. 77, p. 165 and p. 303 by William Strutt, Dixson Library, State Library of New South Wales; p. 20, p. 25, p. 68, p. 92, p. 121, p. 125, p. 176, p. 180, p. 185, p. 241, p. 243, p. 248, p. 268, p. 273, p. 279 and p. 347 from the La Trobe Australian Manuscripts Collection and La Trobe Picture Collection, State Library of Victoria; p. 37 and p. 146, Mortlock Library, State Library of South Australia; p. 89, Royal Botanic Gardens, Melbourne; p. 143, p. 202, p. 210, p. 222, p. 262 and p. 361 by Monty Watkins; p. 351, National Library of Australia, Canberra.

PLATE SECTION: Plates I, II, IV and V by Ludwig Becker, Plate III by William Strutt, La Trobe Picture Collection, State Library of Victoria; Plate VI, portrait of Burke by William Strutt, Private Collection; Plate VII from William Strutt's *Victoria the Golden: Scenes, Sketches and Jottings from Nature 1850–1862*, reproduced with the permission of the Library Committee of the Parliament of Victoria.

First published in Great Britain 2002

First published in Australia by Text Publishing Co Ltd 2002

Bloomsbury Publishing Plc, 38 Soho Square, London W1D 3HB

The moral right of the author has been asserted

A CIP catalogue record for this book is available from the British Library

ISBN 0 7475 5677 6

10 9 8 7 6 5 4 3 2 1

Printed by Clays Ltd, St Ives plc

To Kevin
For winching me out of more creeks than I deserve

Contents

Burke and Wills' Route x

1
Terra Australis Incognita 1

2
Marvellous Melbourne 19

3
The Fertile Island Theory 31

4
An Affair of Cliquery 46

5
A Trifle Insane 56

6
The Honour of Victoria 73

7
No Tea, No Fire 87

8
Ruinous Work 102

9
An Excess of Bravery 120

10
The Dead Heart 140

11
A Sense of Perspective 155

12
Anticipation of Horrors 171

13
Never More Severely Taxed 192

14
Beneath the Veil 206

15
The Awful Truth 217

16
Dig 232

17
This Extraordinary Continent 255

18
From Inertia to Overkill 275

19
The Continent Crossed 295

20
From Absolute Necessity 307

21
An Unmanly Action 322

22
A Bloodless Triumph 336

Epilogue 353

Acknowledgments 362

Select Bibliography 364

Index 369

This is one of the earliest known photographs of the Dig Tree. Taken around 1911, it shows the original message carved into the trunk and the remains of the stockade William Brahe built to protect the expedition's supplies.

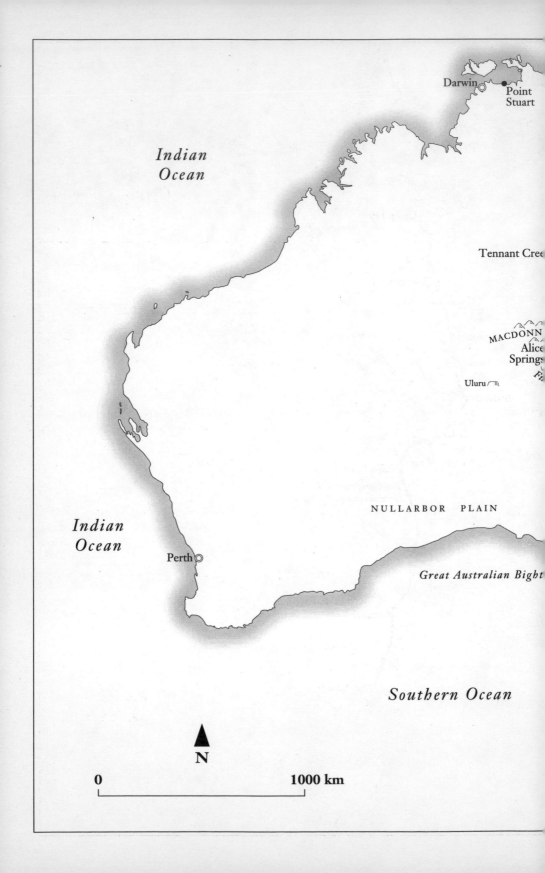

Indian
Ocean

Darwin ⊙   • Point
              Stuart

Tennant Cree

MACDONN
Alice
Springs

Uluru ⌂   Fw

NULLARBOR   PLAIN

Indian
Ocean

Perth ⊙

Great Australian Bight

Southern Ocean

▲
N

0   1000 km

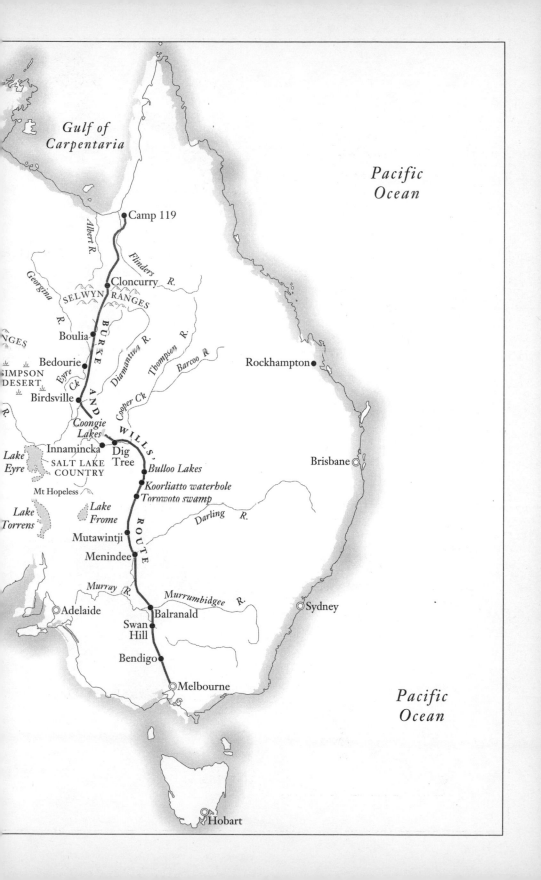

Gulf of
Carpentaria

Pacific
Ocean

Camp 119

Albert R.

Flinders R.

Georgina R.

SELWYN RANGES

Cloncurry

BURKE AND WILLS' ROUTE

Boulia

Diamantina R.

Thompson R.

Barcoo R.

Rockhampton

Bedourie

SIMPSON DESERT

Eyre Ck

RANGES

Birdsville

Cooper Ck

Coongie Lakes

Innamincka

SALT LAKE COUNTRY

Dig Tree

Bulloo Lakes

Brisbane

Koorliatto waterhole
Torowoto swamp

Lake Eyre

Mt Hopeless

Lake Frome

Darling R.

Lake Torrens

Mutawintji

Menindee

Murray R.

Murrumbidgee R.

Adelaide

Balranald

Sydney

Swan Hill

Bendigo

Melbourne

Pacific
Ocean

Hobart

One

Terra Australis Incognita

'Let any man lay the map of Australia before
him, and regard the blank upon its surface, and then let
me ask him if it would not be an honourable achievement
to be the first to place foot in its centre.'
Charles Sturt, 1840

When Captain James Cook stood on the deck of the
Endeavour in March 1770 and felt the hot dry winds filling
her sails off Australia's southern coast, he declared that the
country's interior would be nothing but desert. Nearly a century
later, the same sultry breeze blew down from the heart of the continent, removing the morning chill from Melbourne's Royal Park.
As the sun rose, a small group of men emerged from the row of
new canvas tents pitched under the gum trees. The warm air in
their faces reminded them of the task that lay ahead.

It was Monday 20 August 1860—the day that Australia's most
elaborate and audacious expedition would set out to solve a geographical mystery that had confounded the European settlers
since their arrival in Botany Bay in 1788. The Victorian Exploring
Expedition was charged with crossing the driest inhabited continent on earth; an island the size of the United States of America,
home to such extraordinary creatures as the kangaroo, the emu
and the duck-billed platypus. What other strange beasts or lost
civilisations might lie hidden in a land that had rebuffed European
explorers for so long?

Despite the early hour, people were already making their way
down Melbourne's elegant boulevards, determined to catch a

glimpse of the men, whom journalists had already dubbed 'pioneers of civilisation and progress, some of who perchance might never return'. The crowds bustled towards the park expecting to see a highly organised operation. Instead, they found a scene of 'picturesque confusion'.

Men rushed about, cursing under their breath as they tripped over the twenty tonnes of equipment that lay scattered on the grass. Artists jostled to find the best view and newspaper journalists elbowed their way through to examine the chaos. The *Argus* reported:

> At one part, might be observed a couple of 'associates', already dressed in their expeditionary undress uniform (scarlet jumper, flannel trousers, and cabbage-tree hat), busily engaged in packing; at another, a sepoy might be seen occupied in tying together the legs of a sheep. Orders were being rapidly issued and rapidly executed, and there was, indeed, every indication of the approach of a movement of an extraordinary character.

Many spectators made straight for the specially constructed stables on one side of the park. They were intrigued by the strange bellowing noises and peculiar odour emanating from the building. Those who managed to thrust their way inside were rewarded with a glimpse of four 'Indian' sepoys, attired in white robes and red turbans, trying to calm a small herd of camels. Mochrani, Matvala, Gobin, Golah Singh, Linda, Tschibik and their companions had been imported to conquer the deserts of central Australia. The animals were the pride of the expedition and enjoyed a level of care normally reserved for visiting English opera singers. In preparation for the journey, they had each been fitted with a waterproof rug, complete with a hole for the hump, along with two sets of camel shoes, 'each made of several folds of leather, and shod with iron', designed for travelling over stony ground. Even river crossings had been catered for. 'If it becomes necessary to swim the camels,' boasted the *Argus*, 'air bags are to be lashed under their jowls, so as to keep their heads clear when crossing deep streams.'

People milled about stroking, patting and getting in the way. Then, as the police tried to evict the inquisitive onlookers, pandemonium erupted outside. A passing horse had smelt the new beasts and, displaying the customary equine revulsion for the camel, it bolted through the crowd, throwing its rider and breaking her leg. Not to be outdone, a camel broke loose and chased a well-known police officer across the park:

> The gentleman referred to is of large mould, and until we saw his tumbling feat yesterday, we had no idea that he was such a sprightly gymnast. His down-going and uprising were greeted with shouts of laughter, in which he good-naturedly joined. The erring camel went helter-skelter through the crowd, and was not secured until he showed to admiration how speedily can go 'the ship of the desert'.

In the centre of the turmoil, standing on top of a wagon, was a tall flamboyant Irishman, with flashing blue eyes and a magnificent black beard. Shouting orders in a strong Galway accent, he was trying (and failing) to impose order on the mayhem below. Expedition leader Robert O'Hara Burke grew ever more impatient as he tried to squeeze too much equipment onto too few camels, horses and wagons.

The expedition was already running hopelessly behind schedule but, as fast as his men tried to organise the stores, more people descended in a frenzy of curiosity. They inspected the rifles and ammunition, sat down at the cedar-topped dinner tables and discussed the relative advantages of the bullock cart versus the American wagon. The expedition doctor, Hermann Beckler, recalled later, 'no member of the expedition could see another, none could work with another, none could call another—such was the crush among the thousands who thronged to see our departure'.

The Victorian Exploring Expedition had been organised by a committee of Melbourne's most important men. In July 1851 Victoria had proudly severed its ties with its parent colony of New South Wales and this grand enterprise was designed to show off the achievements of a new and ambitious colony. Every eventuality was catered for using the latest inventions. One 'hospital camel' was fitted with an enclosed stretcher, which would 'afford capital accommodation for invalids, should sickness unfortunately visit the party'. In order to cope with dry conditions, each man carried a 'pocket charcoal filter, by means of which he will be able to obtain drinkable water under the most unfavourable circumstances', and should anyone get lost, the party carried 'an abundance of signals, from the rocket and the blue light to the Union Jack and the Chinese gong'. As the *Age* remarked, 'Never did an expedition set forth under, on the whole, brighter auspices. Everything that could possibly be furnished, as in any way useful or auxiliary to the expedition, has been given it.' The problem was—where to put it all?

By lunchtime the crowd had swelled to around 15,000, a good turnout for a city of 120,000. An impromptu band was formed and a carnival atmosphere swept through the park, compounding the general disarray and giving the proceedings 'a very gay and animated appearance'. Whispers began to circulate that certain 'entertainments' could be procured in the bushes around the edge of the park and a 'sly grog shop' opened up behind the camel stables.

By mid-afternoon an expedition member confirmed one of those rumours by appearing amongst the crowd 'a little too hilarious through excess of beer'. Burke had already dismissed two of his party for disobedience and he now fired ex-policeman Owen Cowan on the spot. The expedition was three men down—and it had not even finished packing.

The only surviving photograph of the expedition leaving Royal Park shows Burke standing in the centre giving a speech to the city's dignitaries.

One man avoided the revelry. Refusing to be interviewed or to have his photograph taken, a neatly dressed young Englishman stayed inside his tent, wrapping his scientific instruments and placing them inside purpose-built mahogany boxes. Surveyor, astronomer, meteorologist and third-in-command, William John Wills packed his nautical almanacs, sextant, compass, theodolite, chronometer, barometer, thermometer, anemometer, telescope, sketchbooks, notebooks, specimen jars and bottles of preserving fluid.

Wills was a born scientist. It was his mission to discover, record and explain the world around him, and now at the age of twenty-six he had the opportunity to cross an entire continent, from the Southern Ocean to the Gulf of Carpentaria. Wills had no doubt that scientific observation would soon dispel the mystique of the Australian interior as surely as it would explain away religion and other superstitions. He expected the journey to last more than two years.

The expedition had been due to depart at one o'clock in the afternoon but 'hour after hour passed in preparation for starting'. After lunch the deputy leader, George Landells, who had special responsibility for the camels, delayed proceedings even further by losing his temper when it was suggested his animals should carry an extra 150 kilograms each. Burke was becoming flustered. With the city's dignitaries waiting to offer the official farewell, he was facing the embarrassing prospect of having to leave with only half his party. Impulsively, and with little regard for the cost, he hired two extra American-style wagons and ordered that the rest of the supplies be loaded at once.

When the column of camels, horses and wagons finally assembled shortly before four o'clock, the mood became patriotic. It was as if the city of Melbourne was saluting its troops as they strode off into battle. Burke returned to his tent, changed into his explorer's uniform and then addressed the crowd. For a man who often had plenty to say, his speech was awkward:

> On behalf of myself and the Expedition I beg to return you my most sincere thanks. No expedition has ever started under such favourable circumstances as this. The people, the government, the committee—they all have done heartily what they could do. It is now our turn; and we shall never do well till we justify what you have done in showing what we can do!

In private Burke was more forthright. 'I will cross Australia,' he told his friends, 'or perish in the attempt.'

As the band struck up 'Cheer, Boys, Cheer', the crowd applauded and the explorers began to march. It was an exotic cavalcade. Dressed in traditional 'oriental' attire, George

Landells took the lead on an enormous bull camel, waving to the spectators and relishing the attention. Burke followed on Billy, his favourite grey horse, and behind him came the Indian sepoys, the scientists, the packhorses and the American-style wagons. The entire procession was half a kilometre long. 'Never have we seen such a manifestation of heartfelt interest in any public undertaking as on this occasion,' the *Argus* declared, 'the oldest dwellers in Australia have experienced nothing equal to it.'

Among the vehicles swaying out of Royal Park was one extra-ordinary contraption. It was a wagon designed so that 'at a very short notice it can be taken off the wheels, and put to all the uses of a river punt, carrying an immense load high and dry on the water'. This elaborate construction revealed the general uncertainty about what lay ahead for the explorers. Some believed the Australian interior would reveal nothing more than a vast desert, others fantasised about mountain ranges, fertile plains, lost civilisations and wild animals unknown to science. A few believed the semi-submersible wagon might be needed to sail across an inland sea. The truth was—nobody knew.

It was 4.30 when the expedition left the park. Ahead lay a journey of at least 5000 kilometres, the equivalent of marching from London to Moscow and back, or making the round trip from New York to Las Vegas. As the rousing speeches faded away and the crowd dispersed, the magnitude of the task became apparent. Several of the wagons became bogged in the soft ground at the edge of the park. One broke down completely just beyond the camels' manure heap.

By the time Burke coaxed his recalcitrant convoy out of Melbourne in 1860, it was the age of overland exploration. Most of the world's great maritime voyages were over and every continent bar Antarctica found itself being poked, prodded and plundered by scientists, missionaries, traders and tyrants. In the course of the nineteenth century Lewis and Clark blazed the Oregon Trail, William Wallace formulated evolutionary theory in south-east Asia, David Livingstone disappeared into the depths of the Zambezi and Friedrich von Humboldt traversed Venezuela, gingerly cataloguing the properties of the electric eel.

Australia revealed its secrets with reluctance. Unlike America, where the pioneers had spread out west as fast as their wagons could carry them, Australia's first colonies were convict settlements. The last thing the British government had in mind was a mass exploration of the surrounding area. This policy of containment was assisted by the foundation of Sydney in 1788 beside the natural prison of the Great Dividing Range. The new immigrants spent the first few decades simply trying to survive, and when they felt secure enough to travel further afield they found they were pinned to the east coast by the towering sandstone cliffs of the Blue Mountains.

Some convicts were convinced that China lay on the other side of the range, others told stories of fearsome warriors, savage kingdoms and dangerous wild animals. These myths were propagated by overworked army officers, keen to emphasise the lurid consequences of escape from the prison farms. But as conditions in Sydney improved, and the fetters of convict society were loosened, pioneers spilled north and south searching for new pastures along the edges of the continent and helped set up the cities of Melbourne, Adelaide and Brisbane.

Despite the opportunity to explore a landmass of 7.5 million square kilometres (about two-thirds the size of Europe), the new settlers showed a marked hesitancy to leave the coast. It seems strange that a new society could cling to the hemline of its adopted continent for so long without knowing what lay in the centre—but with a small population and plenty of fertile soil, there was little incentive to travel inland. Even today, more than 80 per cent of the Australian population live within thirty kilometres of the coast.

As the towns grew into cities, people came to regard 'the bush' with a mixture of apathy and apprehension. They might never have seen a koala or a wombat in the wild; the nearest they came to a kangaroo was when they walked over the skin rugs in their English-style cottages. The subtle olive-greens and silver-greys of the eucalypt forests seemed pallid in comparison. Settlers like John Sherer in the 1850s regarded the Australian landscape as a source of tedium and discomfort:

> There can be no walk, no journey of any kind, more monotonous than one through the bush…there is no association of the past connected with it…Imagination is at a standstill—fairly bogged, as your body may be in a mud swamp. There are no sacred graves…no birthplaces of great men. Nothing of this kind; all is deadly dull, uninspiring hard work.

The first attempts to penetrate further inland were often individual excursions by ambitious farmers. They took off into the unknown, armed with little more than a swag, a rifle and a healthy dose of enthusiasm. Little by little, these unsung heroes of Australian exploration extended their knowledge of the surrounding countryside. They might discover abundant grasslands and giant forests or stumble over nuggets of gold. But as they fumbled further afield, the fertile coastal safety net gave way and the landscape assumed a more menacing aspect.

In 1858, a farmer known as Coulthard set out alone to find new pastures to the north of Adelaide. His mummified body was later discovered by a government expedition. Before he died, he scratched a last message into his empty water bottle:

> I never reached water…My Tung is stkig to my mouth and I see what I have wrote I know it is this is the last time I may

have of expressing feeling alive & the feeling exu is lost for want of water My ey Dassels My tong burn. I can see no More God Help

It was only when the politicians realised that there was money to be made from the new grazing lands that a full-scale assault on the inland began. The countryside was attacked with military-style expeditions using columns of horses and bullock carts to carry enormous quantities of supplies into the bush. Drawings from the early nineteenth century show men wearing starched collars and impressive moustaches, clinging to their European traditions with admirable, if misguided, tenacity. After a hard day in the field, the officers would retire to their separate quarters and dress for dinner. In the middle of nowhere, they sat down at large oak tables, ate their three-course dinners with silver cutlery, sipped their wine and wiped their chins with spotless white napkins.

By the 1830s, the most imperious of all the government explorers, Surveyor-General Sir Thomas Livingstone Mitchell, was marching around New South Wales doing battle with the complexities of its river systems. Apart from being notoriously bad-tempered, Mitchell won recognition for opening up huge areas of grazing land in the far north-west of the colony, but when it came to unravelling the south-eastern rivers he faced a series of humiliating defeats.

Many of the waterways were boomerang-shaped, and just when Mitchell was convinced he knew where they were heading, they had a bizarre tendency to curve inland and flow in the 'wrong' direction. This led Mitchell's great rival, Charles Sturt, to conclude that rivers like the Murray and the Murrumbidgee must eventually drain into an ocean in the middle of the continent. Why else, he reasoned, did seagulls mysteriously appear from the interior in certain years? Sturt was so confident that he pioneered the technique of building wagons that could be

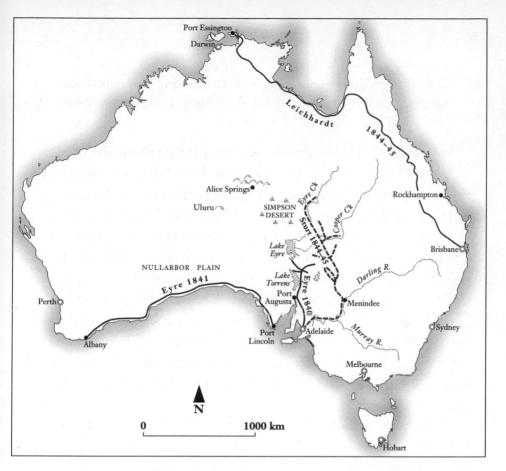

While Eyre and Leichhardt explored Australia's coastal fringes, Sturt penetrated the interior in his quest for the inland sea.

converted into small boats. With backing from the South Australian government, he set off from Adelaide in 1844, heading north on a 'voyage' towards the centre of the continent.

For a man convinced he was about to 'launch into an unknown sea and run away towards the tropics', it was a heartbreaking journey. The grass turned to rock and the cool winds of the coast were replaced by searing blasts of air slicing across the treeless plains. As Sturt continued north, the waterholes dried up and the colour green seemed to vanish from the spectrum. At every turn he was confronted by vistas of sand, salt and clay. After 600 kilometres, his party became trapped between an expanse of gleaming white salt lakes and towering red dunes, 'the most forbidding that our eyes had wandered over', he concluded.

Tormented by mirages, Sturt continued north-west. With a commendable sense of irony he described himself 'as lonely as a ship at sea', stuck in a giant maze of sandhills, 'which looked like the ocean swells rising before us'. Not only had he failed to find the inland sea, he and his men were now marooned in one of the most unforgiving landscapes Australia possesses. 'The truth flashed across my mind,' he wrote, 'that we were locked up in the desolated and heated region that we had penetrated, as effectually as if we had wintered at the Pole.'

After an agonising summer, entombed in a small rocky gorge he named Depot Glen, Sturt mustered his last reserves for a final journey north. He emerged to find his way was barred by 'gibber plains'—enormous expanses of bare earth covered in nothing but small purplish-red rocks.

The area became known as Sturt's Stony Desert and it was to plague Australian explorers for decades to come. Geologists believe it is the relic of an ancient plateau that has been eroded over millions of years to leave belts of rocky plains intersected by sand dunes. The earth is rich in iron and it is the process of oxidation that gives the desert its distinctive colours. The average rainfall is less than 130 millimetres per year. During a drought, there is not a sign of life anywhere.

Sturt's party stumbled onward. As the stones sizzled in the sunlight, it was like crossing a giant barbecue. Within hours their boots were in tatters. The expedition's dog lost all the skin from its paws. Sturt didn't realise it, but he was travelling at the height of one of the fiercest summers ever to be recorded.

The expedition was saved by the kind of geographical miracle that Australia sometimes reserves for those with sufficient perseverance. A chain of waterholes lined with coolibah trees seemed to appear from nowhere. The pools were linked by a series of channels to form a delicate ephemeral river system. This precious water was known to the Aborigines as Kini-papa. On 9 November 1845, Sturt named it 'Cooper's Creek' after a South Australian judge.

It was only a temporary reprieve for the exhausted explorers. Every time Sturt tried to leave the creek, the countryside reverted to a waterless wasteland. A terrible drought gripped the country. Even the local Aboriginal tribes were struggling to survive. There is no water, they told Sturt—'the sun has taken it'.

After months of torment, Charles Sturt's disappointment turned to despair. Sick with scurvy and exhaustion, he conceded defeat and turned south on 11 November 1845. The surveyor abandoned his small wooden boat on the edge of the desert—and with it his dreams of an inland sea.

With so much of Australia's landmass unexplored, the continent proved irresistible to European scientists and adventurers who had run out of discoveries closer to home. Ludwig Leichhardt turned out to be an exceptional explorer. Educated in Prussia, he arrived in Australia in 1841, determined to learn everything about his new environment. His training in zoology, botany, geography, geology and meteorology was so extensive that even Thomas Mitchell was impressed and hired him as a naturalist for several journeys around northern New South Wales.

The Major was less enamoured when, in 1846, he learned that his protégé had led a privately funded expedition from Brisbane to the British settlement of Port Essington, north of the site of Darwin. While Leichhardt blazed a trail through 4800 kilometres of largely uncharted territory, Mitchell was at home polishing his sextant and waiting for government funding for the same journey.

Leichhardt returned to Sydney a hero but his glory was short-lived. His second expedition ended prematurely when heavy rain set in, bogging his wagons and giving his men a 'dose of fever'. Undeterred, he set off again from Roma (to the west of Brisbane) on 4 April 1848. It was a substantial party with seven men, fifty bullocks, 270 goats, seven horses, tents, rifles, ammunition and tonnes of supplies—yet it vanished into the wilderness and was never seen again. To this day, no verifiable trace of the expedition has ever been found.

Leichhardt's disappearance provided another incentive to investigate the mystery of Australia's centre. The New South Wales government asked surveyor Augustus Gregory to search for the lost scientist. Before he left, the methodical and cautious Gregory wrote to Thomas Mitchell asking for his advice. The Major refused 'in a most discourteous manner'.

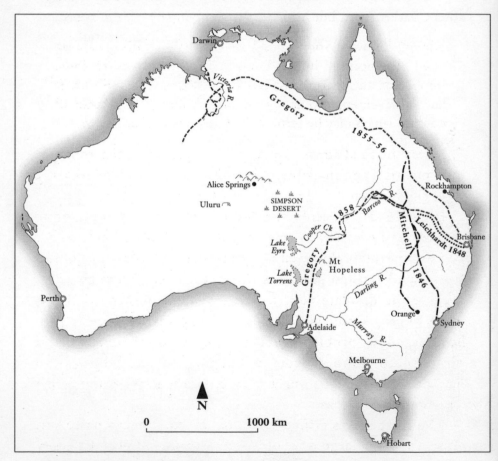

After Mitchell discovered the Barcoo River in 1846 and Leichhardt disappeared in 1848, Gregory forged a route through the deserts to Adelaide.

Gregory was one of the first explorers to dispense with the trappings of comfort, travelling instead on horseback with a minimum of supplies. Between 1855 and 1858, he made a series of ambitious expeditions around the fringes of the central Australian deserts, but his efforts were frustrated by the lack of water. As Gregory explored the north-west of the continent, even major rivers like the Victoria, which settlers hoped might turn out to be Australia's Mississippi, splintered into thousands of rivulets and drained away into the arid land beyond. Gregory's last hope of reaching the core of Australia was a watercourse he had named after Charles Sturt, but it too evaporated amongst the dunes:

> Having followed Sturts Creek for nearly 300 miles, we have been disappointed in our hope that it would lead to some important outlet to the waters of the Australian interior. It has, however, enabled us to penetrate far into the level tract of country which may be termed the Great Australian Desert.

It was the final straw. Gregory gave up chasing the ghosts of lost scientists and invisible rivers—instead he decided to test a theory of his own.

In the 1840s, the explorer Edward Eyre had tried to penetrate the centre of Australia by travelling due north from Adelaide but he was repeatedly thwarted by an impassable 'horseshoe' of salt lakes. Eyre's furthest point was a peak he named Mount Hopeless because the desolate view from the summit destroyed all his hopes of progressing any further. Gregory was convinced that if he attacked the problem from the opposite direction, he could travel south down Cooper Creek, via Mount Hopeless to Adelaide, thus establishing a route from the heart of the desert back down to the coast.

The journey was difficult even for an experienced party but, after crossing a large tract of barren terrain, Gregory emerged triumphant on the southern side of Mount Hopeless. It was the closest anyone had come so far to crossing the 'Great Australian

Desert', but it had not quite solved the puzzle. There was still about 1300 kilometres of unexplored country between the Cooper and the north coast of Australia. Gregory's assessment of its potential was hardly enthusiastic:

> The universal character of the country along the boundary is level sandy desert or worthless scrub without any sign of change in advancing into the interior beyond that of increasing sterility, caused by the greater aridity of the climate, while not one single stream emanates from this inhospitable region, to indicate ranges of hills, better soil or climate.

Since Gregory's expeditions were largely funded by the New South Wales government, his pessimistic conclusions might have been exaggerated in order to deter land speculators from deserting the Sydney market. Nevertheless, his reports fuelled the popular perception that the Australian interior was nothing more than 'a scene of awful desolation, a sterile solitude, without a trace of verdure or a sign of life'.

Stories of Australia's 'dead heart' grew until the hellish descriptions of an immense impenetrable void seduced prospective explorers, eager for the heroic challenge of taming such an implacable enemy. The catchcry 'There's nothing out there' started in the mid-nineteenth century, and it is a myth that permeates urban Australian culture to this day.

It wasn't just the Australian deserts that repelled the European settlers. The northern regions had been just as unpopular ever since the vagabond explorer William Dampier landed on the north-west coast in 1688 and reported that:

> The land is of a dry sandy soil, destitute of water…the woods are not thick nor the trees very big…We saw no sort of animal, nor any track of beast, but once. Neither is the sea very plentifully stored unless you reckon the manatee and turtle as such.

After this derogatory assessment, no one bothered with the north or west coast for some time. It wasn't until the British became suspicious of the French poking around in the area that they dispatched, first Matthew Flinders (the man who gave Australia its name) and later Phillip Parker King, John Wickham and John Stokes (accompanied by Charles Darwin) to survey the northern coastline.

Each naval expedition found itself beset by the same problems. Unable to penetrate the estuaries and swamps, the sailors found only 'a continuous mass of mangroves, mosquitoes, mud and mosquitoes'. The natives seemed equally unhospitable. In 1839 Commander Wickham nearly lost two men who had gone ashore to fix the ship's compass. As they made their repairs, a party of Aborigines appeared, wielding their spears in an unfriendly manner. With great presence of mind, the men folded their arms and began a vigorous demonstration of the sailor's hornpipe. So bemused were the warriors that they threw down their weapons and roared with laughter while the sailors danced for their lives on the beach below. The area, east of Darwin, was later named Escape Cliff.

These miserable reports of hostile tribes, predatory crocodiles and over-enthusiastic insects were unlikely to inspire colonisation—but with an eye to the area's strategic location on the edge of south-east Asia, the British made a couple of half-hearted attempts to establish settlements near the present-day city of Darwin. In the 1830s and 1840s, small groups of unfortunate soldiers and civilians were dumped on the north coast, told to uphold the honour of the empire—and then left to fend for themselves. Most traders sailed straight past them, preferring the established ports of Singapore and Indonesia to these pestilent naval garrisons. In the tropical heat, the new communities were soon strangled by fever. After visiting the settlement of Victoria on the Cobourg Peninsula in 1848, Thomas Huxley described it as, 'the most useless, miserable, ill-managed hole in Her Majesty's dominions'.

By 1860 nearly two-thirds of Australia remained unexplored. The oldest continent on earth seemed to have evolved an ability to repel the new immigrants for longer than almost anywhere else on earth bar the polar ice-caps. It was almost as if the unreachable centre was taunting the cities developing around its perimeter. The desert remained oblivious to nearly a century of European colonisation. Its indigenous inhabitants lived and died as they had always done and, on the banks of Cooper Creek, the old coolibah trees stood unmolested, their roots responding to the floods and droughts that had dictated the rhythms of the interior for thousands of years. But the tranquillity would not last forever.

Two

Marvellous Melbourne

'Nothing will ever be attempted if all
possible objections must first be overcome.'
Samuel Johnson

Dr David Wilkie was an explorer of the armchair variety, a distinguished city physician who had never ventured further
than the odd country picnic. So it was somewhat surprising when,
in 1857, he suggested that Victoria mount a grand expedition to
search for Ludwig Leichhardt and unlock the secrets of Australia's
enigmatic core.

When Wilkie announced his plan to the November meeting of
Melbourne's Philosophical Institute, it was met with bewilderment.
The members debated the idea and then responded as they would
many times over the next three years. They formed a committee
and ordered a report on the matter.

The Philosophical Institute had been formed in 1855. It was
the sort of semi-social, semi-scientific organisation that inevitably
sprang up amongst the educated classes in cities throughout the
British empire. A few of its members were professionals, a few
were self-taught amateurs and the rest were either enthusiastic
eccentrics or committed social climbers. They normally confined
themselves to obscure papers on such subjects as 'The Nature of
Whirlwinds' or 'The Acclimatisation of the Llama', but the idea of
a transcontinental expedition appealed to their sense of importance.
Perhaps it was time for the infant colony of Victoria to prove itself
with a daring bid to open up the centre of the continent.

Despite a generous thirty-two members, the new Exploration

Committee, headed by Melbourne's mayor Dr Richard Eades, boasted just two men with practical experience in the art of geographical discovery: the naturalist William Blandowski, who had led some small scientific collecting parties, and the government botanist Baron Ferdinand von Mueller, who had been with Augustus Gregory in northern Australia.

When Wilkie's plan was shown to Gregory, the explorer dismissed it as 'almost hopeless'. Mueller then suggested that a light party should be sent out from Melbourne to the Darling River on a sort of apprenticeship journey for fledgling explorers. It

SQUARING Yᴱ CIRCLE.

Representing many of Melbourne's most powerful men, the Royal Society was often lampooned by satirists sceptical of its scientific credibility.

could establish a depot just beyond the settled areas and the experience gained could be used to mount a more ambitious expedition at a later date. This new idea confused matters further. After much deliberation, the Exploration Committee only succeeded in producing another long and ultimately inconclusive report.

A month later, on 22 December, a group of men with top hats and mutton-chop whiskers could be found hanging around on Melbourne's Collins Street, loosening their starched collars and cursing the Christmas heatwave. The members of the Philosophical Institute had gathered for their meeting—only to find the violinists from the Philharmonic Orchestra had beaten them to it. Tempers flared as the musicians 'fiddled away happily' inside and the institute's secretary searched for alternative accommodation.

The anger over the lecture halls mix-up set the tone for the rest of the meeting. Mueller's report provoked a series of furious arguments. 'How could Victoria hope to cross the entire continent when it had no explorers and no one with any experience to lead the party?' shouted the institute's secretary John Macadam, a man of many professions including doctor, pathologist, chemist and university lecturer. 'How many men would venture on a larger expedition until they had gained some experience on a smaller one?' 'Dozens! Dozens! Dozens!' screamed Blandowski. 'Two stockmen—yes, two stockmen, by Gott—would gallop across the whole distance and be back in five weeks!'

Ignoring the chairman Dr Richard Eades' pleas for calm, the committee continued to fling amendments in every direction. Some wanted a return to Wilkie's proposal, others wanted an expansion of Mueller's plan, and Blandowski disagreed loudly with everyone.

It was the discovery of gold that gave Victoria the financial luxury to argue about exploration. In 1851, several large nuggets were found near Ballarat and then Bendigo, north-west of Melbourne. The strikes had a magnetic effect on the population.

The countryside was soon crawling with men pushing wheel-barrows down muddy tracks towards the goldfields. By 1853 a thousand ships a year were arriving in Melbourne. Lieutenant-Governor La Trobe despaired as everyone from bank clerks to police officers headed for the hills. 'Cottages are deserted,' he complained, 'houses are to let, business is at a standstill, and even schools are closed. In some suburbs not a man is left.' The *Argus* couldn't resist poking fun, printing a mock dispatch from La Trobe to his colonial masters:

> My Lord,
> As nearly all my officers have 'sloped' for our extravagantly rich diggings, I am obliged to write my despatches with my own hand; besides having to clean my own boots, groom my horse, and do a little amateur wood chopping. I have no clerks and no constables. High and low are at Mt Alexander and, between ourselves, are doing more real work in a day than they used to spread comfortably enough over a month…
> Yours, in a hurry, as I fear the chops are burning.

Those who left the city to make their fortune soon discovered that life in the diggings was not what they had expected. Once the surface nuggets had been removed, mining was a back-breaking slog in the mud with a pick and shovel. Most people lived in filth under makeshift tarpaulins strung out between the few gum trees that remained standing. Food and supplies were sold at vastly inflated prices and many miners made only enough to drink themselves senseless at the sly-grog shops, which popped up like mushrooms around the shanty towns.

Those who did strike it lucky returned to the city to

demonstrate that there was no one more generous than a successful miner with a few drinks under his belt. One digger bought the entire stock of champagne from a Melbourne hotel, emptied it into a horse trough and invited all and sundry to drink it; another donated a full set of solid gold horseshoes to be put on display in the city centre. Onlookers were astonished to find that they had been fitted and used.

Gold transformed life in Melbourne. Imposing sandstone buildings resplendent with columns and carvings began to appear around the city centre. A huge public garden was opened next to the River Yarra. It boasted a bandstand, a menagerie, a dance floor and a theatre. At weekends visitors could watch re-enactments of the burning of Moscow or the eruption of Vesuvius, and at night there were spectacular fireworks displays. Outings to the theatre became popular, particularly among miners looking for an excuse to pick up women. The venues and the shows were as lavish as they were vulgar. One of Melbourne's favourite theatres was renowned for its saloon bar dubiously named 'The Saddling Enclosure'.

By the end of the 1850s gold had catapulted Melbourne from a primitive muddy port to the most magnificent colonial city in the southern hemisphere. Victoria's population jumped to half a million people, many of whom were engaged directly or indirectly in the production of one third of the world's supply of bullion. Melbourne was, claimed the celebrated polymath Archibald Michie, 'as comfortable, as elegant, as luxuriously lit, as any place out of London or Paris'.

As Victoria's wealth spiralled, so did its scientific and cultural aspirations. The growing sense of sophistication brought with it a feeling of shame that large portions of the continent were unmapped, unnamed and—to European eyes—unclaimed. Melburnians might marvel at aeronauts ascending to the skies in giant balloons, or wonder at the African lions in their latest travelling zoo—but no one could say for sure what lay between the city and the north coast.

In this era of opulence the centre of Australia was an insult to the colonial mind; a rebellious outlaw that refused to be parcelled up and tied down by lines of latitude and longitude. The newspapers began to call for a resumption of the colony's early enthusiasm for exploration, with one columnist lamenting, 'That the interior of this continent should still remain shrouded in mystery, is a national reproach to the Australian communities in general but especially to Victoria.'

Victoria, however, was the least likely of all the Australian territories to solve the continent's geographical conundrums. It was the smallest and southernmost mainland colony, hemmed in by New South Wales and South Australia. Since there was no room for territorial expansion, it had little experience in exploration. Yet the pride that Victoria felt in its self-proclaimed status as 'the most advanced of the Australian sisterhood' fuelled the idea of a grand scientific enterprise. The *Argus* wondered why such an 'advanced' colony was not striving to make her mark, by opening up an overland route to the north coast:

> In all probability the time is not too far distant when we shall wonder at the timidity or the apathy and the ignorance displayed. A ghastly blank will no longer stare us in the face when we bend our eyes upon the map of this continent, and the track of the explorers, winding over that white plain, may become one of the highways of commerce dotted with centres of population, and vital with the ebb and flow of a periodic tide of travellers.

Despite the rowdy disorganisation of the Philosophical Institute, the idea of a transcontinental expedition had taken root amongst the rich and powerful in Melbourne society. When the shouting died down at the meeting on 22 December 1857, it was decided that the project should be tackled with new resolve. The institute formed another Exploration Committee, this time with a mere twenty-five members. Their job was to turn the rhetoric into reality.

The first requirement was money. Politicians were duly approached but most were uninspired by the idea of dispatching a group of scientists into the wilderness for the good of humanity. As far as official funding was concerned, the expedition was placed on the backburner. Here it seemed destined to

William Stawell was an influential figure in Melbourne. He exploited Burke's weaknesses to implement his own Machiavellian plans for the expedition.

remain, until a saviour stepped forward in the unlikely guise of Mr Ambrose Kyte.

Kyte was an Irish businessman of questionable but successful methods. He once had his arm set in plaster so he could later disown a signature on a contract he was unsure he wanted to honour. One of Kyte's greatest ambitions was a good name and a knighthood, so he set about establishing himself as a philanthropist. In August 1858 he approached Sir William Foster Stawell with a generous offer for the Philosophical Institute.

Stawell was a lawyer with a commanding gaze and inexhaustible reserves of energy. After emigrating to Australia, he went on to hold nearly every public office in Victoria, from attorney-general to chancellor of Melbourne University and commander of the Royal Yacht Club. For now, he was Victoria's chief justice, president of the Philosophical Institute and a member of the Exploration Committee.

Kyte offered £1000 towards an expedition, provided his fellow colonists subscribed at least another £2000. He wanted his donation kept anonymous, no doubt intending to reveal it when the expedition had succeeded and the impact would be all the greater. Stawell tipped off the *Argus*, which announced the scoop the following morning:

> We are authorised to state that a gentleman of Melbourne has proposed to give the sum of one thousand pounds towards the promotion of a judicious scheme of Australian exploration... the mystery of our Interior is one of the most perplexing and at the same time one of the most interesting of the unsolved problems of physical geography. Hitherto every effort to penetrate it has failed, and Australia presents still the singular spectacle of a great land fringed with a belt of population and industry and yet we possess less positive knowledge than we have of the remotest interior of Africa.

Suddenly the idea of crossing the continent didn't look so far-fetched after all.

Australia was richer than it ever had been but it remained dependent, by necessity if not inclination, on Great Britain. It looked across the globe for government, manufactured goods, export markets and a constant supply of eligible young women. But there was a perpetual time lag since the clipper ships took two to three months to bring news from Europe. Farmers had to wait the best part of a year before they discovered the price for last season's wool clip; mining companies produced tonnes of copper, only to find that, once it reached Europe, everyone was looking for nickel; settlers rushed home to visit a sick relative and found themselves in the nearest graveyard.

In other parts of the world these problems were being solved by a dramatic new invention—the overland telegraph line. In 1844, the first cables were laid between Washington and Baltimore. Suddenly messages could be relayed over hundreds of kilometres with the click of button. Investors and entrepreneurs were quick to embrace the new technology and soon the planet was festooned with an ever-expanding wire network. When engineers began to plan undersea cables, no corner of the globe seemed inaccessible. In these early days, enthusiasm often outstripped expertise—the line from Dover to Calais worked for a just few hours and then went dead, leaving its backers with huge losses.

It was the discovery of gutta-percha (a natural latex) to protect the cables that pushed the technology forward. By 1853, Britain could wield its influence through the copper wires as far afield as Germany, Austria, Russia and Turkey. Plans were under way to link America and Britain. The new communication system was particularly useful in times of conflict and when the Crimean

War broke out in 1854, Australia realised how isolated from the rest of the world it was. Wild rumours circulated that the Russians were about to invade, and at the prospect of this rather unlikely offensive, calls mounted for a cable link to Europe.

The governor of South Australia, Sir Richard MacDonnell, petitioned the British government for assistance. Its response was to dispatch Charles Todd, a London astronomer with a passion for anything electrical. His task was to link the towns along the South Australian coast, giving Adelaide an early-warning system against an enemy attack. Todd arrived to find that private enterprise had outstripped government bureaucracy, and the cable was already in place. He turned his attention to building a line between Adelaide and Melbourne. A small dynamic man, Todd supervised every last detail of his projects. Fond of bad jokes, he would ride from camp to camp announcing to anyone who would listen, 'Without the T, I would be Odd.' Few disagreed with him.

By 1858, all three of Australia's major cities were linked, and Todd began to indulge his ultimate telegraphic fantasy. He wanted to connect Australia to Europe. Like a giant web, the cable network was already being spun throughout Asia—but which route should it follow to reach the remote cities of Adelaide, Melbourne and Sydney? The cost of undersea cabling was about £1000 per kilometre, so it seemed sensible to bring the cable ashore on the northern coast of Australia at its closest point to south-east Asia, then take it directly south. That is—unless you worked for a cable manufacturing company.

Entrepreneur Francis Gisbourne had been involved with the plan to connect New York and London. Now he saw even larger profits in the southern hemisphere. Gisbourne arrived in Australia with an ambitious scheme to bring an undersea cable ashore on the east coast, thus maximising his revenue from the vast amounts of wire needed to go from south-east Asia all the way to Brisbane.

The idea horrified the South Australians. Adelaide was the first port of call for the European clipper ships. It was the gate-keeper of all the news from around the globe and the government made a handsome profit from disseminating the latest reports to the other states. Everyone from businessmen and politicians to homesick settlers had an insatiable appetite for information. Journalists would charter pilot boats to meet the incoming clippers, and then race each other back to the tele-graph station with the latest stories. The competition for transmission slots was so intense that one enterprising reporter enraged his colleagues by ordering passages from his Bible to be telegraphed. Having tied up the line with Deuteronomy, he then composed his European news summary.

For Adelaide, an east-coast telegraph line via Brisbane to Sydney would mean isolation and financial disaster. Governor MacDonnell commissioned a report from Charles Todd who, unsurprisingly, stated that an overland route through the centre of the continent south to Adelaide was the most satisfactory option. MacDonnell communicated these sentiments vigorously, if not speedily, to the British government.

The undersea line via Brisbane never eventuated. It was not the British who wrecked the scheme, but the intransigence of the Australian colonies. Francis Gisbourne returned home a disap-pointed man. Not only had his American cable fallen to pieces after twenty-seven days, but he found that the Australian colonies had 'opinions of their own, a most discouraging factor, even to themselves'.

Gisbourne left behind him a titanic struggle between the war-ring factions. Western Australia wanted the telegraph line to come ashore in Albany on the south-west coast. Brisbane and New South Wales were adamant that the eastern option was preferable and Victoria wondered how it could divide the pack and secure the prize for itself. While the overland route seemed the most logical solution, there was one problem. No one had actually travelled from one coast to the other—so who could say exactly where the telegraph should go?

At Melbourne's Philosophical Institute the issue of the telegraph wires began to influence the more astute members of the Exploration Committee. Soon it was secretly splintering into opposing factions. Scientists like Ferdinand Mueller still envisaged a slow well-equipped party furnished with distinguished scientists and artists to record the natural riches of the Australian interior. Politicians and businessmen such as Sir William Stawell were more concerned with the strategic benefits of controlling the telegraph line, and with the possibility of an overland trade route linking Melbourne with south-east Asia. A swift gallop across the continent to establish a suitable site for a northern port would suffice. Pastoralists wanted to find out if there was fertile soil in the centre of the continent that could somehow be annexed to Victoria. They lobbied for a party led by an experienced bushman who knew a decent chunk of pasture when he saw one.

With money pouring into Victoria's coffers from the goldfields, population pressures increasing and the overland telegraph on the way, the desire to solve the riddle of central Australia was stronger than ever. The reasons to cross the continent were numerous and compelling—but they were also contradictory and the history of exploration has shown that a successful expedition depends on clear objectives.

Three

The Fertile Island Theory

'Land will not reveal itself easily or quickly. It must be
sought for patiently, over time, by many people, employing
a wide range of skills and sensibilities. Discovery is a long,
drawn-out process, which can have no final conclusion.'

Ray Ericksen

If Thomas Embling had achieved his aims, Australia might now
be teeming with zebra, antelope and buffalo, not to mention
herds of quagga and flocks of South American curassow. A close
friend of Sir William Stawell, Embling was a politician and an
entrepreneur with a reputation for eccentricity and spectacular
sideburns. He saw Australia as a vast wilderness waiting to be
filled with the best in fauna and flora from around the planet.

Among Embling's obsessions was a determination to solve the
puzzle of the 'Australian Sahara' and establish an overland trade
route with Asia using camels. An ardent contributor to the newspapers, he wrote in 1858:

> Our desert could be crossed in 10 days, north to south, and all
> we need is to leave in Europe that curse of our race—namely,
> doing only as our fathers have done, from wearing a black hat
> and black woollen garments, to trying to cross the desert on a
> horse.

Embling wasn't the first man to realise the potential of the
camel in Australia. In 1846, a resourceful English grazier by the
name of John Ainsworth Horrocks set out from Adelaide with an
imposing bull named Harry. 'I have great hopes,' he wrote to his

sister, 'the journey suits my temperament as I want a more stirring life.'

Horrocks' adventure turned out to be a little more stirring than he anticipated. Harry soon revealed his darker side by grabbing one of the expedition goats in his mouth and 'would have broken his back if a man had not quickly rescued it'. Later that afternoon the camel attacked the cook, biting his head and 'inflicting two wounds of great length above his temples'. A few days later Horrocks was loading his gun when, 'the camel gave a lurch to one side, and caught his pack in the cock of my gun, which discharged the barrel I was unloading, the contents of which first took off the middle fingers of my right hand between the second and third joints, and entered my left cheek by my lower jaw, knocking out a row of teeth from my upper jaw'.

As he lay in agony in the wilderness, Horrocks scrawled a note for posterity, apologising to his family and patrons. 'It is with extreme sorrow I am obliged to terminate the expedition…had it been earlier in the season and my wounds healed up I should have started again.' The injury turned septic and Horrocks died a few days later—the only explorer to be shot by his own camel.

It was Ambrose Kyte's offer of £1000 and the renewed public interest in exploring that prompted Thomas Embling to reignite his campaign for the introduction of the camel. At the same time a horse-trader by the name of George Landells was about to set sail for India and was looking for a lucrative return cargo. Landells offered to bring back two dozen camels to be used for exploration or as the basis of a breeding program.

At a public meeting on 31 August 1858, Embling and Stawell announced that Victoria's chief secretary John O'Shanassy had agreed to finance Landells' scheme and was also considering funding for the proposed expedition. Importing the camels was seen as a strategic masterstroke. It would give Victoria the decisive advantage over other less adventurous colonies whose explorers continued to lumber around on horses and in bullock carts. Editorial after editorial extolled their virtues. 'The camel, with a load of five to six hundred pounds upon its back,' the *Argus* enthused, 'will with the greatest facility proceed at a rate of forty or fifty miles, and if necessary, will go without water for a period of from ten to fourteen days...What might not be expected from an exploring party equipped with these ships of the desert?'

The camels had been ordered but the Exploration Committee still had to raise the £2000 necessary to supplement Kyte's offer. Despite rousing speeches on the value of exploration, most people were too engrossed in their daily lives to care about what lay in the centre of the continent—much less pay for the privilege of finding out.

The Philosophical Institute responded by forming yet another committee, headed by Sir William Stawell. Ostensibly the Exploration Fund Committee was an independent body, yet all but one of its members also served on the Exploration Committee as well. This led to several farcical situations when one body had to 'resolve' a contentious issue with the other. At least it made sitting on the fence a little easier. It was, after all, the position of choice for most members of the institute.

The *Herald* suggested that Victoria should approach South Australia and New South Wales to see if they were interested in 'a grand combined effort to complete the exploration of this continent'. The South Australians, fearful of losing their monopoly on the overland telegraph, had been openly scathing since the expedition was first suggested. 'Victoria has hitherto done nothing in the work of exploration,' scoffed the *Register*, 'and with the customary ardour of a neophyte she is now projecting labours which no veteran would willingly undertake.'

New South Wales regarded the plan with a polite lack of interest—as did most of the citizens of Victoria, who between them contributed an average of just £100 per month to the expedition's coffers. The Exploration Fund Committee meetings fell away from three times to once a week and by December 1858, they stopped altogether. The project seemed unlikely to survive the lethargy of a Melbourne summer, let alone the heat of the Australian desert.

It took the achievements of a diminutive Scotsman in South Australia to rouse the slumbering Victorians. John McDouall Stuart might never have come to Australia had he not been so small that he was rejected for full army service. At 1.67 metres tall and weighing less than sixty kilograms, he was not considered fighting material, and he turned to civil engineering instead.

One of at least eight children, Stuart was born in Dysart, Fifeshire, in 1815, the son of an army captain. He and his siblings spent their early days running wild, exploring the honeycomb of smugglers' caves that ran through the cliffs near the harbour. When Stuart was just twelve years old this happy childhood was shattered when both his parents died in quick succession. His older brothers went away to study at university and his sisters were sent to boarding school in Edinburgh. Although Stuart was cared for by an old housekeeper in the same city, he rarely saw the rest of his family. From that moment on John McDouall Stuart struck a lonely figure, always an outsider who never managed to re-establish a home of his own. One incident in particular seems to have sealed his destiny.

By 1838, Stuart was living in Glasgow. Early one September evening he was on his way to visit his fiancée at a small cottage on the edge of town. The Scotsman had met the young woman through his friend William Russell—she was Russell's cousin.

Now he had finished his studies as a civil engineer, Stuart wanted to find out if she would be willing to emigrate to Australia with him. Rounding the corner he looked up to see his future wife locked in an embrace with another man. As Stuart stared at the scene in horror, he realised the man was none other than Russell. He turned away and headed for the docks.

Stuart caught a boat to Dundee and secured a passage on the *Indus*, bound for Australia. He sailed the next day, never realising that William Russell was also due to leave for Adelaide and had called around to see his family on the eve of his departure. The kiss was nothing more than two cousins saying goodbye. (Two years later the young woman wrote to Stuart enclosing her engagement ring and explaining what had happened—but by then the young Scotsman had closed his mind to all thoughts of female companionship or marriage.)

Stuart had always suffered from poor health and the voyage to South Australia did nothing to improve his frail constitution. A fellow passenger recorded that, 'on the voyage out Mr Stuart was somewhat delicate, having two rather severe attacks of vomiting blood'. (His later symptoms and constant stomach problems suggest that he was suffering from a duodenal ulcer.) Another noted: 'He was a great reader, comparatively silent, very stubborn, yet withal an agreeable companion, and was rather a favourite amongst his fellow passengers.'

Those who met Stuart after his arrival in South Australia in January 1839 spoke well of him but, still suffering from the pain of his broken engagement, he shunned Adelaide society and headed for the solitude of the bush. He soon found work with a survey team, mapping out plots of land for new settlers. He slept in a makeshift tent, worked six days a week and received a wage of two shillings and ten pence per day plus rations (not including fresh vegetables).

There is a peculiar quality to the Australian bush that

permeates the consciousness of anyone patient enough to endure the heat, the dust and the insects, and who can look beyond its initial disguise of pallid uniformity. It is a fascination fuelled by the intense transparent light and the overpowering sense of space. The explorer Ernest Favenc understood this. 'Repellent as this country is,' he wrote, 'there is a wondrous fascination in it, in its strange loneliness, and the hidden mysteries it might contain, that call to the man who has known it, as surely as the sea calls to the sailor.' So it was with Stuart. Like many explorers he was a social misfit, craving escape from the conventions of society and never comfortable with emotional commitment. Most of his friends were either children or animals and he was so ill at ease staying in the city that he took to sleeping in the garden whenever possible.

In 1844, when Stuart heard that the surveyor-general Charles Sturt was planning an expedition towards the centre of Australia, he jumped at the chance to join the party as a draughtsman. As the gruelling journey towards Cooper Creek took its toll, 'little Stuart' surprised everyone with his stamina and resourcefulness. He once saved the party by tracking a flock of pigeons to one of the few remaining waterholes in the area. Then, when the chief surveyor James Poole died from scurvy, Stuart took over, earning high praise from his leader who recorded the 'valuable and cheerful assistance I received from Mr Stuart, whose zeal and spirits were equally conspicuous, and whose labour at the charts does him great credit'.

The expedition with Charles Sturt cemented the desert landscape in Stuart's imagination. At a dinner to celebrate its return he told guests:

It might be thought by many present that their journeys through the scorching desert of the North were unrelieved by any agreeable change. This was a mistake. They had all along the pleasure which enlightened men know how to appreciate,

An unusual portrait of John McDouall Stuart dressed in his 'exploring clothes'.

of admiring the stupendous works of Nature; and they were
ever and anon buoyed by the hope that their explorations
would result in an extension of knowledge.

From now until the end of his life, Stuart was to return again
and again to the Australian wilderness.

Charles Sturt's reports of unrelenting misery did not inspire
the South Australian government to fund further exploration.
Between 1845 and 1858, John McDouall Stuart tried his hand at
land speculation and sheep farming but he had little business
acumen and most of his ventures ended in failure. It was only
when wealthy businessmen James and John Chambers and
William Finke hired him to find agricultural land in and around
the Flinders Ranges that the Scotsman found his real vocation.

Surveying new grazing runs allowed Stuart to spend most of
his time in the bush, which was probably just as well as he had a
reputation for 'intemperance' whenever he went back to town.
Stuart was a classic binge drinker. He could function perfectly
well for weeks out in the bush, but as soon as he came within a
sniff of a whisky bottle he drank until he dropped. The fourteen-
year-old son of one of Stuart's friends recalled:

> Oh, he is such a funny little man, he is always drunk. You
> won't be able to have him at your house. Papa couldn't. Do
> you know, once, when he got to one of Papa's stations, on
> coming off one of his long journeys, he shut himself up in a
> room, and was drunk for three days.

Away from the bottle, Stuart had an uncanny knack for discovering good pastures in rough country. It was a valuable talent.
Many South Australians had disappeared to the Victorian goldfields and only the prospect of rich grazing land would entice
them back to rejuvenate the local economy. As well as the paucity
of labour, a presumption known as the 'Fertile Island Theory'
was hampering agricultural development. It predicted that the

salt lakes Edward Eyre had found around the north of the state would stifle any further territorial expansion, leaving South Australia isolated and enclosed by an impenetrable natural barricade.

In 1858, Stuart's patrons Finke and Chambers decided to send their surveyor to disprove the 'Fertile Island Theory'. Stuart was delighted. It was the perfect opportunity to try out his new tactics for dealing with hostile country. Like Augustus Gregory, Stuart rejected Charles Sturt's strategy of hauling cumbersome wagons and heavy supplies from camp to camp. He planned to move as fast as possible with just a few horses. It was a risky scheme that could easily backfire in bad conditions but it would allow Stuart's party to cover more ground and cut down the time they needed to stay out in the desert.

Taking advantage of the cooler weather, Stuart left the settled districts in June 1858 with an assistant, George Foster, and a young Aboriginal guide. The trio rode north towards the salt-lake country through the Flinders Ranges. These soaring red escarpments and cavernous gorges stretch for 300 kilometres, before stopping in a series of sheer rock walls that stand like battlements guarding the desert country beyond. The view from the edge of the bluffs is one of the most arresting in Australia. To the south and east, the giant rock undulations run down like waves until they break gently above Port Augusta. To the north and west, there is nothing but desiccated brown earth running towards a string of sharp white salt lakes on the horizon.

This scorched landscape stretches all the way to Lake Eyre, a salt lake covering around 5800 square kilometres with an annual rainfall of less than 125 millimetres. Surrounded by the Tirari Desert, the area has remained largely immune to the taming influence of fences, roads and homesteads. Travellers through the ages have found it an unsettling environment. The explorer Cecil Madigan wrote in 1940:

There are other barren and silent places, but nowhere else is there such vast, obtrusive, and oppressing deadness. One does not need to understand the past history of the region; the ghostly spirit brooding of the past is inescapable, haunting, menacing. Death seems to stalk the land. The vast plain that is the lake is no longer a lake. It is the ghost of a lake, a horrible, white, and salt-crusted travesty.

Thirst can never be quenched there, it can only be aggravated; eyes are blinded by the flare, throats parched by the bitter dust. All signs of life cease as the dead heart, the lake, is approached. The song dies on the drover's lips; silence falls on the exploring party. It is like entering a vast tomb. Gaiety is impossible. One fears to break the silence. There is the indefinable feeling of the presence of death.

It takes a certain type of courage to clamber down from the fertile plateau and set out into the haze with just two companions, six horses, a month's supplies and a compass. Stuart did not hesitate.

He rode north-west across the plains, searching for a mythical freshwater lake referred to by the Aborigines as Wingilpin. The northern settlers told stories of a giant oasis surrounded by gum trees and mobs of kangaroos—there were even rumours that the lost scientist Ludwig Leichhardt had been killed on its shores. Whenever Stuart asked the local tribes where the lake was, they would point in the direction he was heading (whatever that might be) and announce that it was 'five sleeps' away.

As the days passed, Stuart began to wonder if the lake was just wishful thinking. With the terrain deteriorating, he complained everything was 'bleak, barren, and desolate. It grows no timber, so that we scarcely can find sufficient wood to boil our quartpot.' But his persistence was rewarded by the discovery of a significant watercourse he named Chambers Creek. The party pushed on further through good grazing country and it began to rain. Cracks in the drought-ravaged soil filled with water and overflowed until

Stuart found himself 'on an island before we knew what we were about. We were obliged to seek a higher place. Not content with depriving us of our first worley [shelter], it has now forced us to retreat to a bare hill, without any protection from the weather.' The next day the floods receded but the horses were still 'sinking up to their knees in mud' and at one point the whole party was forced to wade 'belly deep' in water. The men made for drier ground and crossed a small range of mountains. On the other side, the whole world turned white.

Stuart had stumbled onto the bleached stony plains that surround the present-day opal mines of Coober Pedy. It is a landscape so alien that it is used as a location for science fiction movies. The town's name comes from the Arabana Aboriginal term *kupa piti*, which means 'white man's hole'. The miners discovered that the only way to deal with the extreme temperatures was to live underground. Today subterranean homes, churches and shops still exist. Outside there is hardly a blade of grass or a tree to be seen, yet in a few areas nearby sheep are raised with some success. Locals joke that they browse in pairs—one to turn the stone over and the other to lick the moss off the bottom. It is hardly intensive farming. Even in the more fertile areas, it takes twelve hectares to support a single sheep and twenty hectares to support a cow.

As he rode through the bleak landscape, Stuart found that the intense light reflecting back from the white rocks caused constant mirages. They were so powerful, he wrote, 'that little bushes appear like great gum-trees, which makes it very difficult to judge what is before us; it is almost as bad as travelling in the dark'. With no sign of better country ahead, the explorers were in a precarious position. They had been away for more than two months. Ahead, they faced a scene of terrible desolation. The horses were lame and the scarcity of game meant that their supplies were almost gone. On 16 July 1858 Stuart swung southwards, admitting that he couldn't 'face the stones again'.

The retreat came just in time. The men were down to their last loaf of damper when they noticed the first signs of fertility returning to the countryside. Soon they were riding through grass 'up to the horses' knees'. Seizing his chance to escape, the Aboriginal guide deserted Stuart and Foster. The ragged pair trudged towards the Nullarbor Plain and once more the countryside degenerated into a 'dreary, dismal, dreadful desert'. 'When will it end?' asked Stuart despairingly in his journal:

> For upwards of a month we have been existing upon two pounds and a half of flour-cake daily...Since we commenced the journey, all the animal food we have been able to obtain has been four wallabies, one opossum, one small duck, one pigeon, and latterly a few kangaroo mice, which were very welcome; we were anxious to find more.

It was five agonising days before Stuart spotted some fresh horse tracks in sand, an indication he was nearing the south coast. From an old hand-drawn map, he judged that they would reach water the next day. Twenty kilometres later the men stumbled into Millers Water, near Ceduna on the Great Australian Bight, just as Stuart had predicted. They were safe.

His journey was an outstanding achievement. He had travelled through more than 1600 kilometres of inhospitable territory using only a compass to navigate and he had mapped out thousands of square kilometres of potential sheep country. The total cost of his journey was £10 for food and £28 for his assistant's wages. The expedition completed Stuart's rigorous apprenticeship. He had been out with one of Australia's greatest explorers, he had honed his bush skills through years of surveying and now, he had completed a major journey with the minimum of equipment. More than most European men alive, he had come to terms with the capriciousness of the Australian desert.

Stuart learned that the outback is governed by irregular

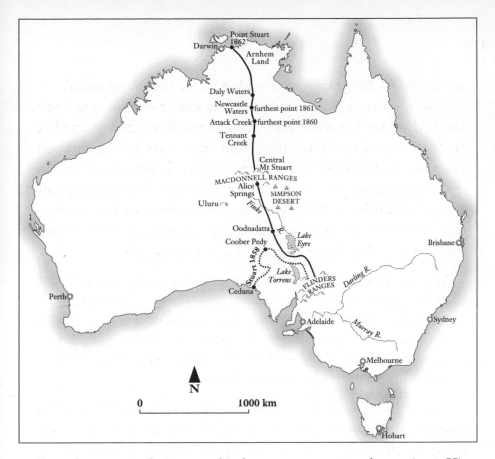

Stuart kept to a similar route on his three attempts to cross the continent. His discovery of mound springs between the Flinders Ranges and Oodnadatta helped him reach central Australia.

climatic patterns that last for years, not months. It is the driest region of the driest inhabited continent on earth, yet it can experience more than 180 millimetres of rainfall on a single day. The temperature ranges from minus 5°C on a winter's night to 45°C on a summer's afternoon. The sky is filled with an overwhelming intensity of heat and light that can be dissolved by the fury of a violent thunderstorm at a moment's notice. Like a giant eraser, the wind skittles across the landscape resculpting the sand dunes and obliterating the footprints of all those who have gone before. Gusts of over 110 kilometres an hour pick up the dust and hurl it around, blotting out the sky and churning the air into a writhing mass of grit. Yet Stuart also realised that the desert was a place of surprise and delight. He learned to savour the fragility of the sunrises, the riotous sunsets and the clarity of the heavens lit up each night by the giant white smudge of the Milky Way.

Stuart seemed oblivious to the desert's detrimental effect on his health. As he travelled home from Ceduna to tell his patrons Chambers and Finke of his discoveries, he called in to see his fellow Scotsman, Robert Bruce, the manager of Arkaba Station. Bruce recalled:

> I turned to see a pallid pasty-faced looking face, crossed by a heavy moustache, and roofed in with a dirty cabbage tree hat, peering through the rails. 'You have the advantage of me,' said I, though the man's voice sounded very familiar to my ears. 'Oh, you know me all right, I'm Mr Stuart,' he responded…'I thought I knew your voice,' I replied politely, 'but what have you been doing with yourself? Your voice is all that is left of you.'

To Stuart's delight, the cattle station had just taken a delivery of whisky. By the end of the evening the normally taciturn Scotsman was boasting about his ancestors from the Royal House of Stuart and delivering rousing versions of 'Auld Lang Syne'. Even Bruce seemed surprised at the amount of liquor such a small man could consume.

Only the desert was more enticing than the whisky bottle. When Stuart's hangover subsided, he continued to work for the Chambers brothers. During 1859 he and three men explored around the northern end of Lake Eyre where they discovered a chain of mound springs running for hundreds of kilometres through some of the most barren areas on the continent. These tiny volcano-like structures occur along faults in the earth's sur-face. They are formed when water, which once fell as rain over the Great Dividing Range millions of years ago, trickles into a giant underground reservoir known as the Great Artesian Basin. Then it bubbles up through tiny cracks in the earth's crust at temperatures up to 43°C, forming tiny oases and unique thermal wetlands like Dalhousie Springs on the edge of the Simpson Desert.

This ready supply of fresh water was the key to breaking through the horseshoe of salt lakes that had defeated Edward Eyre. The geological faultline led Stuart to rivers that beckoned towards the interior. Now more than ever he was determined to 'lift the veil' that hung over central Australia, and cross the continent from coast to coast.

Four

An Affair of Cliquery

'Why explore? It is as well for those who
ask such a question that there are others who
feel the answer and never need to ask.'
Sir Wally Herbert

When John McDouall Stuart returned to Adelaide in July
1859, he found the drawing rooms of the rich and the
powerful more accessible to him than ever before. South
Australia's politicians were delighted. Stuart had broken the stranglehold of the 'Fertile Island Theory' and proved that sizeable
patches of fertile land lay beyond the salt-lake country to the
north. It opened up vast agricultural opportunities and strengthened the case for bringing the overland telegraph line down to
Adelaide.

Sensing the public mood for further expeditions, William
Finke and James Chambers offered to make Stuart available for an
attempt to cross the continent. Their terms were simple: the government would have to cover part of the cost and offer a bonus for
reaching the north coast. Governor Richard MacDonnell was
enthusiastic. On 19 July, he wrote to the South Australian treasurer, William Younghusband, saying, 'It would settle forever the
practicability of carrying the wire, as well as sending horses for
export to India by that route…I strongly recommend immediate
action.' The treasurer was not so sure. He was eager for glory but
reluctant to pay for it. Perhaps, he suggested, the gold-rich
colonies of New South Wales and Victoria might like to make a
contribution?

But New South Wales was still not interested in exploration. Even though much of the 'ghastly blank' was technically within its jurisdiction, the Sydney government had plenty of land and was committed to building an expensive railway network. The Victorians also declined, only less politely. Months of caustic Adelaide newspaper editorials, pouring scorn on their exploratory efforts, had made them more determined than ever to mount their own expedition.

South Australia was forced to switch tactics. In August 1859 it announced a prize of £2000 for the 'first person who shall succeed in crossing through the country lately discovered by Mr Stuart, to either the north or north-western shore of the Australian continent, west of the 143rd degree of east longitude'. Closer inspection of this 'generous' offer reveals it was little more than a crafty ploy to induce the Victorians to plan their route for South Australia's benefit. If they wanted the prize they would have to travel through the country 'lately discovered by Mr Stuart', which was just the territory Adelaide needed to open up the overland telegraph.

Whatever the motives that lay behind it, the prize succeeded in jolting Melbourne's Philosophical Institute out of its summer somnolence. When the Exploration Committee meetings resumed, there was renewed enthusiasm for crossing the continent, but now the original scientific and philanthropic intentions were replaced by politics, intercolonial rivalry and greed. It had become a race between South Australia and Victoria—with £2000 waiting for the winner.

Still short of money, the Exploration Fund Committee tried to speed up proceedings by starting a false rumour that Ambrose Kyte's offer of £1000 was in danger of lapsing. The *Argus* predicted that Stuart would win the race before Victoria had even saddled its camels.

With Melbourne society alive with talk of northern ports,

acres of pastoral land and the chance to build a telegraph line, Victoria's new chief secretary William Nicholson realised there was more to the proposed expedition than a few jars of pickled animals and a couple of new flower species. On 20 January 1860 he announced that parliament had agreed to make £6000 available for the purpose of exploring central and northern Australia. Shortly afterwards the Philosophical Institute received another boost. It was granted a royal charter and became the Royal Society of Victoria, housed in a new building on La Trobe Street.

On 23 January, the Exploration Fund Committee dissolved itself and the Exploration Committee managed to slim down to seventeen members. It now comprised five doctors, four scientists (including Ferdinand Mueller, John Macadam and geologist Alfred Selwyn), the chief justice, Sir William Stawell, the surveyor-general, Charles Ligar, his deputy, a vicar, a journalist, an ironmonger, a publican and a pastoralist, Angus MacMillan. Stawell was appointed chairman. There were still only three men (Mueller, MacMillan and Selwyn) who had any experience of exploration. With only this shallow pool of expertise to draw upon, the committee began to choose an expedition leader.

Victoria was hardly bursting with suitable candidates. In fact, by 1860 Australia itself was somewhat deficient in battle-hardened explorers. To everyone's relief, Thomas Mitchell had retired and was now annoying the British with his constant demands for a knighthood. Charles Sturt had returned to England a physical wreck and Ludwig Leichhardt had disappeared altogether. Augustus Gregory was the obvious choice and, although the leadership was informally offered to him, he accepted an offer from Queensland to become its new surveyor-general.

In the absence of any seasoned contenders, the naturalist William Blandowski, who had been so vociferous at previous meetings, put his own name forward. He had a reputation for controversial behaviour. A few months earlier he had decided to settle a few personal scores by naming several grotesque species of fish after particular members of the Royal Society. Dr Richard Eades was assigned to a specimen with a 'receding forehead and a large belly' and the Reverend John Bleasedale was given a fish described as 'slippery, slimy…lives in the mud'. When the names were published, Blandowski realised his career was unlikely to progress much further. He sailed to Europe soon afterwards.

Ferdinand Mueller was unwilling to lead the expedition himself but he did have a candidate in mind. Major Peter Egerton Warburton was an ex-army officer who had taken up the post of police commissioner in South Australia. In 1857, he was dispatched to recall a surveying team led by Benjamin Herschel Babbage. In recovering the errant party, Warburton had made several valuable discoveries of fertile country north of Adelaide. His triumphant return was overshadowed by his malicious public criticism of the ponderous, yet thorough Babbage, and by his failure to stay out in the field through the hot season. The newspapers branded Warburton a coward for coming home rather than 'summering out' in the desert. 'Really,' thundered the *Register*, 'we are compelled to enquire what was the precise object of the Major's trip. Was it to explore or enjoy?' Despite this withering appraisal of Warburton's 'ticker', several committee members supported his candidacy, including Mueller and the prominent artist and naturalist Ludwig Becker. But there were two reasons why the rest of the Royal Society refused to endorse Warburton.

The Major disliked working with camels. And he was South Australian. The idea of a 'crow-eater' in charge of a Victorian expedition was unthinkable. Chief secretary William Nicholson was especially reluctant to see a government-funded project led by a rival colonist. To Mueller's dismay, Warburton was sidelined. Then in a bizarre departure from protocol, the committee decided to advertise the job of 'Expedition Leader' in the press. The *Herald* was appalled. 'Men of science, of enterprise, and with some knowledge of the ways of the world,' it exclaimed, 'do not relish the notion of being advertised for, as the keeper of a registry office advertises for a butler, housemaid or a cook.'

The general consensus was that the advertisements had been designed to offend Warburton and to put off applicants from other states, particularly those of a 'lower class' like John McDouall Stuart. The Exploration Committee's secretary John Macadam hid the advertisements in the 'Public Notices' column rather than 'Positions Vacant', and then 'forgot' to place them at all in Sydney or Adelaide.

VICTORIAN EXPLORATION EXPEDITION — Gentlemen desirous of offering their services for the LEADERSHIP of the forthcoming EXPEDITION are requested to put themselves in communication with the Honorary Secretary of the Committee on or before the 1st day of March ensuing.

By Order of the Committee.

JOHN MACADAM, M. D., Honorary Secretary, Fitzroy Cottage, Fitzroy-square. Royal Society, Victoria-street Melbourne, January 30, 1860

This unorthodox method of finding an expedition leader was really a devious manoeuvre to ensure that Burke was offered the post.

The resulting applicants ranged from mediocre to downright hopeless. Of the fifteen men who replied, only four had any experience of adventurous travel. None had ever led a major expedition, although one, Gustav von Tempsky, was proud to say he had 'drilled and fought Indians, Blacks, White and Redskins' during his thirteen years in America. The others ranged from dreamers and lunatics to armchair travellers and military men. Warburton refused to respond at all. The whole process, he told the committee, was 'repugnant' and 'incompatible' with his position as a police commissioner.

Melbourne was soon awash with rumours that the appointment was simply a matter of personal favour to be handed out by the most powerful faction within the Royal Society. The *Argus* was disgusted:

> We might ask what confidence can be placed in any body of men who could blunder so egregiously at the outset with regard to the appointment of a leader...and who if the reports of their late meetings and the announcement made in the their late extraordinary advertisement, are to stand for anything, do not up to this time, know what they are going to send an expedition to explore.

Pummelled by scathing editorials and intense public dissatisfaction, the Exploration Committee sank further into an abyss of indecision. Reports of drunkenness and factional infighting at meetings were leaked to the press and by March 1860 the situation was becoming desperate.

While the Victorians bickered, news arrived from South Australia that John McDouall Stuart had set out with two men from Chambers Creek on 2 March. His aim was to find the centre of the continent and then continue to the north coast. If there was to be a race, it seemed that one side had already started.

In Melbourne, the Exploration Committee continued to flounder. On 8 March, the *Argus* warned that the expedition was in danger of collapse. 'The exploration committee are in an embarrassing position. Time presses. The season of the year in which the expedition should set out is rapidly passing away, the camels have not yet arrived; no leader has been appointed.' The committee's response was to form a sub-committee, which drew up a shortlist of possible leaders including most everyone who had applied for the post—plus Warburton, who hadn't submitted his name at all.

Among the candidates was a police superintendent from Castlemaine and Beechworth, Robert O'Hara Burke. Although there is no record of a personal application for the post, Burke's name was put forward by a senior officer, P. H. Smithe, who assured the committee he was:

> a most active man and very strong—most temperate in his habits—and is kind and gentler in his manners—but possessing a strong will—ambitious and had been accustomed to command since boyhood…In conclusion, I am confident from my knowledge of Mr Burke that there is not another gentleman in this Colony possessing so many of the qualifications necessary to the success of the undertaking in question as my friend Burke.

It was said that Burke had powerful backers within the Royal Society but, since he had no previous experience whatsoever, he was initially passed over in favour of Gustav von Tempsky, who was questioned at length by the committee. A report was prepared. No decision was made.

To break the deadlock, Ludwig Becker came up with the idea of an 'exploring exam'. Keen to promote Warburton's case he persuaded the committee that each of the candidates should be called in like schoolboys to answer questions on astronomy, surveying, navigation, map-making and metrology. Since Warburton was the only man with practical experience, he was bound to win, but quite how Becker thought a man who would not answer a public advertisement could be persuaded to take a classroom test was a mystery. The scheme was soon abandoned. Just as it seemed as if every dilatory tactic had been explored, the committee made an announcement. It had decided not to make any further decisions for another three months.

The most plausible justification for this declaration was that since the camels were yet to arrive, there was no hurry to appoint a leader. The second excuse was laughable. All the remaining applicants were to be given three months to learn the art of 'taking lunars'—that is, navigating by the stars. The committee was effectively admitting that not one of their otherwise 'suitable' candidates could find his way home through the bush. By now, most of Melbourne was convinced that the selection process was rigged; a candidate had been promised the appointment and he was being given time to brush up on his navigational skills.

In April, the Royal Society held its annual dinner. It was a feast of fine wine and self-congratulation. Endless toasts were drunk and long speeches were delivered invoking the Roman emperors, the glory of Victoria and the achievements of the Royal Society. In the early hours everyone rolled home red-faced and thoroughly pleased with himself. Melbourne's gentlemen had been discussing an expedition for the best part of three years, yet they still had no camels, no leader and no route mapped out.

By the time news of these antics reached South Australia, John McDouall Stuart had been heading north for nearly three months. The *Register* couldn't resist a dig at its neighbour:

> Only let the Victorian explorers look out for their laurels. It is quite possible and by no means improbable that at this moment the problem of the interior is solved and that John McDouall Stuart will be back in time to show the camels a beaten track through the heart of the Australian mainland.

It was the arrival of the camels that finally stirred the Exploration Committee into action. On 16 June 1860 a small but expectant crowd gathered at Railway Pier in Melbourne. The crisp morning air was choked with steam as a large crane chugged into life and lowered a giant sling towards the decks of the *Chinsurah*, just in from India. People strained for a glimpse as a camel, quivering in fear, was placed inside the cradle. Under the watchful eye of George Landells, the beast was lifted into the air, swung round in a great arc and lowered to the ground. When all twenty-five camels had disembarked safely, Landells took them to St Kilda beach where, to the amazement of the families strolling along the foreshore, he trotted them up and down on the sand.

By lunchtime, the camel dealer was ready to show off his purchases to a wider audience. Resplendent in the traditional red and white robes of an Indian cameleer, he marshalled the animals into a procession and jogged triumphantly through the streets of Melbourne. The ride was disrupted for a moment when a young 'pet' camel scattered the crowd by 'by taking a preliminary canter on its own account, and performing some most extraordinary antics to the terror and confusion of certain elderly ladies who stood gazing with astonishment at the novel importation'.

The citizens of Melbourne were immensely proud of their new purchases. 'Years hence, Australia will boast of its race of camels as England does now of her horse...they certainly are magnificent animals,' bragged the *Argus*. There was a sense of wonder that these exotic creatures cavorting through the city would shortly lift the 'veil of the centre'. So many people turned out to witness the parade that the police had to clear the way to the parliament stables where the camels would recuperate from their long journey.

The new arrivals and their sepoy handlers soon became local celebrities, attracting so many visitors that the *Argus* worried they might not make it to the desert at all. Hundreds of people took to gathering at the stables, dropping their cigarettes amongst the straw and plying the sepoys with beer and brandy. All this unexpected hospitality was apt to make them a little 'absent minded' when it came to matters of safety.

With the camels ready to go, there was no excuse to delay appointing a leader. The impasse was broken at a meeting of the Exploration Committee on 20 June 1860. The three candidates left in the race were Warburton (despite the fact he had not applied), Gustav von Tempsky, and the Irish police officer, Robert O'Hara Burke.

Crucially, Warburton's principal supporter, Ferdinand Mueller was sick and stayed away and several other committee members were so disgusted by the 'base and shameless personal motives at work' that they boycotted the meeting. As a result, discussions centred on von Tempsky and Burke. When the last vote was taken, no one supported Warburton and just five committee members chose von Tempsky. The clear winner with ten votes was Police Superintendent Robert O'Hara Burke.

The Victorian Exploring Expedition finally had a leader—a man who had never travelled beyond the settled districts of Australia, who had no experience of exploration and who was notorious for getting lost on his way home from the pub.

Five

A Trifle Insane

'All things considered there are only two kinds
of men in the world—those who stay at home
and those who do not.' Rudyard Kipling

In 1854, it was common in the town of Beechworth to see a tall
athletic horseman thundering past the weatherboard cottages,
sending mud flying in all directions. With his long black beard
flowing in the wind and a daredevil glint in his bright blue eyes, he
would gallop twenty kilometres to the local magistrate's house, leap
from his horse and swing on the garden gate until he had enraged
its owner beyond words. Only then would the police officer ride
home, remove his uniform, and retire to a bathtub in his garden.
Superintendent Robert O'Hara Burke did not care for the heat.

Newspapers greeted Burke's appointment with a mixture of
relief and incredulity. Most commentators were pleased that a
Victorian candidate had triumphed over the 'foreigners' but others
were baffled. Did the policeman possess any relevant qualifications for the post?

Until recently Burke had been unknown in Melbourne society
but, as reporters soon discovered, his past was as intriguing as his
current bathing habits. He was born in Ireland in 1820, the
second son of a distinguished family of landowners, and he grew
up in the privileged surroundings of the St Clerans estate in
Galway, cared for by his devoted nurse Ellen Dogherty.

At the age of twenty, Burke chose a military career but he
shunned the British forces, opting instead for the predominantly
Catholic Austrian army—a highly unorthodox move given the fact

he was a Protestant. After securing an introduction to Prince Reuss's Seventh Hussars through the British ambassador in Vienna, the young Irishman became a cadet in 1842, and by 1847 he had been promoted twice and was posted to Italy. Life in the regiment was tough. The soldiers wintered out in muddy fields, living under canvas in freezing conditions, often with little to do except play cards and keep an eye on the bands of Italian rebels roving the countryside. But the army also had its perks. Once on leave, Burke travelled to the great European cities and, dressed in the braided uniform of his elite regiment, found that doors opened into an altogether more glamorous world.

The young Irishman cultivated a rakish image, indulging himself in the pursuits expected of a young officer: hunting, gambling, dancing, gambling, chasing women and gambling. He acquired a particular reputation as a favourite with the opposite sex and legend has it that he acquired the large scar on his cheek by fighting a sabre duel to defend his honour. Burke was intelligent, musical, well-read, and could flatter anyone he chose in French, Italian and German. With another promotion at the end of 1847, he seemed to be on the brink of a glittering career. Yet just a few months later First Lieutenant Robert O'Hara Burke was facing ruin at the hands of a military court.

As his regiment prepared for action in Sardinia, Burke went absent without leave and set off through Recoaro in northern Italy to the spa towns of Grafenburg and Aachen in Germany. Rumours circulated that he was ill with constipation but it seems more likely that a mountain of gambling debts provided the real incentive to leave.

By the time he returned to his regiment early in 1848, he was facing a court-martial and a possible jail sentence. Fortunately, a preliminary inquiry found he had run up his debts through 'carelessness' rather than deceit. Burke was allowed to resign—his punishment was the dishonour of a shattered reputation.

Burke presented this portrait to Julia Matthews whom he first met in 1858, when he proposed to her for the final time.

With his military career over, Burke turned to the police force and joined the Irish Constabulary in County Kildare. He quickly made a name for himself as a 'powerful young man' whose 'great feats as an athlete were the theme and conversation of all who witnessed them'. But Burke found the life of a country policeman monotonous and the salary inadequate—it hardly compared to the excitement and sophistication of Europe.

A transfer to Dublin's mounted police failed to curb Burke's restlessness. He hung around in the city's bars, where stories of gold and adventure in Australia cut through the haze of tobacco smoke and fired his imagination. As a member of the gentry, he was more fortunate than most—family connections gave him strings to pull, and he had no reservations about giving them a sharp tug in order to escape his provincial existence. In time-honoured fashion Burke accumulated an impressive portfolio of references from men who barely knew him, but nevertheless proclaimed he was 'a man with unusual and extensive knowledge of the world'. Thus armed, he set sail for Australia.

By the time he landed in Melbourne in 1853, Victoria's gold rush was in full swing and the colony was in desperate need of police officers to impose order on the chaos. So many fortune seekers had arrived that most miners were struggling to make a living. Burke soon realised that gold mining was not the guaranteed route to wealth he had imagined. He fell back into a police career and was made an acting inspector at Beechworth, 225 kilometres north-east of Melbourne.

The position was not an easy one. When Burke arrived it was the administrative centre of the Ovens Valley region, which was dominated by the gold-mining industry. Crime was rife and ethnic disagreements between the European and Chinese immigrants promoted a simmering sense of unease in the valleys. Bushrangers menaced the highways, cattle rustlers stalked the plains and petty thieves harassed the shop-keepers. The pubs were crawling with diggers drowning their sorrows or picking fights. On a good evening, they might even manage both. It was a district that became famous for hardened criminals—the Kelly gang was to terrorise the area in the late 1870s until Ned Kelly was caught and committed for trial at the Beechworth courthouse.

For now, Acting Inspector Burke was preoccupied with reforming his demoralised officers, who spent most of their time extracting bribes from the local ruffians and drinking the proceeds at one of the sly-grog shops in the area. He was also left to deal with endless petty offences such as 'riding furiously while intoxicated' and 'public drunkenness'.

As the local police chief Burke was also the town prosecutor. Given the number of magistrates who reprimanded him for his inattention to detail and propensity to lose important paperwork, it was a role he obviously found irksome. In fact life in Australia was proving to be depressingly similar to the one he had left behind in Ireland. The only compensation was the salary. At £700 a year, it was three times what he would have made back home.

Away from the bright lights of Europe, Burke ceased to maintain his dashing image. Despite his rank, Burke did not appear to possess a full police uniform and he was known to rush around borrowing clothing from his colleagues whenever a local dignitary was due in town. On or off duty, he didn't care what he looked like, and was often seen wearing check trousers, a red shirt and a threadbare jacket covered in patches. Underneath a peculiar sombrero-type hat, his hair was unkempt and his face obscured by a black beard, over which he was sometimes said to dribble saliva.

But the real gossip centred on Burke's bathing habits. Neighbours whispered he was 'as fond of water as a retriever', and that he often spent hours lying in his outdoor bathtub, wearing nothing but his police helmet, reading a book and cursing the mosquitoes. In the heat of summer the local constables were startled to find their inspector stretched out in the water working on his police reports. In order not to embarrass his housekeeper, Burke constructed a screen with a trapdoor in it so that food and drink could be passed to him as he reclined. Several people wondered if he was perhaps 'a trifle insane'. Burke did nothing to counter the impression. Once he tired of administration, he would leap from his bath and indulge in frenetic bouts of exercise—taking long walks in the forest by himself or setting about the local trees with an axe. At least he undertook these activities fully clothed.

Despite this behaviour Burke proved himself a popular and capable police chief. He had a knack for imposing strict discipline yet remaining friendly with his subordinates. While improving the efficiency of the Beechworth force, Burke still found time to share stories and jokes with the locals and became famous for his extravagant tales of adventure in Europe. He took an active part in town life, joining the local orchestra and helping to establish a Literary and Science Institute. He was so well-liked that, when he later applied for a transfer to the town of Castlemaine, the residents of Beechworth petitioned him to stay on.

Whatever freedom Burke had to indulge his eccentricities in the Australian bush, the tedious life of a country policeman failed to satisfy his aspirations for adventure. He told colleagues that he was desperate for 'something to take the sting out of him'.

Then, in 1854, Burke's younger brother James became the first British officer to be killed in the Crimean war. His heroic death was reported in the *Age*:

> As he leapt ashore, six soldiers charged him. Two he shot with his revolver, one he cut down with his sword, the rest turned and fled. Then he had charged a group of riflemen with headlong gallantry. As he got near he was struck by a ball, which broke his jawbone, but he rushed on, shot three men dead at close quarters with his revolver, and cleft two men through helmet and all into the brain with his sword. He was then surrounded and while engaged in cutting his way with heroic courage through the ranks of the enemy, a sabre cut from behind, given by a dragoon as he went by, nearly severed his head from his body; and he fell dead, covered with bayonet wounds, sabre gashes, and marked with lance thrusts and bullet holes.

Burke was profoundly affected by this glorious (if exaggerated) account and could often be found staring at his brother's portrait and weeping. The tragedy continued to weigh on his mind, for in March 1856 he obtained leave of absence and left to join the British army. He arrived in Liverpool to find his services were not required. The fighting was over and a peace treaty had already been signed.

Disappointed, Burke returned to Australia and by the end of 1856 he was back in his old position at Beechworth where he found life just as mundane as before. With the gold now beginning to run out, the only real excitement was a riot staged by European and American miners who set about trying to drive their Chinese counterparts away from the diggings. At gunpoint, they herded their Asian neighbours like sheep until some fell down a gorge into the Buckland River. When Burke heard of the trouble, he took twenty men and rode the eighty kilometres to Buckland in just twenty-four hours. As they neared the scene, there was talk of an ambush but Burke refused to turn back. Placing himself in front of his men, he charged into the miners' camp—only to find it deserted. The unrest was over. Just as he had missed the height of the gold rush and the fighting in the Crimea, Burke turned up at Buckland a little too late to take part in the real action. It seemed he had a talent for bad timing.

It wasn't until 1858, when a travelling theatre company came to town, that life began to liven up in Beechworth. Its star performer was a sixteen-year-old actress described by the critics as 'sparkling, gay and bewitching'. Julia Matthews was born in London, the daughter of a music teacher and a sailor turned artificial-flower maker. Their daughter was precociously talented and made her debut in Sydney in 1854 in a play aptly named *Spoiled Child*. She had been entrancing audiences ever since.

As a music and theatre lover, it was no surprise that Burke went to see Julia perform, and even less of a surprise that he fell uncontrollably in love with her. Each evening his passion increased as he sat transfixed in the front row. On her last night

Julia Matthews was a seductive actress and singer who captivated Burke until he was prepared to risk everything to win her love.

he went backstage and asked her to marry him. Even by Burke's standards, it was an outrageous proposal. He was a thirty-eight-year-old Protestant police officer and she was a Catholic actress less than half his age (actresses in those days being considered of dubious reputation however scrupulous their conduct).

The offer horrified Julia's mother, who saw Burke as yet another 'Stage Door Johnnie'. Her daughter was already earning the vast sum of £60 per week (of which Julia received just 2s 6d) and Mrs Matthews envisaged a long and lucrative career, not an early wedding to a country police officer. But her opposition could not deter this lovestruck Irishman. On the ingenious pretext of tracking a gang of dangerous horse thieves, Burke spent the next few weeks charging around Victoria to watch his beloved's every performance. Julia may have been susceptible, but all the Irish charm in the world could not persuade her mother, who took her daughter back to Melbourne to star in a new opera. Burke had no option but to return to his lonely life of bachelorhood in Beechworth.

In the weeks that followed, neighbours noticed that his cottage was filled with music. He had bought a piano and was playing out his grief through Julia's songs. Later, when the heartbroken policeman remembered that his next-door neighbour was expecting a baby, he worried that his constant practising might be disturbing the family. He gathered up as many blankets as he could and draped them over the piano to dampen the noise, then continued playing the same songs for hours on end. When the baby was delivered, Burke told the proud father, with tears in his eyes: 'Ah, if I had such ties as you have, I think I should be a happier and better man.'

The Irishman's life had stalled. In November 1858, he transferred to the larger Castlemaine district, where along with two hundred others from the town, he subscribed two shillings and sixpence to the 'Exploration Fund'—little knowing that one day he would be leading the expedition. In the meantime, he fell in with a new group of friends including the town jailer John Castieau.

Castieau's boisterous diary of life in Castlemaine reveals a long series of rowdy parties and poker games often conducted 'at my friend Burke's house'. On Sundays, the two men would set out for walks in the countryside to clear their heads, before Burke began to grumble that the journey was too arduous or the weather too hot and insist that they retire instead to the pub for lunch. On one occasion they conducted running races in the beer garden with Castieau reporting later, 'Came home and was so sick I could eat no dinner, my racing days are over!'

The opportunity to escape presented itself with the arrival in Castlemaine of a railway tycoon named John Bruce. Like Ambrose Kyte, Bruce was a businessman of dubious methods. He often used the local police to quell disturbances staged by his disgruntled workers and, in the course of his dealings with Burke, was impressed by his 'manliness of character and determined energy'. The two men became friends and it wasn't long before Bruce began to smarten up his protégé and introduce him to the 'right people' in Melbourne. When the Royal Society announced it was looking for an expedition leader, Bruce encouraged Burke to apply.

It was a tantalising prospect and Bruce made it seem all the more attractive by embellishing the endeavour with stories of fame, glory, knighthoods and grants of land. In fact few explorers ever received much financial reward for their efforts. Only one, the irascible Sir Thomas Mitchell, received a knighthood and that was only to keep him quiet. But for a disillusioned policeman desperate for an opportunity to distinguish himself, this was the chance to fulfil all his dreams. After all, what woman could resist an offer of marriage from a rich and famous explorer?

The idea of Burke leading any expedition anywhere at all was ludicrous. He was neither a surveyor nor a scientist and had no exploration experience. His talent for getting lost was legendary, prompting his bank manager, Falconer Larkworthy, to observe:

> It was said of him as a good joke but true nevertheless, that
> when he was returning from Yackandandah to Beechworth he
> lost his way, although the track was well beaten and fre-
> quented, and did not arrive at his destination for many hours
> after he was due. He was in no sense a bushman.

Beechworth's police officers often had to retrieve their chief
from 'his latest confusion' and the *Mount Alexander Mail*
revealed, 'he could not tell the north from the south in broad
daylight, and the Southern Cross as a guide was a never ending
puzzle to him'. How would he cope in the wilderness with no
roads or signposts? How could he travel in a straight line when
he couldn't even measure latitude and longitude?

There was also a question mark over Burke's temperament.
He had energy and passion in abundance, but was such an exuberant daredevil the right man to lead a large party of men into
unknown territory? Did he have the tenacity of Charles Sturt,
the methodical persistence of Augustus Gregory or the eye for
detail of Ludwig Leichhardt?

Exploration might seem a glamorous occupation, but it was
often a laborious test of stamina and organisation. Burke was
popular, charming and intelligent but excitable, impulsive and
headstrong. He responded to situations emotionally and seemed
to lack the composure to think through the consequences of his
actions.

So why was such an unlikely candidate chosen to lead the
most prestigious project Victoria had ever undertaken? The
answers lie buried deep in the preoccupations of a colonial
society convinced of its own superiority, and in the Machiavellian
motivations of a small group of rich and powerful men who were
developing a strong influence on the expedition.

The higher echelons of Melbourne society had been weaned
on a diet of British class-consciousness. Many commentators

accepted Burke's appointment because he came from an ancient and honourable family and was 'accustomed to command'. Never mind that he could hardly read a compass—he had the right blood flowing through his veins and as far as the *Herald* was concerned that was enough:

> We may add here that a brother of Mr Burke's, an officer in the Royal Engineers, made himself very conspicuous for his gallantry at the beginning of the Crimean War and is celebrated in Russell's history of the campaign. Such is the man, his qualification and his antecedents. That these are such as will induce public confidence in Mr Burke there cannot, we think be any doubt.

One reporter was impressed with Burke's physical attributes. 'He was tall, well-made with dark brown hair; his broad chest was decorated with a magnificent beard; he had fine intelligent eyes, and a splendidly formed head'. Another described him as 'a gentleman in the prime of life' who was 'a perfect centaur as to horsemanship'. Then, there was Burke's dashing history and his mysterious scar, all of which proved immensely appealing to the ladies of Melbourne. The chief justice's wife Mary Stawell gushed:

> When we first met Mr Burke we called him 'Brian Boru'; there was such a daring reckless look about him which was enhanced by a giant scar across his face, caused by a sabre cut in a duel when he was in the Austrian service; he had withal a very attractive manner.

In 1859 Burke had joined the Melbourne Club, allowing him access to the rich and powerful. He quaffed red wine with men like Sir William Stawell, who was as impressed by Burke as his wife had been, and would become a strong advocate.

As the leadership battle dragged on through April and May of 1860, Gustav von Tempsky embarked on a rigorous training program, improving his cardiovascular capabilities and poring over astronomical formulae. Burke took a rather different approach. He was normally to be found in the bar of the Melbourne Club losing vast quantities of money at cards but winning plenty of friends. At times his debts reached up to £450—nearly two-thirds of his annual salary.

As Burke's losses mounted, John Bruce and his associates manipulated matters shamelessly in the background, leaning on friends, calling in favours, even conspiring to stack the Exploration Committee with members sympathetic to the cause.

The Late Dr. Macadam.

John Macadam, secretary of the Royal Society, was influential in the leadership battle to ensure Burke's victory.

Their most important conquest was Sir William Stawell. Once he had indicated his support for his fellow Irishman, several committee members including Georg Neumayer and John Macadam followed suit.

Burke's cosmopolitan past was also proving a powerful asset. He hailed from Galway so he identified with the Irish contingent, and his fluent German went some way to mollifying the scientists on the committee. Best of all, he was not South Australian. Despite his lilting accent and his Irish ancestry, Burke's seven years' service in the colony made him as Victorian as the next man.

Burke enjoyed every minute in the limelight. Perhaps in his more romantic moments he imagined himself like the knights of old—he had been given a quest, a chance to prove himself and perhaps to secure the woman he loved. In the meantime he set about reversing the effects of his somewhat dissolute leadership campaign. Reports began to appear in the newspapers of a red-faced man jogging around Melbourne's Royal Park. It was Burke, tackling 'the severest of physical privations' to ready himself for the journey ahead.

On 4 July 1860 a ragtag assortment of prospective explorers queued outside the headquarters of the Royal Society. Seven hundred men applied to join a venture that would 'constitute for long years if not ages to come, the highest glory of the colony of Victoria'. Many men offered to go for minimal wages; some said they would go for none at all.

Their applications ranged from grubby scrawled notes to an eleven-page dossier detailing supplies, equipment, possible routes and probable dangers. Many of the letters were from stockmen and drovers who boasted of their capacity to work for days without food, ride the wildest of horses, shoot the wariest of kangaroos and 'deal' with the 'most difficult Aborigines'. One typical applicant, Edward Wooldridge, claimed to be ready for every hardship:

> I've often cooked my own dinner at the end of a pointed stick promoted for the occasion to the office of toasting fork. It may be suggested to an explorer that the very food itself is often wanting; be it so in such a case, my stomach would doubtless grumble but I would endeavor to bear the privation with equanimity.

Wooldridge needn't have bothered. The inspection process was a charade. Burke spent just three hours looking at three hundred of the applicants then dismissed them all in favour of men with the 'right' connections. He ignored candidates like Robert Bowman and William Weddell, both of whom had travelled through the Australian deserts with Augustus Gregory and had excellent references from their former employer.

Twenty-five-year-old William Brahe was chosen largely because his brother was a friend of Georg Neumayer. Since arriving in Australia in 1852, the young German had worked on the Victorian goldfields, where he was well known for his skill in driving wagons on the muddy roads. John Macadam recommended sailor Henry Creber as a useful man in case an inland sea was discovered. Robert Fletcher's father was a friend of several committee members. Blacksmith William Patten and labourer Thomas McDonough knew Burke back in Ireland, Patrick Langan met him in Castlemaine and Owen Cowan was a fellow Victorian police officer.

Once the men had been chosen, the Exploration Committee decided that the expedition should leave by the end of August 1860. But with just a month to go before departure its route had still not been finalised. It had been assumed that Burke's party would leave from Melbourne and make for the north coast via Cooper Creek, but at a meeting on 17 July 1860, events took an extraordinary turn.

It emerged that some committee members favoured a bizarre scheme to load the camels back onto the *Chinsurah* and sail them halfway round Australia to an inlet known as Blunder Bay on the north-west coast. The expedition would then traverse the continent southwards to Melbourne. The plan was endorsed by George Landells, who was suspected of plotting with the *Chinsurah*'s owners to split the profits from the voyage. Burke also spoke in favour of the Blunder Bay option and in the absence of Sir William Stawell, who favoured Cooper Creek, the Exploration Committee agreed to support the new route.

When Stawell awoke the next morning to find the headline 'To Blunder Bay', plastered all over the newspapers, he was furious. The chief justice immediately called another meeting and, in a withering address, insisted the resolution should be overturned. As usual, he got his way. On 27 July, an announcement was made that Burke would leave from Melbourne. The Exploration Committee issued Burke's official instructions, which started clearly enough:

> The Committee having decided upon 'Coopers Creek' of Sturt, as the basis of your operations, request that you will proceed thither, form a depot of provisions and stores, and make arrangements for keeping open a communication in your rear to the Darling, if in your opinion advisable; and thence to Melbourne, so that you may be enabled to keep the Committee informed of your movements, and receive in return the assistance in stores and advice in which you may stand in need.

After that, however, the orders became vague and confused:

> The object of the Committee in directing you to Cooper's Creek, is, that you should explore the country intervening between it and Leichhardt's track, south of the Gulf of Carpentaria, avoiding, as far as practicable, Sturt's route to the west, and Gregory's, down the Victoria to the east.

To this object the Committee wishes you to devote your energies in the first instance, but should you determine the impracticability of this route you are desired to turn westward into the country recently discovered by Stuart, and connect his furthest point northward with Gregory's furthest Southern Exploration in 1856 (Mount Wilson)...

Should you fail, however, in connecting the two points of Stuart's and Gregory's furthest, or should you ascertain that his space has already been traversed, you are requested if possible to connect your explorations with those of the younger Gregory in the vicinity of Mount Gould, and thence you might proceed to Shark's Bay, or down the River Murchison to the settlements in Western Australia.

The instructions effectively allowed Burke to go wherever he chose. The next paragraph admitted as much:

The Committee is fully aware of the difficulty of the country you are called on to traverse, and in giving you these instructions has placed these routes before you more as an indication of what is deemed desirable to have accomplished than as indicating any exact course for you to pursue.

These baffling orders only reinforced the growing sentiment that the Exploration Committee was not capable of organising a Sunday picnic. The rumours surrounding Burke's appointment had intensified until he was forced to defend himself, insisting he had used 'only fair and honourable means' to secure his position. But the *Age* still suspected the public was not being told the whole story:

If Mr B's scientific attainments are equal to the task, let the public know them, if they are not, the public will protest against a piece of cliqueism in which the interests of the country are again sacrificed to please and serve the purposes of an unscrupulous and dangerous party.

Some columnists predicted that the expedition would be a disaster. One forecast that lives would be lost.

Six

The Honour of Victoria

'The wild charm and exciting desire that induce an
individual to undertake the arduous tasks that
lie before an explorer, and the pleasure and delight
of visiting new and totally unknown places, are
only whetted by his first attempt.'
Ernest Giles

On its first day, the Victorian Exploring Expedition with its
twenty-six camels, twenty-three horses, nineteen men and six
wagons travelled just eleven kilometres. It was seven-thirty in the
evening on 20 August 1860 before the cavalcade straggled into
Essendon on the outskirts of Melbourne. The camels stood incon-
gruously on the green in front of the church and, smelling their
arrival, all the local horses promptly bolted.

The laborious business of unpacking then began. No one knew
where anything was, who was responsible for what, or how the
camp should be organised. To compound matters, the wagons still
hadn't arrived. Even Burke was not sure what was going on.
Spectators recalled him marching around the camp, telling his
men that if he found anyone guilty of disobedience or idleness 'he
would nail the culprit up by the ears to the nearest gum tree'.

As the Irishman tried to impose some sort of order, an elderly
man approached him and introduced himself as Dr Wills—the
father of the expedition's young surveyor, William John Wills.
Grasping Burke's hand, the doctor launched into a plea for his
son's safety. 'If it were in my power, I would even now prevent his
going…If he knew what I am about to say, he would not, I think

The chaotic first night's camp at Essendon. Burke is in the centre in his cabbage-tree hat. Landells is just to the left of him. Becker stands in front of the tent.

be well pleased; but if you ever happen to want my son's advice or opinion you must ask it, for he will not offer it unasked. No matter what course you may adopt he will follow without remonstrance or murmur.'

'There is nothing you can say will raise him higher in my estimation than he stands at present,' Burke replied. 'I will do as you desire.' With tears in his eyes, the doctor turned away.

Twenty-six-year-old William Wills had been appointed surveyor with a minimum of fuss. Since neither the leader nor the deputy could navigate, he held an unusually important position, but as the protégé of Professor Georg Neumayer, he was proposed and seconded without debate.

Wills was born in Totnes, Devon, in 1834. Nicknamed 'Old Jack' or 'Gentleman Jack' as a child because of his rather serious outlook on life, he contracted 'remittent fever' at the age of seven and suffered afterwards from a slight speech impediment. Always precocious, Wills spent his spare time helping out at his father's medical practice. 'In all cases his caution was extreme,' wrote Dr Wills senior, 'and we had no fear of his making mistakes. The ordinary operations of extracting a tooth, or breathing a vein when a bumpkin presented himself as a patient, he speedily mastered.'

After passing his school exams with ease, Wills went to London where at the age of seventeen he demonstrated his extraordinary sense of direction by unravelling London's Hampton Court maze in less than ten minutes. Friends described him as a serious, unassuming young man whose affable manner belied his strong opinions. Wills had intended to study as a surgeon but he was never truly enthusiastic about medicine and soon turned to the purer sciences of maths, geometry and physics, where he excelled in every subject.

It was the lure of gold that drew the Wills family to Australia. Dr Wills wanted to emigrate with his two eldest sons and secure the family's financial future, but in the end William and his younger brother Tom went on ahead, sailing for Melbourne on the *Janet Mitchell* in 1852. Wills was fascinated by his new surroundings. He kept a daily log of the weather and sea conditions as well as learning how to set the sails and catch his own supper:

> Monday, November 1st. Begun the month well, caught a fine young shark this morning. It was about five feet long. We soon cut him up between us. I got a fine piece about 3 or 4 pounds and some one who did not like it gave us about as much more, so I cut it in slices and put plenty of butter, pepper and flour and bake it as you would a hake, and it is first rate.

Wednesday, December 1st. Small breeze this morning, which soon increased to a gale. I was up furling top gallant sails only half dressed after breakfast. Had to double reef our top sails and furl main sail, main spencer, spanker, jib and cross jack. The sea here looks beautiful but the waves do not look as large as I expected owing to the swell being so gradual. It is amusing to see the birds pitch about on the waves.

The brothers arrived in Australia in January 1853 at the pinnacle of the gold rush. They were shocked by the exorbitant prices and the shortage of accommodation. Nineteen-year-old Wills was not impressed. 'I do not like Melbourne in its present state,' he complained, 'you are not safe out after sundown...there were two or three men taken out of the river drowned and several attempts at robberies while we were there.' Determined to leave town as soon as possible, William and Tom found work as shepherds near the town of Deniliquin, 250 kilometres away. After a three-week walk to start work, the brothers soon settled in and seemed to relish their new lifestyle. Wills told his family:

> We are very comfortable in a hut by ourselves, 4 miles from the home station, and with between 13 or 14 hundred rams to look after; by far the smallest and easiest flock on the station. The hut is a very nice one built of split wood roofed with bark. I assure you we make ourselves quite comfortable here...We are very well off in the way of food; as much mutton as we like and we can make sure of getting a duck, pigeon or cockatoo at any time almost without going out of sight of the hut, besides plenty of fish in the creek. There are also plenty of mussel fish.

He got to know the landscape, the animals, birds, and even the finer points of sheep farming. It wasn't long before the Australian bush had captured his imagination:

You cannot think how glad I am that you let us come out here. If you had only let us come out without a shilling it would have been worth more than a thousand pounds in England, one is so free. This is a beautiful country, the more I see of it the better I like it.

In August 1853, Dr Wills joined his sons and took them to the gold-mining town of Ballarat, where he set up a surgery amongst the wooden shacks and maze of muddy trenches. Wills junior started a successful business analysing specimens of quartz and gold but his father recalled that 'he was ever pining for the bush.

Engrossed by his scientific studies, Wills was unaware of the public interest in the expedition and reluctant to pose for an official portrait.

The "busy haunts of men" had no attraction for him. He preferred the society of a few to that of many, but the study of nature was his passion. His love was fixed on animals, plants, and the starry firmament.'

Wills soon began to dream of exploring further afield. In 1855, he walked 160 kilometres in the hope of joining an expedition led by a Dr Catherwood. Before he left he told his mother not to worry about the dangers because, 'if everyone had such ideas we should have no one going to sea for fear of being drowned, no one would go in a railway train for fear the engine would burst, and all would live in the open air for fear of houses falling in'. The expedition was a fraud. By the time Wills caught up to him, Dr Catherwood had bolted, taking with him several hundred pounds in public subscriptions.

In 1856 Wills found work as a junior surveyor measuring out new leases, but science was still his major obsession. While many young men were out in the pubs and brothels of Ballarat, Wills was poring over books such as *Chambers' Mathematics* or *The Twelve Planispheres*. While they blew their wages on liquor and prostitutes, he collected astronomical tables and scientific instruments.

Wills' studies convinced him that it was science, not God, which would explain the universe and everything that happened within it. As his opinions about life crystallised, his letters home reveal a rather sanctimonious young man, quite sure of his beliefs, and not afraid to express them:

My dear Mother,
I have at length found time to write to you. You will no doubt say it ought to be a long letter after so much delay, but I am afraid you will be disappointed as it is quite against my nature; you know how I hate writing. In the last letter I received from you, you asked me to send Bessie any information I could, I can assure you I shall be most happy to do so and to encourage a taste for science as much as in my power.
I would recommend you to let the children learn drawing.

I do not mean merely sketching, but Perspective Drawing, with scale and compasses, for it is a very nice amusement, and they may some day find it very useful. There is another thing that would do them a deal of good if they should have a taste for it: this is Euclid. Not to learn it by heart, but to read it so as to understand it. In fact Mathematics generally, and Euclid and Algebra in particular, are the best things young people can learn, for they are the only things we can depend on as true. There is no disputing that Christians and all heathens and Mormons; all, no matter what their faith agree in Mathematics. In nothing else do all men agree, in nothing else can there be perfect truth. Of course I leave the Bible out of the question.

But I suppose I must tell you some thing about your undutiful Son. I am now learning surveying with Mr Fred Byerly—a nice man indeed. In fact I could not have had a better master had he been made to order, for he is a first rate Surveyor, and we are exactly *suited* as regards *general ideas*, which, to tell the truth, is a *very rare chance for me*. The only point we are at issue on is of course religious, as he believes rather strongly in Mesmerism and Clairvoyance. He belongs to the Sect they call New Church or Swedenborgians and certainly, leaving Clairvoyance and Spiritualism out of the question, I think theirs is the most rational and Charitable Religion I have met with. They are greatly opposed to the Lutheran doctrine of justification by faith alone.

But to resume, I am at present getting £150.00 a year and board, but I hope in twelve months to have a party of my own, and then I shall get double as much. Surveying is just the sort of life for me—nearly always in the bush marking out land for sale or surveying unknown parts. It is very different from Surveying in England.

Glenaruel is 15 miles from Ballarat. I saw Tom and the Doctor two or three days ago; they were quite well. I hope you are all so. Give my *love to all*; if I do not mention names no one can be jealous.

Wills' reward for his diligent scientific study came in 1858, when the head of Melbourne's new Flagstaff Observatory, Professor Georg Neumayer, offered him a post as an assistant. Neumayer was the archetypal eccentric scientist. His passion for measuring the earth's magnetic fields was so engrossing that he found it difficult to converse on any other subject. Evidently Wills found the subject just as fascinating because he moved into the observatory to spend more time on his experiments.

For two years Wills did almost nothing but work. Even his leisure time was devoted to improving his mind by taking brisk walks or swimming in the bracing waters of Port Phillip Bay. On occasion he allowed himself an outing to the opera and although he admitted he sometimes enjoyed dancing, none of his letters ever mentioned women. Instead his correspondence revolved around education, science, literature and above all religion, something he rejected ever more vehemently as his rationalist beliefs grew stronger.

Wills was thrilled when he discovered he had been chosen as the expedition's 'Surveyor and Astronomical Observer'. He told his mother:

> You need not work yourself up to such a state of excitement at the bare idea of my going, but should rather rejoice that the opportunity presents itself. The actual danger is nothing, and the positive advantages very great. Besides, my dear mother, what avails your faith if you terrify yourself about such trifles? Were we born, think you, to be locked up in comfortable rooms, and never to incur the hazard of mishap? If things were at the worst, I trust I could meet death with as much res-ignation as others, even if it came tonight. I am often disgusted at hearing young people I know, declare that they are afraid of doing this or that, because they might be killed. Were I in some of their shoes I should be glad to hail the chance of departing this life fairly in the execution of an hon-ourable duty.

The boy who scanned the horizon from the crow's nest of the *Janet Mitchell* was now about to cross an entire continent. Wills saw it as an opportunity to put all his scientific skills to the test and he was determined to conduct a thorough survey of the unknown country that lay ahead.

When he joined the expedition, Wills hardly fitted the classic image of a burly explorer. His friend Richard Birnie described him as having 'a light clean, agile frame…and a handiness such as is often seen in a young girl'. On the other hand Wills was 'plucky as a mastiff, high-blooded as a racer, enterprising but reflective, cool, keen and as composed as he is daring', with 'not a jot of effeminacy'. His professional colleagues knew him to be an intelligent, dependable, abstemious young man with a talent for surveying and a strong sense of duty. Without realising it, the Exploration Committee had chosen the perfect foil for Robert O'Hara Burke.

On the day of departure, Wills was oblivious to the pomp and ceremony going on around him in Melbourne's Royal Park. He spent several hours ensuring his equipment was properly loaded and arrived in Essendon a few hours later to find that Burke had already disappeared. His deputy George Landells was in charge of the camp. He shouted orders in his strong Northumberland accent and fussed around the camels. As well as the precious imported animals, Landells was also in charge of six other camels, purchased by the Exploration Committee on the spur of the moment for £50 from local circus impresario George Coppin. Untrained and undersized, they were already proving a hindrance to the smooth running of the expedition.

Landells had been a popular choice as deputy leader. As soon as the camels arrived he had become quite a celebrity, impressing everyone including Burke with his mastery of the animals and his ability to communicate with the Indian sepoys. Aware of his value, Landells played hard to get. Whilst declaring publicly that his

only desire was to ensure the expedition was a success, he submitted a long list of conditions to the Exploration Committee.
These included a £600 salary and a guarantee that he would be
'entirely charged with all matters relating to the treatment,
loading and working of the camels, and to be responsible for their
health'. In addition the expedition would have to carry 270 litres
of rum for the camels for 'medicinal purposes'.

The committee was in a difficult position. Landells had asked
for a salary £100 a year greater than Burke's and by insisting on
full control of the camels he was undermining the authority of
the expedition leader. Burke continued to support Landells and,
in a dramatic gesture, he refused to allow the committee to
increase his own salary to £600 as well. Under increasing pressure to appoint someone, the Exploration Committee capitulated
to Landells' financial demands and, although they could not officially grant him authority over the camels, they told the
Englishman in private that where the management of the animals
was concerned he could expect Burke to follow his advice
without question. By pandering to Landells' conditions, the committee implicitly admitted that Burke was incapable of
commanding all aspects of the enterprise. It broke the cardinal
rule of 'one ship, one captain' and placed the two inexperienced,
highly-strung men on a collision course from the beginning.

Using Landells to import camels to Victoria may have been a
daring move by the Royal Society but their introduction came at
a cost. Landells had trekked for thousands of kilometres in the
midst of the Indian Mutiny to select the best animals available.
He spent double his budget and arrived back in Melbourne seven
months later than planned. The delay meant that the expedition
had missed the cool winter season.

Conventional wisdom held that it was better to travel between
April and September when the temperatures were bearable and
water was more plentiful. But Landells was unconcerned. He

reassured the committee that his camels could perform in any climate, provided they were lightly loaded at the beginning of the journey to conserve their energy for the more demanding desert stages later on. The committee went along with his advice. In its haste to beat Stuart it ignored the wisdom of all Australia's most experienced explorers and ordered the expedition to head out into the unknown during the height of summer. Burke had neither the knowledge nor the patience to resist.

Landells brought six men with him on the expedition. The first, John Drakeford, was to serve as a camel handler and cook. He had worked in Africa and claimed that he could have explored with Livingstone but 'chose not to'. The second man, John King, was a small shy character, who had been discharged from the army in India for 'fever of a bad type'. No one was quite sure if he had completely recovered.

The other four were 'sepoy' camel handlers. Their exact origin and religion is confused by the fact that they were often classified as simply 'Indians' or 'Afghans', but the expedition's artist Ludwig Becker described Samla as a Hindu, Dost Mohomet and Esau Khan as Muslims, and Belooch as a Parsee. They were paid two shillings a week—less than a third of the wages of the other men.

It was late in the evening before the first of the wagons rolled into Essendon. Much of the gear that had been loaded just a few hours earlier now had to be unpacked all over again. Men grappled with unfamiliar equipment, struggled with unruly animals and discovered that everything took longer than they had anticipated. As darkness settled around the campsite, John Drakeford prepared supper. Soon large metal pots bubbled over campfires and the men began to line up with their tin plates and mugs.

It was Charles Ferguson's job to supervise the camp. Officers were not expected to trouble themselves with day-to-day matters, so a reliable foreman was required. 'Reliable' was hardly the first word that came to mind when describing Ferguson. 'Rogue' might have been more appropriate.

Ferguson was an American from Ohio. He had fought and plundered his way through the Californian goldfields before chasing his dreams to the diggings in Victoria. When Australia's most famous rebellion broke out at Eureka in 1854 as the miners revolted over the cost of their licences, Ferguson found himself being arrested and handcuffed to one of the ringleaders, Raffaello Carboni. Once he had talked his way out of the resulting criminal charges, Ferguson went on to dabble in cattle trading and horse breaking. A vocal critic of Australian cuisine, he later started up an American-style steak restaurant in Ballarat. Presumably the Australians were equally unimpressed with American food—the enterprise went bankrupt after just a few months. He found himself breaking horses once more, claiming he could 'reduce the wildest colt to perfect submission' within three hours.

Ferguson was in the goldfields of Kiandra in New South Wales when he heard of the Victorian Exploring Expedition. It is unclear just how he came to join the party since his autobiography is a dubious catalogue of extravagant tales. By his own account, he was so essential to the operation that both the Exploration Committee and Burke invited him to join up. Ferguson claimed that on his way to Melbourne, he fell and sprained his ankle just outside the town of Albury. Determined to complete his journey, he hijacked a cart at gunpoint and forced the driver to take him the rest of the way.

Whatever the reality or the lawfulness of Ferguson's travel arrangements, he turned up in the city eager to join the expedition. After bargaining hard over his pay, he signed up as foreman on a salary of £200 per annum. Not everyone was impressed with

Ferguson. Just before the expedition departed, one of Burke's fellow police officers warned him, 'You'll have to shoot that man yet.'

By any standards the expedition was a disparate group. Fletcher, Creber and Cowan had been sacked before the party left Royal Park, leaving five Irishmen, four 'Indians', three Englishmen, three Germans and an American. None had any real exploration experience. As the men began to size each other up, it became clear that the party was an uneasy fusion of personalities and motivations. Burke's mission to reach the north coast first had become an obsession. Just before leaving Melbourne, he told his friend Charles Saint, 'I have only one ambition, which is to do some deed before I die, that shall entitle me to have my name honourably inscribed on the page of history. If I succeed in that I care not what death, or when I die.'

In contrast, his surveyor William Wills along with the artist Ludwig Becker and the expedition doctor Hermann Beckler were expecting a genuine scientific examination of the continent. Landells cared little for either pursuit, as long as his own reputation remained intact, and it soon became clear he was volatile, stubborn and easily upset. Ferguson was a loose cannon and the remaining men were little more than enthusiastic amateurs. It was not a combination calculated to achieve that most elusive of exploration goals—a cohesive group of men who would pull together in times of trouble.

Oblivious to his responsibility for cultivating team spirit, Burke had already deserted his officers to satisfy a more powerful urge. As his men struggled to set up their first camp in Essendon, the Irishman galloped back to Melbourne to see Julia Matthews perform one last time at the Princess Theatre.

In the days before the expedition's departure, Burke's infatuation with Julia had only intensified. On 18 August 1860, he called together two of his confidants—Richard Nash, the government

storekeeper, and John Macadam, the Royal Society's secretary—
to ask them to witness the following document:

> This is my last will and testament. That I Robert O'Hara
> Burke do here direct Mr R. Nash in case of my death whilst in
> charge of the Expedition to pay all monies belonging to me
> (after just debts have been defrayed) to Miss Julia Matthews
> (Actress) now of Melbourne and presently engaged at the
> Princess Theatre in this colony. And all other of my effects to
> the said Julia Matthews.

For an unmarried gentleman to leave all his worldly goods to an
actress less than half his age was a shocking gesture. Only Burke's
closest friends including Sir William Stawell knew about the will,
and since it had the potential to cause considerable scandal they
all agreed not to discuss the matter further.

After the performance Burke went backstage to declare his
love yet again. He presented Julia with a miniature portrait of
himself and asked her to marry him, even offering to give up the
expedition or postpone its departure if she would become his
wife. To Burke's distress, Julia refused to give an immediate
answer but after further persuasion she agreed to reconsider the
offer once he returned. There was, at least, some hope.
Newspapers noted that it wasn't until the next morning that the
leader returned to his camp in Essendon. Robert O'Hara Burke
set out the next day with a lock of Julia's hair in a pouch around
his neck and reputedly with one of her tiny kid gloves in his
pocket. His quest had begun.

Seven

No Tea, No Fire

'I feel that failure would, to me, be ruin;
but I am determined to succeed, and count on
completing my work within a year at farthest.'
Robert O'Hara Burke

As Burke led his cavalcade through the towns and villages to the north of Melbourne, the 'Australian Sahara' must have seemed a million miles away. The rain was heavy and prolonged. Some days the hailstones were the size of billiard balls. At night, frost crept into the valleys, freezing the water in the billycans and leaving the camels dejected and shivering. The men huddled around their campfires, smoking and sipping tea—but no matter how close they sat to the flames, their flannel trousers and woollen tops never really dried out. The canvas tents were saturated, and their sodden equipment was twice as heavy to lift.

Every day the roads deteriorated and the wheel ruts deepened. While the camels slithered through the bogs, the wagons ground to a halt. The expedition was in black soil country, a seemingly innocuous geographical feature, which is still responsible for many an abandoned vehicle across Australia. In dry conditions the dark earth bakes like concrete but rain transforms it into a natural skating rink. In the worst areas, the wagon wheels disappeared and the drivers were forced to wade into the quagmire, dig the axles free and lay branches in the wheel ruts to provide traction. If that didn't work, they had to unhitch the horses from the wagons behind and attach them to the stranded vehicle. This back-breaking routine resulted in an average speed of between one and five kilometres an hour.

The camels' progress was faster but equally precarious. The horny pads on their feet were designed for deserts, not swamps, and they slipped constantly. Fearing for their safety, Landells ordered that they were not to be ridden, prompting Ludwig Becker to complain that 'it is very tedious and tiring work to lead on foot a camel through such ground and at the same time taking good care that no branch overhead or on the ground interferes with walking or rather skating'. On 22 August as the party headed for the village of Lancefield, sixty kilometres from Melbourne, Becker trudged for ten hours through the mud. That evening he wrote in his diary: 'No tea, no fire; we slept in the wet.'

Ludwig Becker had not expected to rip his hands to shreds leading camels and loading boxes each day. He was an officer, a biologist and a painter charged with recording the expedition's progress for posterity. He was also an early victim of the Royal Society's muddled objectives. Scientists and trailblazers tended not to mix. Even Captain James Cook struggled to contain his displeasure when he saw the botanist Joseph Banks heading for the *Endeavour* with trunks full of scientific instruments, an entourage of servants and a couple of pet greyhounds. Scientists travel slowly—their deviations infuriate the pioneers determined to conquer as much new territory as possible before the supplies run out. In general, the magnitude of an explorer's tolerance towards a scientist was inversely proportional to the hostility of the terrain being traversed. Augustus Gregory grew so frustrated with the botanist Ferdinand Mueller that he vowed never to take a scientist out in the field again.

With its enormous procession of wagons and camels, the Victorian Exploring Expedition had all the appearances of a genuine scientific survey party. Indeed, many Royal Society members were still under the impression that a thorough investigation of the continent was about to take place. Others realised that Burke's appointment as leader had already destroyed any veneer of scientific credibility. If it hadn't been for the Royal Society's German contingent, Burke would have dispensed with the scientists altogether. But as a compromise he agreed to take Ludwig Becker to serve as 'artist and naturalist' and Hermann Beckler, a doctor and amateur botanist who could fulfil a dual role.

Hermann Beckler was born in the Bavarian market town of Höchstät in 1828. After studying medicine in Munich, he arrived in Australia in 1856. Inspired by the travels of his compatriot Ludwig Leichhardt, Beckler dreamed of a career as a biologist

Hermann Beckler, doctor and botanical collector, feared that the expedition's scientific achievements would be 'few and ambiguous'.

and botanist. For many years he tried to establish a medical practice to fund his passion but he struggled to earn a living, let alone undertake any journeys of his own. After a poorly paid but otherwise rewarding stint collecting specimens for Melbourne's botanical gardens, Beckler secured the backing of Mueller and applied to join the expedition. He wrote in his application that, in addition to his duties as a medical officer, he 'would be gratified to serve further in the capacity of botanical collector'.

Beckler's appointment should have been straightforward but there was some anti-German feeling in the press at the time. The appointment of a foreigner 'bestows little credit upon the scientific qualifications of our own people' sniffed the *Leader*. Since Beckler couldn't afford a medical licence, he had to suffer the ignominy of having his abilities vetted by Professor McCoy from the Royal Society and Victoria's chief medical officer. Both pronounced him 'a well educated medical man' and the controversy subsided but it left Beckler in a defensive mood as he embarked on the expedition.

The only member of the Royal Society to join Burke's party was Ludwig Becker, the man who suggested all the leadership candidates should sit an 'exploring exam'. Born in Darmstadt in 1808, Becker was a charming eccentric who spent several years in the goldfields armed with a sketchpad and a pet bat. He was the kind of 'universal man' whose armoury of talents delighted friends like Lady Denison, the wife of Tasmania's lieutenant-governor:

He is a most amusing person, talks English badly but very energetically. I have sometimes great difficulty in keeping my countenance when I see him struggling between the rapidity of his ideas and the difficulty of giving them utterance, repeating to himself...and helping all out with an abundance of most expressive gesticulation; but I would not for the world let him see me laugh, poor man, for he is rather shy and sensitive; but with all that he is very pleasing. He is one of those universal geniuses who do anything; is a very good naturalist;

geologist etc., draws and plays and sings, conjures and ventril-
oquises and imitates the notes of birds so accurately that the
wild birds will come to him at the sound of the call. He is very
fond of children, amuses and astonishes us to a great extent by
his conjuring tricks and ventriloquism, and being very oddish-
looking besides, with a large red beard.

Becker might have been an entertaining genius but he was
always broke. He dabbled in the production of drawings and litho-
graphs for various scientific publications in Melbourne and,
when he got desperate made a little extra by drawing likenesses
and caricatures.

Burke was not impressed by Becker's character or his talent.
He saw the fifty-two-year-old German as an encumbrance foisted
on him by Mueller. After all, if a middle-aged scientist could
cross the continent, Burke could hardly claim it was a colossal
physical achievement. It was only the influence of Victoria's governor Sir Henry Barkly that persuaded Burke to accept the
appointment at all.

The Royal Society's instructions to the scientists were as
daunting as they were unrealistic. Hermann Beckler was expected
to keep a diary of all the flora he observed, collect specimens in
various stages of development, detail plants used by Aboriginal
tribes as food and medicine, and undertake as many side-trips as
possible to record the maximum number of new species. Ludwig
Becker was to sketch the general terrain (with particular reference to watercourses and mineral formations) and collect and
sketch specimens of all mammals, birds, fish and fossils found en
route. Presumably he was expected to forgo sleep—the instructions also suggested he should pay particular attention to
nocturnal mammals.

William Wills bore the heaviest burden. By day he was to
keep detailed records: of distance travelled, general terrain,
watercourses, water quality (including samples), geological

formations, soil types (including samples), and occurrence of minerals or gems (including samples). He was to sketch specimens, draw updated maps daily, measure compass variations and record meteorological conditions, including rainfall, temperature, wind speeds, whirlwinds, thunderstorms, dust storms, mirages, refraction and magnetic observations. By night, while Becker was up collecting bats, Wills was expected to make astronomical observations including the 'paths of meteors' and the 'patterns of twinkling stars'.

Just in case Wills found himself with an idle moment, he also

Ludwig Becker was appointed against Burke's wishes as naturalist and artist. Forced to work in secret, he nevertheless produced a series of exquisite paintings and sketches.

had to navigate the party across the continent. He was, after all, the only member of the party fully conversant with taking star sightings and the only man practised in using a compass and sextant. Undeterred by this impossible workload, Wills soon devised a way of working as he rode:

> Riding on the camels is a much more pleasant process than I anticipated, and for my work I find it much better than riding on horseback. The saddles, as you are aware, are double, so I sit on the back portion behind the hump, and pack my instruments in front. I can thus ride on, keeping my journal and making calculations; and need only stop the camel when I want to take any bearings carefully, but the barometers can be read and registered without halting. The animals are very quiet, and easily managed, much more so than horses.

Not everyone found the camels so appealing. According to Charles Ferguson the merest sniff of the new creatures caused havoc along the route:

> The caravan caused no little commotion in traversing the settled portion of the country embraced in the first few hundred miles. Cattle and horses along the route stampeded from terror at the sight, and even at the smell of the camels, wafted on the breeze in advance of their appearance. It was said that some wild horses on the ranches ran thirty miles before stopping, such is their instinctive aversion to and terror of the camel.

With the rain continuing to pelt down, no one was giving much thought to science. On the third day one of the sepoys, Samla, resigned. As a Hindu he was not allowed to eat the salt beef that was a staple of the explorers' diet. The poor fellow had suffered in silence for two days on bread and water, before asking Landells if he could be discharged. Ludwig Becker watched as Samla 'touched with his fingers mother Earth and then his forehead, and blessing Mr Landells and the men near him, this good man went his way towards Melbourne, his eyes full of tears'. Four of the original recruits had now left. Burke's response was to hire general labourers on a casual basis. Three men, Brooks, Lane and McIlwaine joined the party after it left Melbourne.

As the expedition inched north, the wagons broke down daily and the semi-submersible dray developed 'an alarming lean to the right'. During the first week alone, it cost £83 in repairs. Everyone who watched the expedition totter past reached the same conclusion: Burke's party had too many supplies and not enough transport. The expedition carried eight tonnes of food but this was not an excessive amount considering it had to last nineteen men between eighteen months and two years. Although Burke had the final say, it was Ferdinand Mueller who drew up the original list of supplies, based on a formula devised by Augustus Gregory. He had discovered that the minimum daily ration required to keep his men healthy was: 500 grams of salt beef or pork, 500 grams of flour, twenty-one grams of coffee or seven grams of tea, eighty-five grams of sugar and a small measure of vinegar and lime juice to prevent scurvy. Mueller's list allowed for much the same nutritional intake but with more variety.

It was the other twelve tonnes that really slowed things down. The mounds of useless equipment were the result of an inexperienced commander with a free hand and an open chequebook. Were twelve sets of dandruff brushes and four enema kits really necessary?

Stores had been ordered in such an ad hoc manner that no one could be sure the expedition had what was essential. Even the prisoners at Melbourne's Pentridge jail were set to work making clothing, harnesses and ironmongery. In addition, there were six tonnes of firewood, 200 kilograms of medications for the camels and horses and enough ammunition to win a small war. Luxuries were well catered for: a large bathtub, an oak and cedar table with two oak stools and forty-five yards of gossamer for fly veils. Yet the party took just two sets of field glasses, two watches and only twelve water bottles.

The most successful explorers keep meticulous records of their stores—their diaries are peppered with calculations about what remains and how long it will last—but Burke did not have the patience for such detailed analysis. Even before the expedition left, he turned the management of the stores over to Hermann Beckler, who was appalled at the indiscriminate acquisition of so much equipment:

> In every respect the preparations reflected the grandiose scale intended for the expedition, but, with the exception of our victuals, our requirements were ordered and purchased on a scale out of all proportion to our means of transport. We could not tell whether this or that article was necessary or superfluous…when I returned to the hotel where Mr Burke and I were staying, he was in the habit of saying: 'What are we going to do with all this? How are we going to move it?'

It had been intended to convey the bulk of the stores by ship via Adelaide and the Darling River as far as Menindee. Royal Society member and steamboat pioneer Captain Francis Cadell offered to provide the service free of charge. This generous proposal would dispense with the need for wagons and save the horses and camels for the more arduous terrain further north.

But just forty-eight hours before the expedition was due to depart, Burke overturned the plan. He decided that transporting the supplies via Adelaide would give the South Australians an opportunity to interfere and delay proceedings. Also, Cadell had supported Warburton in the leadership battle and Burke didn't want to entrust the stores to a staunch opponent. The alternative was to carry everything by wagon at vast expense. Beckler protested, yet Burke was adamant. He wanted full control and he was prepared to drag twenty tonnes of equipment along

750 kilometres of unmade roads to get it. Every day for the next fifty-seven days, the men of the Victorian Exploring Expedition had to live with Burke's decision, which meant more work, more mud and less sleep.

After the first few chaotic days a routine began to emerge. Each morning the men woke at dawn to the sound of a Chinese gong echoing through the gum trees. They crawled from their clammy woollen bedrolls and stoked up the campfire. As smoke filled the air, tea was brewed and they breakfasted on hunks of damper filled with salt beef. If the horses and camels had been tethered or kept in paddocks the night before, little time was wasted catching them, but if they had been hobbled or let loose, it might require a walk of a few kilometres to recapture them before loading could begin.

As the rain dripped through the trees, the damp leather harnesses were stiff and slippery, and the buckles difficult to tighten. It took between two and three hours to organise the packs, then hoist them onto the horses and camels using a pulley system slung over a tree branch. Often it was 9.30 before the main party set off, with Burke and the horses up ahead, followed by Landells and his camels, and the wagons grinding along behind.

The party travelled for up to twelve hours a day, coaxing their animals along the rutted tracks and stopping only for lunch and the odd smoko. The men were exhausted by the time they reached camp but they still had a couple of hours work ahead, feeding and watering the animals, unloading the supplies and mending broken equipment. By nightfall the tents were pitched, the campfire was crackling, the stew was bubbling and loaves of fresh damper sat swelling in the camp ovens. The officers retired to their tents to write up their journals and the men sat in the flickering light, smoking and telling yarns.

After a week, the expedition had only covered 100 kilometres and was camped at the hamlet of Mia Mia. Since it was a Sunday and the wagons were still bogged some kilometres behind, Burke allowed a rare day of rest. Always anxious to avoid paperwork, he gave Becker the task of sorting out the expedition's accounts. The artist spent the day crouched in his tent copying out receipts and fending off curious spectators.

For many small towns, the arrival of the expedition was the most exciting event in years. Settlers travelled from far and wide to inspect the glamorous cast of characters they had read so much about in the newspapers. One spectator reported:

> As we approached the Mia Mia hotel, we saw a long line of strange looking animals squatted alongside a fence, with their legs doubled under them, and looking for all the world like so many immense fowls, trussed for cooking. Occasional peculiar snorts emitted by the animals had a strange effect on our horses, and though we had ridden them so hard already, they seemed quite disposed to turn round and rush home again.

The next day, as the explorers attempted to strike camp, an even larger crowd of 'bedazzled spectators' gathered to watch them set off towards Swan Hill. That day Hermann Beckler noticed for the first time that the countryside was changing:

> There is nothing more interesting than this sharp frontier between the coastal land and the inland, continental regions. The alteration in the terrain, often quite sudden, shows such an extreme change in physiognomy that one might well believe one was no longer in the same country…In a word one now finds oneself in the inland, and however far one penetrates into the heart of the continent, the landscape of the coastal fringe is left behind forever.

The small farms gave way to the more ancient panorama of the Terrick-Terrick Plains. Becker was now in open country:

> The effect when one sees extensive plains for the first time is somewhat very peculiar: the plain looks like a calm ocean with

green water; the horizon appears to be much higher than the point the spectator stands on, the whole plain looks concave. On you go, miles and miles, a single tree, a belt of timber appeared at the horizon affected by the mirage; you reach that belt of small trees, a Wallaby, a kangerooh-rat disturbs for a moment the monotony, and a few steps further on you are again on the green calm ocean.

The expedition may have presented an impressive tableau as it marched across the plains, but tensions were already apparent. The dynamics of a successful outfit depend to a great extent on its leader. If the commander establishes a routine and a realistic set of responsibilities during the early stages, each member remains motivated while they learn about the party's strengths and weaknesses. Cohesion and camaraderie follow, establishing a valuable reserve of goodwill for harsher times later on.

Nurturing this delicate process is difficult at the best of times and, in the case of Burke's party, the Exploration Committee had already planted the seeds of dissension by giving Landells 'special responsibility' for his 'ships of the desert'. Burke had little patience with either the camels or the scientists but provided they maintained a reasonable pace he was happy to ignore them as far as possible. He rode on ahead, leaving Landells, Wills, Beckler and Becker to travel on foot dragging their reluctant animals through the mud.

With the rain running down their shirts and little communication from their leader, morale sagged and feelings of resentment began to germinate. Burke aggravated the situation by retiring to the nearest pub or farmhouse in the evenings, instead of camping near his men. It was Landells and Ferguson who dealt with the everyday problems of loose horses, stray camels and overloaded wagons.

Landells was worried that Burke was in too much of a hurry. The camels had little time to graze and even at this early stage the heavy conditions were beginning to take their toll. Beckler confirmed his fears. 'Within five days the camels began to show the effects of continual rain, the gradual change of feed and camping in the open. They developed catarrhs and diarrhoea and their faeces contained their hitherto customary feed, gram [an Indian fodder], in an undigested state.'

The problem was that Burke had so much to prove. The Melbourne newspapers had jeered at his lack of experience and as the expedition passed near Bendigo, the *Advertiser* increased his sense of insecurity by reserving its only complimentary remarks for the noble shape of his head. Landells was singled out as a real leader:

> Mr Landells is a quiet unassuming man, who improves very much upon acquaintance. He is of course the most capable man of the party, from the extensive experience of travelling in India and his thorough acquaintance of the camels upon whom the success of the expedition greatly depends, and he seems to be the only man of the lot thoroughly at ease. A robust man with a large dark beard and black peaked California hat, and with the air of a leader about him, is pointed out to us as Mr Burke. He has a large well-shaped head, which is not unlike that of the lamented Leichhardt.

That night the town's dignitaries threw a party for the explorers, and Burke took the opportunity to defend himself, hoping that 'the public would be patient and allow them full and fair trial, for success could not be at once attained in such an enterprise'. He and Landells retired at ten o'clock but several of the men stayed on drinking to 'make a night of it'. Packing the camels took a little longer the next morning.

So far the reception from settlers along the way had been friendly, although not everyone appreciated the camels' tendency to scatter livestock and the wagons' capacity to destroy the flooded roads. Word had spread that Burke was a man in a hurry with 'money to burn' so the locals retaliated by charging outrageously for fodder and accommodation en route. Costs began to escalate as goods became more expensive to the north of Bendigo. Suddenly the settlements began to thin out, leaving just a scattering of shepherds' huts and a few Aboriginal camps. Hermann Beckler climbed a small hill to take in the surreal beauty of the natural landscape:

> It was a magnificent panorama which affected the observer not by any delightful or varied detail, but by the horizontal areas of various gentle hues and unbroken, one could almost say mathematical, lines. At a distance of about six miles to the south-south-west lay an isolated cone of rock called The Pyramid; a well chosen name. On the other side of the Pyramid the country was divided horizontally by lines of trees and in the far distance lay Mount Korong, hardly distinguishable in the haze. To the north-west, the unbroken line of a distant horizon defeated the eye that tried to contain it. This expanse looked arid and burnt. Towards the horizon a sombre grey-blue colour covered most of the land. Closer to us, the yellow-brown earth was spotted with countless small, dark bushes and the remnant stumps of burnt grass-trees. Here, too, the plain was divided into horizontal strips by narrow lines of low scrub whose effect made the expanse look even greater. The play of sunlight and clouds produced wonderful effects on the wide plain; light and shadow alternated in quick succession as in a diorama. Miles of land were lit up, only to be cast into deepest shadow within a few seconds. Huge clouds sailed across the sky and their shadows rolled over the land like the tatters of a gigantic, torn veil.

The weather deteriorated again and Burke was forced to schedule another rest day after the entire expedition became saturated on a thirty-four-kilometre trek towards Mount Hope. The wagons got stuck and, on his way back to retrieve them, Charles Ferguson got lost, fell into a pit and knocked himself unconscious. It was several hours before he came to and managed to rejoin the expedition.

When the bedraggled party arrived close to dark at John Holloway's station to the north of Pyramid Hill, Becker found to his relief that extensive preparations had been made for their arrival. 'The comfort our inner and outer man experienced was very great, the hospitable roof protected each of us against the all night lasting torrents.' Beckler helped to revive the animals and noted that 'Landells gave the camels tidy doses of rum to warm them; the expedition members too partook and enjoyed the stimulant with rather more enthusiasm than the camels!'

The next day the scientists caught up on their journals while Burke entertained his hosts at the piano with a selection of love songs he had learned from Julia Matthews. That evening the god-fearing Holloways insisted on a small service to pray for the expedition's safe return. Mrs Holloway presented Burke with some religious tracts and Wills seized the opportunity to return the compliment by ridding himself of his Bible.

Three days later, on 6 September, the party reached Swan Hill on the Murray River, 320 kilometres from Melbourne. Here Burke intended to rest for a couple of days and prepare for the next leg of the journey towards Menindee, but his composure was shaken when he arrived to find an urgent telegram waiting for him. It warned that a warrant was being sought for his arrest.

Eight
Ruinous Work

'He who does not travel does not know the value of men.'
Moorish proverb

Nearly all Swan Hill's 140 residents turned out to greet the explorers as they rode in triumph past the town's twelve buildings. Burke's euphoria was short-lived. He dismounted to find the telegram threatened him with imprisonment for a dishonoured personal cheque for £96. A bounced cheque was a serious matter. It could endanger Burke's standing with the Royal Society and particularly with Sir William Stawell. In panic, he scribbled two letters to his friend Richard Nash, apologising and explaining that he had not expected 'that infernal cheque' to be presented for at least six months. Burke asked Nash to stand security for his debt (which he did), but since his letters would take several days to reach Melbourne he had no way of knowing if the matter had been resolved.

Swan Hill was not a happy town for explorers. Thomas Mitchell named it in temper after the birds kept him awake at night. Burke's stay was plagued by indecision. He fretted about the cheque and worried that gossip about the expedition's sluggish progress and soaring costs would find its way back to Melbourne. The wagons were still three days adrift, their drivers were demanding more pay by the hour and Burke was becoming more and more disorganised. Charles Ferguson remarked later:

> He was kind and generous to a fault but let anything happen out of the routine he was confused, then excited until finally he would lose all control of his better judgement. Then again

when he had made up his mind to do something he never considered the consequences. He had thorough discipline and no one dared to presume to contradict him.

The arrival of the Royal Society's Georg Neumayer only increased Burke's paranoia. The professor joined the explorers in Swan Hill as part of his survey of the earth's magnetism. He intended to travel with the party towards Menindee, a small settlement by the Darling River.

During the next five days, Burke wrote four dispatches to the committee, each one more defensive than the last. Desperate to prove he was economising he announced that 'any man in future joining the party will supply themselves with clothing at their own cost and any additional article of clothing requested by any member of the party will deducted from their pay'. The best-equipped expedition of its age was now asking its men to pay for their own trousers.

Nearly three weeks into the journey, Burke began to realise that his party was being crippled by the weight of its supplies. He pondered his dilemma. The committee was insisting that he get rid of the wagons as soon as possible but, having refused Cadell's offer of river transport, how else was he to carry all his supplies to the proposed depot at Cooper Creek?

Having placed himself in an impossible situation, Burke needed to cover his back. He called his officers together to secure their support, then wrote to the committee justifying their 'joint decision' to retain the wagons as far as Menindee:

> I am well aware that our baggage is cumbersome and that a time will I hope soon come when we shall be obliged to have the greater part of it behind us, but to do so now, before having established our Depot upon the Darling, where every article may be of the greatest service, would I think be a most dangerous injudicious proceeding.
>
> If I had lost this opportunity of conveying the stores, it

would have retarded the progress of the expedition and might prove fatal to it; it would be impossible for us to move them without assistance; within the next month or six weeks the road will be impracticable for drays for want of feed and water and will continue so in all probability for the next eight or ten months.

The idea of a depot on the Darling River was new. In suggesting it, Burke was deviating from his instructions to form the expedition's base camp at Cooper Creek. So was the Darling camp an addition to the original plan or a replacement for it? Burke most likely realised that it would be as much as he could do to drag his entire outfit as far as Menindee. After that, he would have to improvise.

While Burke scrambled to protect his reputation, the rest of the party enjoyed Swan Hill's hospitality. The camels were the star attractions, especially amongst the local Aboriginal children. They seemed 'intoxicated with joy and excitement' at the sight of the 'big emus with four legs' and scampered about 'with the delight of school children at their first circus'. The expedition had been travelling through the territories of Aboriginal people including the Boonwurrung, Yorta-Yorta, Taungurong, Wadi-Wadi and the Woiworung. Only Ludwig Becker paid them any attention. He noted down scraps of their languages, recorded their traditional songs and documented the local customs he saw along the way:

Several natives sat on the ground, among them was a couple of women whose faces were painted in such a manner as to give the head the appearance of a skull, when seen from a distance; round the eyes was drawn with white paint, a circle, an inch broad, and the hair of one woman tied up closely and covered with a piece of cloth, while the other lubra had her hair painted or rather smeared over with the same white colour, giving her head a still more skull-like appearance. I found that this mode of painting the faces is a habit met with as far as the Darling; it is a sign of mourning for relations...

The expedition's last day in Swan Hill, 11 September, turned into something of a party. Picnics were laid out near the camp and the braver souls took rides on the camels. It was late afternoon before they made it to the Murray River pursued by a cheering crowd. That evening Beckler declared that their riverside campsite in the heart of Wemba-Wemba Aboriginal country was the most beautiful so far:

> The delightful thing in this landscape is the graceful grouping, the roundness and opulence of the trees and shrubs. The peace, the tranquillity that is poured over this landscape and the parklike neatness of the whole area so satisfies our innermost souls that we revel in beholding it. Not one barren spot, no stony ground (scarcely even a solitary stone), no tree skeletons, barely even single dead tree-trunk disturb the impression of a landscape filled with exuberant life.

Swan Hill seemed reluctant to relinquish the explorers to the desert—the next morning there was another rowdy farewell as the party was bombarded with old boots and handfuls of rice for good luck. One observer noticed that Burke wiped his eyes and seemed 'visibly affected by the genuine kindness he had met with from all ranks'.

The party that crossed the Murray was very different from the one that had rolled out of Melbourne three weeks earlier. Only fourteen of the original nineteen members remained. At Swan Hill, Burke discharged the sepoy Esau Khan, who had become too ill to work. He also let go Brooks, Lane and John Polongeaux, a Frenchman, whom he had enthusiastically hired near Bendigo a few days earlier. Four new men joined the expedition. Alexander MacPherson was a blacksmith and saddler, William Hodgkinson a journalist, and Charley Gray an ex-sailor.

Robert Bowman had previously accompanied both Augustus and Charles Gregory on expeditions in northern and central Australia. Bowman had tried to join the expedition in Melbourne. Aside from the Gregory brothers he was probably the most experienced explorer in Australia and a valuable addition to Burke's outfit.

With so many people coming and going, it was difficult to establish any sense of unity. In particular, the men disliked their high-handed foreman Charles Ferguson. Sensing that there was an 'underhand current' working against him, the American made things worse when he publicly dismissed his subordinates as 'knowing nothing of hard work...ignorant of bush life, and conseqently wholly unfit for an expedition of any kind'. When Ferguson began to complain about his pay, Burke retaliated by attempting to reduce his salary even further. A row ensued in which the foreman threatened to resign. Burke backed down. Ferguson stayed on.

It took the remodelled party three days to reach the hamlet of Balranald in New South Wales. The journey had been dogged by bad weather yet again and the roads were now so bad that the wagon drivers insisted their loads be reduced or their horses would collapse in their harnesses. The result was an impromptu public auction. After hauling his supplies at great expense for more than 400 kilometres, Burke chose to sell off a valuable selection of his equipment in the middle of nowhere. Some things (two full sets of blacksmiths' tools, assorted firearms, the camel stretcher) had always been superfluous but many explorers would have regarded other items as essential. In particular, supplies of lime juice were jettisoned, which had been purchased to prevent scurvy.

To cut costs further, Burke decided to discharge six more men at Balranald, yet for all his military training, he had trouble confronting anyone with bad news. Wills recognised that he was 'human and tender hearted as a woman' but hid it with a 'brusquerie wholly external'. Instead of paying the men and letting them go, Burke fudged the issue. He told Becker, Ferguson, Brahe, Langan, McIlwaine and Belooch to stay behind at Balranald, assuring them he would send for them later on.

For several hours the camp was on the brink of mutiny. Ferguson challenged his leader to a fight and had to be restrained. At first, Burke insisted that he wanted the American to stay, but later he called Ferguson aside and told him, 'I cannot on my conscience deceive you. You surmised right; it was just as you thought. I intended to leave you before but I could not tell you of it.' Burke then offered to retain Ferguson and Langan at reduced salaries. When they refused, he issued their wage cheques—but since shopkeepers and bank-tellers knew that the expedition was in financial trouble, no one was willing to cash them.

Burke must have changed his mind again because a few hours later Becker, Brahe and Belooch rejoined the main party and no more was said about their dismissal. He was, however, determined to rid himself of Ferguson, Langan and McIlwaine, who chased the party for thirty-five kilometres to beg for enough money to return to Melbourne. When the trio turned south, they were united in their threats to sue Burke for wrongful dismissal. Revealing a prodigious talent for denial, Burke wrote later to the committee: 'In conclusion, I beg leave to state that the best possible spirit animates both officers and men, and that we shall do everything in our power to bring the enterprise to a successful conclusion.'

This debacle did nothing to improve the Irishman's reputation. In Balranald, the general opinion was that he was 'thoroughly deficient in experience'. Settlers noticed that 'Camping places were not selected until after dark, sometimes till after midnight, when it could not be seen whether there might be any food for the cattle [camels] or not. At every camp, lots of tools, axes and spades were left.' As the expedition left for Menindee, Beckler confided that 'Mr Burke became somewhat impatient at this point, both with the slowness and with the very difficult progress of the wagons. He therefore decided to travel ahead with the expedition party and the camels and leave the wagons to follow under my supervision.'

The plan was a disaster. Against local advice, Burke decided that instead of following the recognised track from Balranald to the Darling River, he would cut across country. Beckler was exasperated. 'Why did we have to experiment just here? It was the "shortest route", the straight line that once again led Mr Burke into temptation.' Burke's route took his party across 'mallee country', a vast undulating tangle of rusty sandhills, anchored by thousands of distinctive multi-stemmed mallee trees. Locals commented that 'no one knows who invented the mallee, but the devil is strongly suspected'.

The terrain was monotonous and confusing. Beckler branded it a 'wild wasteland...oppressive to the highest degree' and 'hell on earth' for the wagon drivers:

> The misery for the horses really began at this point...they were required to draw their wagons through wild desert and through deep loose sand and pathless mallee scrub...The wagon wheels sank deep into the soil as did the horses and we were often forced to come to the aid of one or the other half-buried wagon wheel with a shovel. After minutes of gradually increasing shouting and yelling, often to the point of despair, the horses were perhaps able to pull together, only then to stop exhausted again a few paces further on. The wagoners all became so hoarse that they could hardly utter an audible word.

While Burke rode on ahead with Wills, the wagons crawled through the heavy sand at just one or two kilometres an hour. The men were so worn out they could barely be bothered to set up camp. One night, a sudden thunderstorm forced Ludwig Becker to share a tent 'rather too temporarily pitched' with Hermann Beckler. When a strong wind sprang up the next morning:

> The first gust carried our tent into the air, together with the two saplings we had used as supporters—it came down again and fell right over me; my head had a narrow escape from being crushed as one of the poles fell alongside of it. The Doctor found himself in the open air and I was nearly suffocated under the pressure of the canvas before I could extricate myself. The scene was one of great confusion, at the same time to me so ludicrous that I could not help laughing, while the Doctor held a different opinion.

By 25 September, just over a week after leaving Balranald, the draught horses were too exhausted to go any further. They were unhitched and driven on to a waterhole, leaving the wagons abandoned in the scrub. Far from saving time, Burke's 'short cut' meant that the forward party had to traverse the mallee country three times in order to rescue the wagons.

No one was surprised when Georg Neumayer announced his intention to return to Melbourne. He had finished collecting his 'magnetic data' and was anxious to return to the city. Since the professor had ridden on ahead for much of the time, he avoided the fiasco of the stricken wagons and formed a largely positive (if misguided) impression of the expedition's prospects. In fact Burke, Wills and Neumayer had become increasingly friendly as they rode across the mallee country together. On 28 September, as Neumayer was packing up, the three men sat up into the night, discussing the possibility of sending a relief vessel to the north coast to meet the expedition. It was agreed that Burke would write to the committee from Menindee if he decided such a ship were necessary.

Despite their new closeness, Burke was relieved at Neumayer's departure. No sooner had he disappeared over the horizon than Burke started to dismantle any remaining vestige of scientific credibility surrounding the expedition. Free at last to do as he pleased without reports being taken back to the Royal Society, Burke confronted the scientists on 1 October. It was the mild-mannered Becker who bore the brunt of his dissatisfaction:

> Before we marched Mr Burke told us that, from today, we had to walk inch for inch, all the way up to the Gulf of Carpentaria, as all the camels and horses were required to carry stores etc. To Dr Beckler and me he said: 'now Gentleman from this time you have to give up your scientific investigations but to work like the rest of the men, as long as you are on the road or not free from camp-duties; at the same time you have to limit your materials and other things required for your investigating, to the utmost, in numbers as well as in weight and size of the parcel.'

Burke told all his men that henceforth they would be allowed just fifteen kilograms of personal equipment each. For the scientists, this meant leaving behind nearly all their instruments—from now on they were little more than glorified camel hands. Hermann Beckler trimmed his medical supplies to a minimum and reduced his personal belonging to the following items:

> Kit bag made of oil-cloth ½ kilogram
> 1 pair of shoes 1½ kilograms
> 3 flannel shirts 1½ kilograms
> 2 pairs of flannel trousers 1½ kilograms
> 1 pair of canvas trousers 1 kilogram
> Bedding, that is:
> 1 double woollen blanket 3½ kilograms
> 1 piece of oil cloth 2 kilograms
> 1 poncho 4 kilograms
> Assorted items:
> Shoes, socks, handkerchiefs, towels, books 4½ kilograms
> Total 20 kilograms

Then, Burke turned on Landells. He insisted that in order to lighten the wagons, each camel would have to carry an extra 180 kilograms. With heavy rain and thunderstorms drenching the campsite, the stores were reorganised yet again. The new regime brought nothing but misery for Becker:

Last night was very cold with hoarfrost in the morning. Having had no sleep for the last two nights but plenty of hard work during the day-time I felt somewhat unwell, however I began work as usual at 5 o'clock in the morning. We commenced saddling and loading the camels and were ready to start by 11 o'clock. As I have said already 400 lbs was nearly each camel's share, mostly consisting of bags of flower and sugar; each of these bags weighed 200 lb, and as each camel had to carry two of them which being fastened together before they were put on the pack-saddle, it is easy to understand that 4 men were required to lift this weight into the air and then let it carefully down on the camel's back; this had to be done a dozen times. It is the most exhausting kind of labour and the new canvas bags soon told upon our fingernails—half of mine were split and bent.

None of us was told how far or how long we had this day, or rather the rest of this day, to travel, and as nothing but tea and biscuit with a little cold mutton was served out early in the morning, and we had no food before starting, I thought, in a few hours we would halt on some waterhole to take there the required nourishment—but nothing of that kind was allowed: we marched on without rest and food for twenty-four miles over high hills covered with a deep, loose sand, and arrived at night at a plain containing some water. I had no food for nearly three days; partly in consequence of my own indisposition, and no sleep for two nights, and had to pull, in the heat of the day, three camels for 24 miles through the most wretched country—it was quite natural I should feel weak. It was about sunset when I asked Mr Landells to stop only 5 minutes so as to be able to recover myself as I felt like fainting. Mr Landells answered: I cannot stop; loaded camels won't rise again when once allowed to lie down; give me your camels, take rest if you require it, and follow at leisure. Fortunately for me that, when leaving the camp, I had picked up a thrown-away empty gunpowder flask, large enough to hold 4 ounces of water, which I had found at noon in a small clay-pan, and these few drops now enabled me to reach Mr Landells camp just in time to hear the order 'now then Mr Becker, look sharp, unload your camels!' and so I did of course.

Becker's suffering was no accident. In a letter to his friend Frederick Standish, Burke revealed:

You should have seen old B——'s face upon my announcing that all the officers would have to act as working men, and that we shall only carry 30 lb weight of baggage for each man. Loading four camels and then marching 20 miles is no joke. The first two days of it nearly cooked poor B——, and I think he will not be able to stand it much longer.

Burke ordered Landells not to let Becker ride at all, but to 'walk him until he gave in', and as part of his cruel campaign, he also barred him from any scientific activities:

Now a direct order was given by Mr Burke, that I had to give up all scientific observations until further orders.—To obey these different commands I was obliged to use the night. When all in the camp were asleep or at rest, I sat them up writing or sketching till midnight; This sort of work robbed me night after night three hours sleep and many times I slept in 24 hours only four. If you further consider that in consequence of the hard and rough work I had to perform during day-time my finger and finger-nails were in a pitiable condition, it is easily understood that under these circumstances pursuing science is rather a heavy task. However, I did what I could and not less.

A beleaguered Ludwig Becker refused to give up. Despite the

'ruinous work' attending the camels, he still managed to complete seven beautiful sketches on his way to the Darling. He had become the unwitting object of a power struggle between Burke and Landells that was fuelled by ignorance and mismanagement. As the expedition approached the Darling River, it threatened to blow the party apart.

George Landells was incensed that the camels were fully loaded before the expedition had even reached the edge of the desert. According to Beckler:

> Landells' basic principle was to watch over and care for the camels as long as possible and not to over burden them, in order to have them as strong and fresh as possible when forced marches, principally resulting from lack of water, would become necessary. This strategy was, without doubt, correct. However, Burke was not just impatient with the progress of the expedition in general but, as he often complained to me, with the camels in particular. Because until now they had run away frequently, because they had moved more slowly than the horses and because they naturally took a greater length of time to load, he no longer placed much confidence in them.

Burke's hostility towards the camels led to a shift in alliances. Landells was left to his own devices and at the same time, both Becker and Beckler begin to mention that 'Mr Wills was left in charge' of certain matters. Burke was sidelining his deputy and confiding more and more in his surveyor.

Late on 2 October the expedition reached Bilbarka on the Darling River. Here Burke learned that a steamer, the *Moolgewanke*, was heading north to Menindee. Better still, it was owned by a certain Captain Johnston and had nothing to do with Burke's enemy Francis Cadell. Seizing the opportunity to rid himself of 'those accursed impediments', the wagons, Burke ordered his men to prepare the stores so that eight tonnes of equipment could be loaded onto the steamer. While this was being done, Burke continued to bicker with his deputy, sending ripples of tension running through the camp. Their latest disagreement centred on the 270 litres of rum that Landells had insisted on bringing as medicine for the camels.

Modern camel experts dismiss the idea of rum as a camel pick-me-up, but there is a story often told in Menindee that Landells wanted the liquor to preserve the camels' feet. It is known that urine with a high alcohol content stiffens leather, and it may have been that the camel driver intended his men to drink the rum and then use their urine to toughen the animals' feet before they reached the stony desert regions. A less elaborate explanation suggests Landells brought the rum so he could sell it on the black market en route.

Whether their urine was put to good use or not, several members of the expedition had already experimented enthusiastically with the rum's restorative properties. Then on 7 October a group of shearers from the nearby Phelps sheep station broke into the expedition's store and helped themselves to as much liquor as they could drink. Stories of drunkenness made their way back to Melbourne and into the *Age*: 'It seems that, among the other bad habits acquired by contact with human beings, the camels are addicted to that of tippling raw spirits, and they have a special liking for rum.' Burke was furious. He confronted Landells and demanded that the rum be left behind. 'Early in the day I heard Mr Burke talking, in front of his tent, very loud to Mr Landells;' Becker wrote, 'the nature or the object of that communication seemed to me to be a disagreeable one to both of them.' Burke accused Landells of pampering the camels, slowing down the expedition and constantly offering the wrong advice. Landells stormed off, saying Burke was a madman who would get them all killed:

> His conduct throughout has displayed such want of judgement, candour, and decision, as at once to destroy my entire

confidence and respect. Indeed, that conduct has been altogether of such an extraordinary character, that I have on several occasions grave doubts about his sanity. His temper was quite ungovernable. He usually carried loaded firearms, and I often was fearful that he would use them dangerously while in a passion.

Accounts differ on how the quarrel was resolved but, whatever the details, the result was melodramatic and undignified. According to Landells, Burke burst into tears and begged his deputy to stay, saying, 'My God! I never thought you would leave me, as I have great dependence in you. Come on: I hope none of the men have seen this.' According to Burke, Landells wanted to return to Melbourne, claiming he had only ever agreed to go as far as the Darling. According to Wills, Landells maintained he had a 'secret agreement' with the committee and would continue only if he had complete control over the camels. When Burke threatened to withhold his pay for 'disgraceful behaviour', Landells backed down and agreed to stay on.

Wills' prominent role in the proceedings revealed his growing influence on the management of the expedition. The surveyor respected Landells' work with the camels but nevertheless decided he was:

nothing of a gentleman, either in manners or feeling...sentimental, good natured, more particularly towards dumb animals, and, as a natural concomitant selfish in the extreme, mildly persevering, and perseveringly mild; but, at the same time, he must always make people dislike him, from his unmannerly diffidence and want of substance.

While the camp seethed with gossip, the camels, all of them, took it into their heads to vanish into the bush. Hodgkinson, King, McDonough and Dost Mohomet set out to find them, but only succeeded in losing themselves. Landells and Belooch then failed to locate either the men or the camels, forcing Burke and Becker to wander around lighting fires and sounding the Chinese gong to guide everyone home. King, McDonough, Dost Mohomet, Landells and Belooch returned that night but Hodgkinson did not come back until noon the next day. No one found the camels.

This enraged Burke so much that he considered abandoning the camels altogether. Becker reported a further series of fierce arguments between the leader and his deputy but was reluctant to record the details. It was only when Burke paid an Aboriginal tracker £5 that the camels were located. 'Them long-neck yarrowman' were grazing just a kilometre away from the camp.

The *Moolgewanke* arrived on 9 October and the supplies were transferred to the steamer. The rum was left behind at Phelps station along with assorted boxes of stores. When the party finally departed for Menindee on 11 October, the atmosphere was tense. Determined to prove he could keep pace with the horses, Landells drove the camels long into the night and poor Becker was once again caught in the crossfire:

It was a most harazing affair; beside this neither myself nor Mr. Landells were sufficiently prepared to go on in this way, we had no food and no water, and the moon was down—but a few matches assisted us in looking for the track. On we went for miles and miles; Mr Landells, staggering in front, was scarcely able to keep himself free from falling asleep; I, behind, pulling the camels and looking out anxiously for our camp-fire…One disappointment followed the other till half an hour before midnight when we reached the long longed for halting-place. We found everyone asleep, however the cook willingly assisted us in getting a drop of tea. It was near two o'clock before our overtaxed limbs were allowed to rest. We had travelled this day 22 miles.

Three days later on 14 October, Becker's horse trod on his foot, 'splitting the nail of the big toe', and 'forcing one half of it through the flesh down to the bone'. The accident left the artist barely able to walk and Burke was forced to allow him to ride one of the horses.

By pushing his animals to the limit, Landells arrived in Menindee on 15 October just twenty-four hours after Burke. He and his exhausted animals pulled up under the shade of the river red gums on the banks of the Darling, and the camel driver went triumphantly to report his arrival. But it was not Burke who awaited him in the leader's tent. It was Wills. The young surveyor calmly told Landells that he was fired.

In a calculated act of humiliation, Landells had been sacked by a junior officer. Landells accused Burke of insanity. The Irishman responded by branding his deputy a scoundrel and challenged him to a duel with pistols. Landells refused, saying he had come to 'fight the desert', not his commanding officer. He tendered his resignation once more, this time in writing. Burke scrawled on the back: 'Since that time I believe that he has been doing everything in his power to obstruct my orders.'

The next morning, as if to prove he could dispense with Landells' expertise, Burke had the camels lined up and fitted with special ropes attached to their nose-pegs. The animals bellowed as one by one they were led towards the slippery riverbank. To Landells' consternation, the camels were about to be swum across the Darling in defiance of his recommendation that they be ferried over by boat. Camels can swim quite well provided they are not too fat. If the hump is too heavy, they tend to overbalance and drown. The men kicked the dirt in embarrassment as yet another argument broke out and raised voices began to echo up and down the river.

Burke deliberately placed Wills in command of the operation, declaring that if such a 'trifling obstacle' as the Darling River was enough to stop the animals, then they 'would be of little use upon the contemplated journey'. As Landells stood glowering on the sidelines, each camel swam across the muddy waters. His humiliation was complete. He packed his bags and made immediate arrangements to travel back to Melbourne. It was Wills who informed the rest of the party of Landells' resignation. By nightfall his position was official—Burke had promoted him to the post of deputy leader.

Landells' departure sent the camp into a frenzy of speculation about what would happen next. Beckler made the first move. Later that evening, he too announced his resignation. 'It was no little matter for me,' he admitted, 'to draw back from a wish nurtured so ardently and for so long as this expedition, to renounce so suddenly what had been a fervent desire.'

The expedition had only been in Menindee two days and already the tumultuous events had provided the settlement with more excitement than it had ever seen before. Rumours swirled down the Darling and resurfaced in newspaper editorials nearer Melbourne:

> The opinion of parties able to judge on the Darling is that Mr Burke will not be able to make any more than 200 miles beyond the settled districts this season, and that he is not the right man for the work he has undertaken. It is stated that instead of making himself agreeable to the men, he harasses them soldier style and in going to camp at night will not allow a man to dismount until he gives the word, although he may be a mile away.

The Victorian Exploring Expedition had disintegrated on the easiest section of the journey and was now lying in tatters on the edge of the desert. The journey of 750 kilometres from Melbourne to Menindee had taken fifty-six days—a horseman could ride it in ten. Of the nineteen original recruits, eleven had resigned or been dismissed. Eight more men had been hired. Five of these had also left. Burke had lost 60 per cent of his staff.

The most significant departure, aside from Landells, was that of the experienced hand Robert Bowman. It seems he could not bear the ineptitude paraded before him daily. Beckler noted that Bowman 'did not like it with us at all and left us after only a few days'. Another account says that Bowman was 'so imprudent on one occasion as to contrast the superior skill of Gregory with the bungling of the Victorian leader'.

Now, perched on the outskirts of European civilisation, Burke faced the challenge of rescuing the expedition before it disappeared behind the 'shimmering veils' of the desert. From now on there would be no tracks, no signposts and no local information, save for the wisdom of the indigenous people who lived along the route. The next stage of the journey would take him to the very edge of the map—to the giant coolibah trees that stood on the banks of Cooper Creek.

Nine

An Excess of Bravery

'The desert is not just a place where greedy men
may find precious metals. It has something more to offer
in making us aware of the ultimate questions in life.'
Manning Clark

Menindee lay in Baagandji Aboriginal territory and took its
name inexplicably from their term *milhthaka*, meaning egg
yolk. There were a few bark huts, a pub, a store and a police station. Only the Darling River brought the area to life. Its 'coffee
and plenty of milk' coloured waters rolled through the sandhills
and life in Menindee settled down to much the same pace.

This was as far as European settlement had penetrated. The
pioneers had come in search of grazing land but, as the climate
grew more fickle and the countryside less productive, farming
became a precarious exercise. It took a particular brand of obstinacy and optimism to believe that imported sheep and cattle
would thrive here. Hermann Beckler was amazed that anyone
would attempt to exploit such an unforgiving environment:

> If one were to show this country to an expert just arrived from
> Europe and tell him that this was good pasture land…he would
> laugh in your face…for the most part it was a miserable
> country of a strangely sombre nature…grasses were hardly to
> be seen. Small gaunt trees made the country seem even poorer
> and half of these were dead.

Menindee owed its continued survival to the riverboat pioneer
Francis Cadell. He set up a fortnightly steamer service and a small

Ludwig Becker's sketch features Thomas Paine's Hotel where members of the expedition spent much of their spare time.

trading post in 1859. When the river was high enough, boats brought supplies up from Adelaide and returned south laden with cargoes of wool. Once the shearing was finished and the fleeces disappeared around the last bend in the river, the only entertainment was to drink rum at Thomas Paine's Hotel, until the heat, the flies and the dust melted into oblivion.

Today the pub has been remodelled by fire and renovation. It is still possible to sit and stare at the faded portraits of Burke and Wills on the wall, but these days the outside world is beamed in via satellite, and the saloon jangles with television commercials and poker machines. The surrounding countryside has been transformed by a series of dams and giant artificial lakes, but ten minutes' walk into the dunes takes you straight back into the same arid land that the explorers found in 1860.

After rain, the light is soft and the land green and smothered in wildflowers. But in the dry season, the sun is blindingly intense. It scorches away the deeper tones to leave behind earth that is not black and brown, but orange and yellow. The grass withers to a jaundiced beige and even the sky is bleached white around the edges. As the summer heat melts the landscape into a quivering canvas of deception, the only solid point of reference is found around the riverbank, where lines of river red gums stand like sentinels guarding the precious water of the Darling. Each October, the time of year Burke's party arrived, a fierce wind blows down from the north-west; a whirling force that sends dust skittering along the water's edge. To stare across the dunes, screwing up your eyes against the dust and the sun, is like gazing at an over-exposed photograph. Only rain will restore the balance.

The expedition had reached Menindee far later than expected. It was the 'wrong time of year' to leave the safety of the Darling River system for Cooper Creek, nearly 600 kilometres away to the north. Summer was beginning to shrivel the waterholes, but Burke was determined to push on. Before resigning, Landells and Beckler had petitioned strongly to wait out the summer on the banks of the Darling. They argued that since the expedition had missed the cool season between April and September, it would be better to stay put where there was access to fresh supplies. But the thought of delaying for another three months only seemed to exacerbate Burke's desire to escape—postponement would be an admission of defeat.

Transport (too little) and supplies (too many) were still the expedition's main problems. To make matters worse, as the men began unloading the rations from the steamer *Moolgewanke*, it was discovered that the dried 'pemmican' meat had rotted. If the whole party was to reach the Cooper, it would take at least a month to procure fresh supplies of dried meat.

It seems incredible that such a lavish expedition should find itself facing logistical problems before it had left the settled districts. Perhaps the answer lay in reducing the party to more manageable proportions? Burke's instructions, however, required him to take his entire outfit to Cooper Creek. If he officially split the party now, it would be in direct contravention of his orders. The alternative was to send a forward party up to the Cooper with half the supplies, then return the pack animals to retrieve the remainder. This was a risky option. Burke had few experienced men, insufficient pack animals and only one qualified navigator. The history of Australian exploration is littered with the corpses of men who underestimated the power, the size and the unpredictability of the outback.

Burke's solution was to extract the 'best' elements of his party for himself and leave the remainder behind to fend for themselves. He decided to take Wills (as his deputy and surveyor), John King (to look after the camels), William Brahe, William Patten, Thomas McDonough, Charley Gray and Dost Mohomet, along with three-quarters of his remaining horses and camels. This would leave the rest of the men plus seven horses and ten camels on the banks of the Darling with a vague promise that they would be called up to the Cooper at a later date.

On 17 October, in a final hollow gesture towards scientific endeavour, Burke asked Becker to join the forward party, saying:

> Do you like to stay in the depot, or to go on with me now to Coopers Creek? If you like to be with the party, you are welcome, but I must tell you, there is no time for scientific researches, nor a horse or camel to ride on, you will have to tramp all the way, and must do the work like the other men.

Burke knew Becker had injured his foot and would have no choice but to refuse. A gifted artist—the only man capable of recording and preserving the expedition's achievements—was being forced to stay in Menindee, an outpost he could have reached comfortably by river steamer. Having discarded the expedition's 'dead wood', Burke retired to the Menindee pub, where he fell into conversation with a local man named William Wright.

Wright was a man of profuse whiskers and few words. With his rough weatherbeaten hands and slow direct manner, he had all the hallmarks of a hardened bushman. Until recently he had managed the nearby Kinchega sheep station, but the business was being sold and Wright was on the lookout for an opportunity. As the two men talked at the bar, Burke discovered Wright had just returned from a 250-kilometre journey towards Cooper Creek and was keen to explore further. Several drinks later, Wright volunteered as a guide and Burke accepted. Accompanying the expedition may have been an excuse for Wright to survey new sheep runs for a new farming operation, so it wasn't surprising that he suggested leaving Menindee as soon as possible. He also recommended keeping the expedition together so the entire outfit could reach the Cooper while the waterholes were full.

Burke took the first piece of advice and ignored the second. He asked Hermann Beckler to take charge of a rearguard camp with just four men: Becker, MacPherson, Belooch and Hodgkinson. Beckler was unenthusiastic but agreed to stay on, at least until a replacement officer could be found. Since the recent altercation with Landells, Burke was edgy and secretive. He knew the locals were sceptical of his abilities and that it wouldn't be long before rumours of his incompetence percolated down to Melbourne. Menindee might be remote but a recall was not out of the question. Public humiliation would follow and his reputation would be ruined.

Burke's overwhelming motivation was to get away as soon as possible—after that his intentions are difficult to decipher. He kept no written records and, crucially, he issued no written instructions to his subordinates. He told Ludwig Becker, 'I intend to look for a road up to Coopers Creek, and how the way is, and about the water; and as soon as I have found a spot where to form a depot, I shall send for you to come up with the others and with such things as wanted.' But did he really mean to fetch up the rearguard party and make a proper depot on the Cooper or was he just setting up a quick dash for the north coast?

If Burke was genuinely planning to reunite his party, he never made it clear whether he expected the remaining men to make

THE GREAT AUSTRALIAN EXPLORATION RACE.

This Melbourne *Punch* cartoon was drawn by Nicholas Chevalier at the height of the inter-colonial rivalry between Victoria and South Australia. The public loved the idea of a race between Burke and Stuart.

their own way to the Cooper with the animals they had left, or whether he planned to send back extra transport to help them. Either way, his strategy made little sense. From now on, many of the expedition's most valuable supplies would be sitting in Menindee, while the men who needed them most were out in the desert.

Perhaps the biggest reason for Burke's decision to leave the Darling so soon had arrived aboard the *Moolgewanke*. It carried South Australian newspapers revealing that John McDouall Stuart had failed in his first attempt to cross the continent. He had just returned to Adelaide after a journey that had taken him to within 800 kilometres of the north coast. He had planted a Union Jack in the centre of Australia, and then continued north, only to be turned back on 26 June 1860 by an Aboriginal ambush near the present-day town of Tennant Creek. Neither side sustained casualties but with food supplies dwindling and his men and horses weakening fast, Stuart decided to retreat. Burke guessed that it would not be long before his rival set out again. In the meantime he had at least a two-month head start over the South Australians and he was determined not to squander it.

The idea of a race had always appealed to Burke. It implied there would be a winner and, more than anything else in life, Burke needed to prove he was a winner. Stuart's failure had given him a real chance of success.

On 19 October 1860, a new incarnation of the Victorian Exploring Expedition left Menindee. There were eight Europeans, two Aboriginal guides and a string of sixteen camels and nineteen horses. Burke must have felt an overwhelming sense of relief as he clattered out of town—the wagons and the scientists were gone, he had escaped any censure from the committee, and he was at least two months ahead of John McDouall Stuart. At last the politics were over and the journey into the unknown had begun. Burke was undaunted by the 600 kilometres of wilderness that lay between him and Cooper Creek. Just before he left Menindee, he wrote to the committee, 'I still feel as confident as ever in the success of the main object of the Expedition.'

Just what was the 'main object' of the expedition? All pretence of scientific research had been abandoned. Somehow, between Melbourne and Menindee, the expedition had metamorphosed into a unit strikingly similar to the lightweight outfit employed by Stuart. Did the impracticability of the enormous original party mean that such a transformation was inevitable, or was it a deliberate policy to whittle down the group once it was beyond the public gaze? If so—was it Burke's idea alone or was there a secret official plan?

The answers lie strewn around in the contradictory objectives of opposing factions in the Royal Society, in Burke's loyalties to certain powerful members of the Exploration Committee and in his desire to play the role of the hero. Science was rarely a route to glory. If Burke was to fulfil his perceived destiny he had to be first across the continent. He was brave, ignorant and had nothing to lose. It would be easy to take advantage of such a dangerous combination.

Early in 1860, a small group of men began to recognise the expedition's potential role in opening up northern Australia for commercial exploitation. Chief amongst them was Sir William Stawell, the man who had secured Burke's position as leader. Stawell had an eye for opportunity and a broad knowledge of Australian politics. He and other committee members such as Thomas Embling, Richard Eades and John Macadam wanted to develop an overland route to a northern port. Aside from the telegraph, it would also allow a direct commercial link to south-east Asia and the construction of a trade centre similar to America's Hudson Bay. And there were other opportunities waiting to be explored.

When Queensland was declared an independent colony in 1860, its newly formed parliament also began drawing up plans for a settlement on the north coast. The scheme was abandoned, however, when it was discovered that a large area of land (now western Queensland) between the 141st and 138th meridians had not been included in the colony when it was first proclaimed. Queensland's governor George Bowen wrote to the Duke of Newcastle, Secretary of State for the Colonies, requesting that the land be added as soon as possible. Newcastle replied that 'the government of South Australia had proposed the annexation to

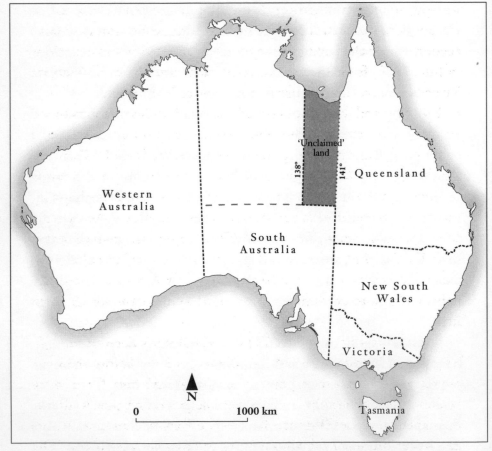

The 'unclaimed land' in the Gulf country was a rich prize for the first colony that could lay claim to it.

that colony of part of the territory which Queensland wanted. Also a certain group of gentlemen in Victoria wanted to form a settlement on the north coast of Australia.'

The leader of the Victorian group was the merchant and Royal Society member Thomas Embling. He was backed by Sir William Stawell.

Stawell was an expert in constitutional law—he had drafted Victoria's constitution in 1850. It would not have escaped his notice that a large portion of northern Australia still technically belonged to New South Wales and that, in the absence of that colony's interest in the area, there was a significant tract of land waiting for the first group to establish a route to the Gulf of Carpentaria on Australia's north coast. This realisation may have accounted for the sudden change to the expedition's instructions in June 1860, from a north-western route towards to the Victoria River to a more direct journey north towards the Gulf.

Embling and Stawell pondered the possibilities and developed an ambitious scheme. They enlisted the tacit support of several other politicians including the chief secretary John O'Shanassy for the expedition to explore more than just the flora and fauna of northern Australia. Victoria was rich but small. Perhaps its future lay in the annexation of a northern territory? An expedition cloaked in scientific respectability might also make a secret push for the Gulf and secure the prize before another colony got a chance. Burke was the perfect leader—bold, enthusiastic and naive enough to go as hard as he could to make the north coast first.

It has always been assumed that it was Burke's decision to split his party at Menindee, a rash gesture to get away before the consequences of his mismanagement caught up with him. Conclusive evidence now shows there had always been a secret plot to divide the expedition. Certain members of the Exploration Committee had never intended the whole party to cross the continent. The proof is contained in a letter, written the day before the expedition left Melbourne, from prominent Royal Society member Alfred Selwyn asking his friend Harry if he wishes to join the expedition as a surveyor. In it, Selwyn admits the party will divide at Cooper Creek.

> My dear Harry,
>
> Would you like to join the Exploring Party? Another surveyor is wanted and I think you would be just the man if your wishes are that way inclined. The pay would be less than you make now and you would of course have to go second to Wills, who is already appointed and be under him while you were together, but that would probably not be for long—*as the party will have to divide after leaving Cooper's Creek and a surveyor be attached to each*—If you like the idea and feel ambition of the honour and I hope glory to be gained by being attached to such a party, let me know by return of post. [italics added]

Selwyn had been looking out for a second surveyor for some time but no one seemed keen to take up the job. One prospective candidate expressed his doubts about Burke's capabilities as a leader:

> Do you think Mr. Burke has all the qualities that a leader ought to have? Everyone gives him credit for being a kind hearted man with plenty of pluck and determination and with great powers of endurance but some who know him predict disturbance in his party from his too hasty temper and say he acts too much from impulse.

Selwyn's response was ominous. 'I have not much faith,' he confided, 'in the success of the Expedition as at present constructed.'

The secret plan to divide the party and allow Burke to 'make a dash for it' is reinforced by a letter to the expedition leader from Georg Neumayer in Melbourne, written on 25 October 1860 a few days after Burke had left Menindee. Obviously Burke and

Neumayer had been discussing the necessity for a second surveyor but Neumayer admitted the plan was proving impossible to implement, 'I tried in vain to get another surveyor sent after you...There is underground work going on—I am sure about it. I have done my duty. You may be sure about it.' The professor went on to say that he had also tried to arrange a ship to meet Burke when he reached the north coast so far without success. But Neumayer's letter never reached Burke, a fact that influenced his plans in two important areas. First, Burke set out knowing that he couldn't rely on a rescue vessel and would therefore have to cross the continent in both directions. Second and more important, he departed under the misguided impression that Neumayer could procure a second surveyor to join the rearguard party in Menindee.

In dividing his party, Burke acted with the full knowledge and official backing of some of the most powerful members of the Exploration Committee. He guessed correctly that all they wanted was for him to reach the north coast first. Given his transport problems on the way to the Darling, Burke probably thought his best chance of success lay in slimming down the expedition sooner rather than later. This accounts for his decision to disobey his official orders and split the expedition at Menindee instead of the Cooper. The desperation of some committee members for Burke to succeed is evident in a packet of letters sent to Burke at the end of October. Royal Society secretary John Macadam urged him on, saying:

> My dearest Burke,
> Every success; all well—one especially—you know who! Everyone wishes you well. The honour of Victoria is in your hands. We know and feel assured that you will vindicate the confidence reposed in you. May God bless and preserve you.

This veiled reference to Julia Matthews was designed to fire up the impassioned Irishman even further. Richard Eades told Burke he expected him to be 'first to cross from sea to sea' and Thomas Embling exhorted Burke to make sure that Victoria triumphed over South Australia. 'The two colonies are in jealous rivalry,' he wrote, 'and I want you to win your spurs.' In a final scurrilous paragraph, he warned Burke to be careful in dealing with the Aboriginal tribes. 'I should like your work not to be sullied with blood as Stuart's is.'

This remark, falsely accusing Stuart of killing Aborigines during his journey north, was part of a smear campaign designed to undermine the Scotsman's credibility. Several members of the Exploration Committee had already recruited their friends in Adelaide to dig up dirt on Stuart. The result was a series of 'tip offs' to the newspapers and a report compiled by the Royal Society's assistant secretary Robert Dickson, which suggested Stuart's last northern expedition might have been a fake. 'His whole trip is still enveloped in impenetrable mystery,' wrote Dickson, adding that the Scotsman was so 'fearfully subject to the Demon Drink' that he spent most of the journey swigging bottles of preserving fluid and drinking alcohol from his scientific instruments. The committee's efforts to rouse Burke were all in vain. The packet of letters never reached him.

In Melbourne George Landells' resignation was causing a major scandal. The camel driver had rushed back to the city desperate to put his side of the story, but in the end Burke won the public relations battle by two newspapers to one. The *Age* was his major supporter. It decided that the Irishman had shown 'firmness and self-reliance' by reducing his party:

> The Exploring Expedition, as it recedes from the confines of the peopled districts, and approaches the solitude of the unknown interior, is gradually casting off the 'Barnacles' which clung to it, so long as its progress was a mere affair of

An Excess of Bravery | *133*

parade and holiday work. The silent wilderness has terrors for the faint of heart; and any excuse is gladly seized on by them, in order to retreat without open concession of cowardice…If Landells found he could not work in harmony with his chief officer, he should have resigned in peace and with dignified self-respect, without seeking to make himself appear an ill-used man, and Mr Burke a crack-brained tyrant.

The *Argus* agreed but the *Herald*, proclaiming itself 'impartial, not neutral', decided this was Burke's fault, stating that 'he had already demonstrated his total incapacity to hold his party firmly in hand, and that of itself is a very grave deduction from his concrete merits as a leader'.

As more revelations emerged, the members of the Royal Society squirmed with embarrassment. Matters reached crisis point with the publication of an 'explanation letter' from Landells, followed by a long and excruciatingly petty dispatch from Wills accusing the camel driver of disloyalty and duplicity:

> Whereupon it came out that Mr Landells has been playing a fine game trying to set us all together by the ears. To Mr Burke he has been abusing and finding fault with all of us; so much so that Mr Burke tells me that Landells positively hates me—when we have, apparently been the best of friends. To me he has been abusing Mr Burke, and has always spoken as if he hated the doctor and Mr Beckler, where as to them he had been all milk and honey. There is scarcely a man in the party whom he had not urged Mr Burke to dismiss.

The *Herald* was appalled:

Mr Wills, both in his present and former communication has nothing more to tell than that there were continual squabbles about the camels. The other petty details of the small personal bickering and tattlings that went on in the camp are utterly unworthy of serious record. Mr Wills ought not to have condescended upon journalising them…the bare fact that such contemptible trifles are occupying attention in the exploring party, shows clearly enough that the spirit of elevated enthusiasm with which it was started has pretty well evaporated by this time.

On his return to Melbourne, Neumayer attempted to subdue the scandal by holding a public meeting to defend the expedition. With the skill of a spin-doctor, he emphasised Burke's 'wisdom' and 'judicious' behaviour. 'There was not one man who was not pleased with the excellent leader placed over him,' he declared. The only concession to reality was an acknowledgment that 'Mr Burke might require some assistance in some scientific matters connected with the journey'.

The committee was by now facing financial problems. An audit revealed that £4500 had been spent to equip the party, one third more than expected. The hired wagons added another £700, which left only enough to pay the men's salaries until the end of the year. To compound matters, the committee had placed just £150 in Burke's bank account, not realising he had been writing cheques at will, which were now bouncing back to Melbourne.

By late October, even the tiny store in Menindee was refusing credit for the back-up party. Beckler and Becker had to search their packs for loose change every time they needed so much as a stamp or a new bootlace. Stawell wrote to Burke warning that 'The Committee was rather alarmed at finding the expense greater than they anticipated.' The Royal Society was forced to approach the government for more funds and the chief secretary William Nicholson had little choice but to grant another £6000.

To Melburnians, the expedition had been reduced to melodrama. Charles Ferguson was threatening to sue for wrongful dismissal and rumours were circulating about the complete break-up of the party. Melbourne could not wait to hear the next instalment.

As Burke's reputation was being dismembered in the city, he was making excellent progress towards Cooper Creek. With Landells and the scientists out of the way, it was a more harmonious group that trekked north hour after hour. Wright and his Aboriginal trackers proved to be able guides and water was readily available. Away from the framework of fences and farmland, the environment was like nothing the men had ever seen before, forcing even Wills to readjust his preconceptions. 'This last season,' he wrote, 'is said to have been the most rainy that they have had for several years; yet everything looked so parched up that I should have imagined it had been an exceedingly dry one.'

A journey unconstrained by the artificial structure of tracks and settlements is free to settle into the rhythms of the natural landscape. It was a survival skill the Aboriginal people had perfected over many thousands of years. North of the Darling, tribes such as the Danggali, the Wiljali, the Bandjgali, the Karennggapa and the Kullila all moved around according to the seasons, the locations of the game and the state of the water-holes. Burke made no attempt to learn these patterns of co-existence. He marched for up to sixteen hours day, often passing excellent water in the afternoon and camping late at night. There were no rest days. For now, the favourable conditions allowed him to get away with his cavalier approach but his rapid progress also gave him a false sense of security.

One hundred and twenty-five kilometres north of Menindee, the expedition passed through the Bynguano Ranges, a striking mountainous plateau that rises high above kilometres of flat waterless plains. Known as Mutawintji or Mootwingee, the area remains sacred for the Wilyakali tribe and many other Aboriginal groups.

To wander from the flat scrubby plains into Mutawintji is to enter a haunting spiritual world. The plants, the trees, the earth, even the smell is different. Deep inside the network of red gorges, the atmosphere of secrecy is overwhelming. The narrow tumbling gullies hide dark silent pools, surrounded by some of the most sacred Aboriginal art in south-east Australia. Rocky overhangs are transformed into magnificent galleries adorned with hand stencils, emu tracks, boomerangs and kangaroos, all drawn in striking red ochres and yellow clay paint.

Mutawintji had been a place of ceremony and celebration for indigenous people for thousands of years before Burke and Wills arrived. With its permanent supply of water and game, it also provided a sort of emergency larder, a place of refuge that was not permanently occupied by any particular tribe. Its resources were never squandered and when better times returned tribes such as the Milpulo, Maljangapa and the Wanjiwalku returned to the plains beneath.

The explorers arrived with a different perspective. They spent just a few hours in one of the richest geological, biological, botanical and anthropological areas in New South Wales. Too busy to appreciate the subtleties before them, they filled their waterbags and left, describing the area as 'dark and gloomy'.

Burke was consumed by his desire to beat Stuart. William Brahe recalled later that speed dominated the expedition's daily routine:

> Delay of any kind chafed Burke. The only angry word I ever had from him was in consequence of it. Some packs had shifted; the horses were delayed. He rode back, asking impatiently what was wrong. I explained, and said 'It's all right.' 'It's not all right,' he exclaimed angrily. 'It's all wrong!' and rode away. In two hours he was back, saying kindly, 'You must be very tired Brahe. Ride my horse for a while.' He would blaze up into a temper very quickly, but soon got over it.

The rest of the men had no choice but to keep up. Wills continued with his special 'camel-back' system to record basic weather, geological and biological information. He amazed everyone with his stamina. Long after the others had crawled inside their bedrolls, he stayed up to take his nightly observations and plot the party's position.

Burke did not keep a diary at all along this stretch of the journey, relying on his deputy to record any geographical features. Wills was surprised at the variety of the landscape they traversed. It alternated between 'as good grazing country as one would wish to see' and dusty clay flats 'so arid and barren...one might almost fancy himself in another planet'.

Ten days after leaving Menindee, on 29 October, the explorers reached a low-lying fertile area known as the Torowoto swamp, 250 kilometres north of Menindee. Like 'river', 'lake' and 'creek', the word 'swamp' implies a degree of dependability that doesn't necessarily exist in inland Australian geography. Maps in these areas can only ever be statistical averages, but this fact had not yet registered with European pioneers. Unaware of the enormous seasonal variations, the early explorers often misread the agricultural potential of the landscape. Many farmers followed these optimistic reports, driving their flocks for hundreds of kilometres towards nothing but drought, dust and despair.

Burke was no exception. Keen to fulfil the expectations of his patrons, he wrote to his uncle with misguided enthusiasm:

> What we have done up to this will cause a great sensation as we have passed some very fine sheep grazing country not before known for which when my report goes down immediate application will be made. We are now encamped upon a creek not before known. Grass nearly fit to mow...

With the journey progressing so well, Burke was increasingly impressed with William Wright's abilities as a bushman. At Torowoto, he decided to make Wright his third-in-command and the next morning he lined up the men and announced his intention to proceed to the Cooper at once. Wright was to return to Menindee with his Aboriginal trackers and retrieve the remainder of the stores. Burke outlined his plan, then offered each man the chance to turn back if they wished. All refused.

As usual Burke did not issue written instructions. In this case they would have been superfluous since Wright was nearly illiterate. Nevertheless, he did send a dispatch to the committee 'explaining' his decision:

> Mr Wright returns from here to Menindie. I informed him that I should consider him third officer of the expedition, subject to the approval of the committee, from the day of our departure from Menindie, and I hope that they will confirm the appointment. In the mean time I have instructed him to follow me up with the remainder of the camels to Cooper's Creek, to take steps to procure a supply of jerked meat, and I have written to the doctor to inform him that I have accepted his resignation, as, although I was anxious to await the decision of the committee, the circumstances will not admit of delay, and he has positively refused to leave the settled districts. I am willing to admit that he did his best until his fear for the safety of the party overcame him; but these fears, I think, clearly show how unfit he is for his post. If Mr Wright is allowed to follow out the instructions I have given him, I am confident that the result will be satisfactory; and if the committee think proper to make inquiries to him, they will find that he is very well qualified for the post, and that he bears the very highest character. I shall proceed on from here to Cooper's Creek. I may, or may not, be able to send back from there until we are followed up. Perhaps it would not be prudent to divide the party; the natives here have told Mr Wright that we shall meet with opposition on our way there. Perhaps I might find it advisable to leave a depot at Cooper's Creek, and go on with a small party to examine the country beyond it.
>
> Under any circumstance it is desirable that we should be followed up. I consider myself very fortunate in having Mr Wills as my second in command. He is a capital officer,

zealous and untiring in the performance of his duties, and I trust that he will remain my second as long as I am in charge of the expedition.

The men all conduct themselves admirably, and they are all most anxious to go on; but the committee may rely upon it that I shall go on steadily and carefully, and that I shall endeavour not to lose a chance or to run any unnecessary risk.

The letter was alarmingly imprecise and ominous in its use of the word 'perhaps'. It failed to clarify whether Wright was to wait until his appointment was confirmed before bringing up the stores or whether he would be receiving extra pack animals to boost his transport arrangements. Burke's accompanying letter to his uncle only increased the confusion:

I shall proceed on from here to Cooper's Creek or the Victoria River as it is sometimes called, and from thence to Carpentaria as straight as I can go and *if* I can go…It is very possible that I may leave half the party behind and push on with the rest if I find I cannot get through with them all.

With the promise that a second surveyor would be sent from Melbourne, Burke might have been justified in assuming that his rearguard party would at least be able to navigate to the Cooper. But he seemed to have forgotten that he had left just a handful of exhausted camels and horses in Menindee—hardly enough to haul tonnes of supplies for 600 kilometres through the desert. Relishing his role as an adventurer in an unknown land, Burke seemed unconcerned about the precariousness of his plan. In the uncluttered landscape of the interior, it was proving all too easy to consign the complications of Menindee and Melbourne to another world.

As Wright dissolved away into the horizon, so did the expedition's last link with civilisation. A man who had been running a sheep station two weeks earlier was now Burke's only lifeline.

Ten

The Dead Heart

'Desert: 1) A dry barren often sand-covered area of land.
2) An uninteresting or barren subject, period, etc. eg cultural
desert. Adjective: barren and uncultivated; uninhabited.'
Modern Australian Oxford Dictionary

The heart of Australia is not dead. Its pulse is just less regular. The seasons do not arrive in convenient quarterly bundles, but stretch through decades in erratic cycles of drought and flood. When conditions shift, they do so in spectacular style, rearranging the landscape with astounding ferocity. The result is a patchwork of boom and bust—an unpredictable environment that demands flexibility and patience.

About one third of Australia receives an average of less than 250 millimetres of rain a year. Geographically, it is classified as desert but, as Charles Sturt had discovered, it is not all wrinkled sandhills and tree-lined oases. The dunes are mixed with expanses of clay, dust, black soil, scrub, salt lakes and stones. This stark collage is broken up by mountains, creeks and even forests, features made all the more astonishing by the bleakness that surrounds them. On occasion the desert creates real surprises: the thermal wetlands of Dalhousie Springs, a huge quartz pillar near Alice Springs, a giant monolith such as Uluru or the most extensive cave system in the world under the Nullarbor Plain. An appreciation of these contrasts entails a shift in perception, an acceptance of emptiness, space and scale. For Burke, trapped in his European mindset and brought up on the green, compact, agricultural landscapes of England and Ireland, they were difficult concepts to grasp.

Today the desert captivates or repels. To some it will always be desolate and barren. For others it is a different form of beauty, simpler and more arresting than any other on earth. Either way, it is deeply affecting, even from within the air-conditioned security of a modern four-wheel-drive. People can still die here from drowning or dehydration. Burke and Wills passed through the landscape oblivious to these brutal possibilities. Their task was relentless, but they were lucky enough to be travelling in an unusually benign season and, contrary to most stereotypical desert treks, they were short of water for just one day on their entire journey.

The eight men toiled northwards towards the Cooper with their camels slapping across the claypans and crunching over the rock-strewn plains. After twenty-three days, on 11 November 1860, they entered an undulating area of stony rises, little realising that the desert was about to perform one of its most startling transformations. The clues were subtle—a faint green sheen on the horizon, the rustle of a lizard in the scrub, a flock of birds in the distance.

After an excess of space and light, the rich green environment that suddenly confronted the party was a revelation. Ahead was Cooper Creek, winding its way through the wilderness like a fat orange snake. The tired and dusty convoy of men, horses and camels plunged down its banks, and threw themselves into the water. The sludgy reddish liquid was cool, refreshing and too good to resist. The men were exultant; they were almost halfway across the continent and in terms of European exploration they were nearing the edge of the map.

Burke and Wills had reached one of the world's most remote and elusive river systems. Modern topographical maps show the Cooper as an enticing maze of blue lines, which thread their way through the dunes to a series of lakes strung out across the desert. But the maps are deceptive. Most of the time the Cooper is a series of transient waterholes fed by a network of sluggish, muddy streams bleeding away in the relentless heat.

Defying convention, the water flows away from the coast. Fed by tropical downpours sweeping over the Great Dividing Range, it creeps inland through thousands of small arterial channels. Sometimes the creeks braid together to form a billabong, before splintering once more to drizzle away and vanish into the earth. All around, the terrain is scarred with channels gouged out by floods that have long since evaporated. Every year the baffling labyrinth changes according to the rainfall patterns, frustrating map-makers and confounding travellers.

Central Australia is dominated by anti-cyclones coming in from the west. These cells of high pressure provide clear skies, intense summer heat and low rainfall. But the region is also subject to the vagaries of the El Niño Southern Oscillation Effect, a complicated weather system that can produce violent bursts of rainfall and floods interspersed with long periods of drought. In an 'average season', the giant Cooper system might flow for just a few hours or a few days, but in an exceptional year torrents of water are disgorged down the myriad channels, cascading into one another, and spilling out into lakes up to 100 kilometres wide. Perhaps just once or twice in a century, the deluge rushes south with such momentum that it sweeps across more than a thousand kilometres of arid land to fill Lake Eyre—one of the world's largest salt lakes. Briefly, the mythical inland sea that fascinated Charles Sturt becomes a reality.

The huge expanse of glaring white salt is overwhelmed by floodwater, and this giant ephemeral oasis becomes inundated with birds and animals. Frogs, fish and shrimps, dormant for years buried in the mud, emerge through the dissolving salt crust and catapult a temporary food chain into action. Mats of floating plants spread over thousands of square kilometres of water and photosynthesise so rapidly that they become too hot to touch.

For several months everything from the pelican to the dingo embarks on a reproductive frenzy, but this outburst of fertility does not last. The blazing sun reasserts its stranglehold, the floodwaters recede and the desert returns.

The Cooper Creek basin is a land of extremes. One season may yield a beautiful chain of waterholes, bristling with life; the next will leave a series of glutinous mud-holes harbouring the skeletons of those unable to find sanctuary elsewhere. Once a drought takes hold it can last for many years. The weak will perish, and the strong must retreat and retreat, until they are

The explorers arrived at Cooper Creek on 11 November 1860, at the beginning of the hot season. Wills noted temperatures 'generally exceeded 100°' with the highest being '109° in the shade'.

clinging to the few remaining permanent billabongs. In summer the temperature is stupefying, soaring through 45°C and combining with furnace-like winds to paralyse all activity. In winter, the mercury can plunge to freezing point. Southerlies penetrate the desert, leaving the earth raw with frost.

Everything here is on a scale the human mind finds either exhilarating or crushing. Writing during her travels through the cattle stations of the area in the 1930s, journalist Ernestine Hill gave this haunting insight into the cruelty of the landscape:

> Three hundred cattle were grouped about the borehead, in horribly lifelike attitudes, except that the eye sockets were empty. They had been dead for three years. Many had died standing and sitting, and sunk down only a little deeper in the sand. Hides and horns were mummified in that dry air. They were denied the mercy of decay.

Yet the Cooper is also a place of great beauty, especially in the cool air and the soft light of the early mornings, or when the vivid sunsets of red, purple, orange and pink streak across the horizon and light up the evening sky. When Burke arrived here at the beginning of the summer in 1860, he found the Cooper resplendent in lush green foliage. Huge river red gums and coolibahs were flourishing along the banks of the creek and grass carpeted the red earth. Little realising how lucky they were, Wills decided the sudden outburst of fertility reminded him of England. 'Imagine a creek or river somewhat similar to the Dart above the weir,' he wrote to his family, 'winding its way through those flats, having its banks densely clothed with gum trees and other evergreens.'

After the relative silence and emptiness of the desert plains, the Cooper was crowded, noisy and brimming with life. While pelicans and spoonbills patrolled the creek, turtles and water rats foraged along the banks. Echidnas snuffled through the grass looking for insects, while parrots, lorikeets and rosellas chattered in the branches above, and goannas and water dragons warmed themselves in the sun. Sliding through the undergrowth were some of the world's deadliest snakes: the king brown, the death adder and, most dangerous of all, the fierce snake, whose fangs could inject enough venom to kill a hundred men.

In the early evening, dingoes, wallabies and kangaroos crept down to the water's edge to drink, and the trees were filled with flocks of cockatoos, shrieking as they bickered over their favourite branch. Even the nights were noisy, as small marsupial mice, possums and bilbies scurried through the grass looking for insects, and the air became choked with the calls of cicadas, crickets and frogs.

Surrounded on all sides by an unforgiving terrain, the Cooper attracted creatures from hundreds of kilometres around to take advantage of the season. Burke and Wills were camped on the same thread of fertility that had for thousands of years kept the land and its people alive.

For the local Aboriginal tribes, the recent rains had produced a feast along the creek. Despite the unpredictability of their environment, indigenous people had lived and thrived around the Cooper or Kini-papa for more than 20,000 years. There were four main groups in the area, each comprised of about five hundred people: the Ngurawola, the Wangkamurra, the Yawarrawarrka and the Yandruwandha. The last two groups were closely related and it was their land that Burke and Wills were exploring as they moved up the creek.

The explorers found a tall, athletic people, who used nothing more than a simple string girdle or a smearing of goanna fat to protect themselves from the elements. Many decorated themselves with necklaces and bangles made from brightly coloured seeds, shells and even human teeth. The men dressed their hair with feathers and knotted their beards into a distinctive loop tied with fur string. On ceremonial occasions they painted their

Danbidleli was a member of the Yandruwandha tribe. As a young man he helped Burke and Wills during their last days on the Cooper.

bodies with red ochre, charcoal and white clay.

Each tribe was headed by elders—men of power and influence, who had reached their position over the course of many years by undergoing various stages of initiation. They rose in status only when they were judged worthy of knowing the stories and myths that accompanied each level of wisdom. The signs of initiation included circumcision, the removal of two front teeth (the lateral incisors) and parallel scars on the torso. The elders enforced strict tribal laws, including complex rules governing marriage and procreation. This ensured that, despite the small size of each tribal group, there was no inbreeding and little incidence of genetic disease.

The strength and preservation of each tribe depended on a complex family structure. The Yandruwandha were divided into several distinct dialect groups. The first were the Murnpeowie Yandruwandha or Tingatinga blacks, who lived around Lake Blanche and up to Merty-Merty station. The second group were the Parlpanadramadra Yandruwandha who lived on the eastern extremity of the Cooper, around the Baryulah waterhole. The third group around the Cullymurra waterhole were the Nirrpi people. The fourth group were the Thayipilthirringuda people, from 'the land of the stone chips' near the present-day outpost of Innamincka.

Within these family groups, each person was assigned to a 'skin group' or *kamiri*, which determined certain aspects of identity and also governed who could marry. In addition, everyone belonged to a particular totem group, a practice common across nearly all Australia's Aboriginal tribes. The Yandruwandha had between twenty-four and twenty-six totemic groups linked to various aspects of the environment such as the kangaroo or *tjukurru* group and the sand goanna or *mangali* group. It was considered taboo to eat the animal that had given you your totemic identity.

All the tribes were nomadic hunter-gatherers, moving around in small groups as their water and food supplies allowed. Possessions were limited, perhaps just a fire-making stick, a dish and a digging implement. Tools and weapons were also kept to a minimum, but the men made stone knives, chisels and adzes, and carved wooden spears, boomerangs, shields and clubs. Women collected local plants and fashioned the stems into string for fishing nets, cradles and bags.

They lived in temporary shelters made of branches and known by the Europeans as wurleys, gunyahs or mia-mias. Sometimes when the seasons were favourable, the people built substantial villages near waterholes, constructing solid beehive-shaped huts, which were thatched and then covered in earth.

As the Cooper provided permanent water, it was the hub of a busy trade route through Aboriginal Australia and long journeys were undertaken to procure goods from as far afield as the Flinders Ranges in South Australia and Boulia in Queensland. Gatherings of more than a thousand men were held to the south at a meeting place known as Kooperamana, where neighbouring tribes traded their prized red ochre for shields, axe heads, wooden bowls and the narcotic shrub, *pituri*.

Traders thought nothing of travelling across hundreds of kilometres of desert for ceremonial or commercial purposes. They were experts at finding water, digging in exactly the right spots in the dried-up creek beds or tracking animals and birds to rock pools and soaks. If all else failed, they could get water from certain roots and plant stems, even a particular type of frog, which was dug up and squeezed judiciously until its bloated body yielded a stream of precious liquid. If a man left his camp to hunt by himself, he would leave behind a small, decorated wooden object known as a *toa*. It depicted the natural features of the area and acted as a message-stick to friends and relatives.

Even if food was plentiful, it was rare for everyone to

congregate in the same place unless there were ceremonies to be held. Then several hundred people would gather in special areas to carry out sacred rituals. At the same time there would be feasts, dancing, singing, rock painting and the opportunity for stories, legends and gossip to be related around the campfire.

Magic formed an intrinsic part of everyday life. Sorcerers could cure illness, change weather patterns and make men and women fall in love. Some could even cast spells powerful enough to cause death. One of the last of the Yawarrawarrka people, a man known as Wilpie, died in 1958 when he was ninety-three. He believed he had been sung to death by a sorcerer from Queensland with whom he had quarrelled the previous year.

For Aboriginal people life is inextricably bound to the land, its features, rhythms, animals and its spirits. Every man is the owner and custodian of his own territory, a birthright passed down to him through the male line. A person's identity is forged by their land. The two are inseparable and removal from that place means spiritual as well as physical destruction.

The Aboriginal philosophy could not have been more different from that of their European visitors. After researching the tribes around the Cooper for many years, historian Helen Tolcher concluded that:

> Time had no past, present or future, but was a single unit within which man moved, either as a spirit awaiting birth, as a human being, or as the spirit of one dead awaiting reincarnation. When they were tired they slept, and when they were hungry they ate; unless the need was urgent a task could be put aside and equally well taken up at dusk, in the morning, or when three floods had passed by. The division of time into regular units had no relevance to this way of life.

It was the land that shaped the needs of the Aboriginal tribes around the Cooper. The desert imposed a spartan semi-nomadic lifestyle, which was cruel when conditions were bad. It was nevertheless sustainable and enriched by sophisticated social structures and by a wide range of cultural activities. The Aboriginal people adapted, survived and prospered in conditions that defeated many who came later.

Unaware of the subtleties of this life, Burke's party travelled through Yandruwandha and Yawarrawarrka territory searching for somewhere to rest and revitalise. The footsore party ambled alongside the creek until it reached a magnificent waterhole, more than a kilometre long, surrounded by grass and teeming with game.

The Cooper is home to more than two hundred species of birds. Its murky waters hide thirteen types of fish including plump yellowbelly (with flesh as sweet as any whiting), perch and bony bream. Down among the tangled tree roots are yabbies—freshwater crayfish, which taste like small lobsters and are now a delicacy around the world. The Aboriginal people made full use of these resources, trapping the fish and squelching their toes into the mud to feel for freshwater mussels or *thukali*. They were experts at mimicking the giant unsuspecting emus, which they lured into woven nets. And, as the writer George McIver noted, they were also skilled at catching the local waterbirds:

The preliminary to capturing whatever ducks he may require is cutting a thick bush. This he places over his head and wades into the water—always at a distance not likely to frighten the birds. If the water is shallow, as is often the case…he will wade towards the birds, and so slowly, with his body underwater and his head concealed by the bush, that the bush which appears to be stationary is all that can be seen by the birds. When near enough, he will grab a duck's leg from beneath, pull the bird underwater, and while there quickly break its neck. The captured bird rarely utters a sound when it is being pulled underwater. In this way he may capture half a dozen or more, if he so desires without scaring the other birds.

Aboriginal people supplemented their protein intake with lizards, marsupials and snakes, but the core of their diet came from a wide range of plants and seeds. Local knowledge and persistence revealed mulga apples, succulent native figs, cucumbers, oranges, lemons and millet. There were coolibah seeds, pigweed and, most important of all, a small aquatic fern, resembling a four-leaf clover, known as nardoo, which grows in swampy country and provides seeds that can be ground into a paste and baked.

After 20,000 years living near the Cooper, the Aboriginal people knew every inch of their land; they understood how it worked and what it had to offer. In the good seasons they ate a nourishing diet, and even during times of drought they could survive on what nature provided. But harvesting the local bush tucker demanded knowledge, skill and patience—qualities conspicuously lacking in the man who now sought to lay claim to the land for European settlement. Burke had no interest in the intricacies and possibilities of his new environment. He had come to conquer, not to learn.

The arrival of the explorers must have been an astonishing experience for the Yandruwandha, as if aliens had appeared from over the horizon. Their land was suddenly being invaded by strange figures mounted on giant four-legged creatures that snorted and spat their way through the sandhills.

Today the descendants of the Yandruwandha have long been displaced from their traditional lands, but they still possess much of their tribal history and language. Stories of the explorers' stay on the Cooper have been passed down through the generations to Arran Patterson and his family. Arran's great-great-great grandfather Kimi was a young man when the expeditioners arrived at Cooper Creek in November 1860.

From the Yandruwandha point of view, the explorers behaved rudely. The waterholes along the Cooper were the equivalent of family homes and, as in most societies, Aboriginal people observed certain protocols when entering the territory of others. It was polite to stop a certain distance away and wait for a tribal representative to approach. He would find out where the stranger had come from, what his business was and, most important of all, what totem group he belonged to. Then, a member of that same totem group would come forward and escort the guest into the camp, where he would be fed and looked after. It was acceptable and even expected that 'foreign' tribes might visit an area for special events, and particular camping places were set aside for outsiders. Provided the proper courtesies were followed, there was no cause for conflict.

The Yandruwandha watched in amazement as these new strangers charged straight towards the water and began paddling around in it. They did not call the men 'whitefellas' but *pirti-pirti*, which means 'red fella'. Presumably Burke and his men were sunburnt after their long march across the desert.

Wills was to notice that the Aborigines often gesticulated vigorously at them whenever they approached a waterhole. The explorers interpreted this as aggression but, a century and a half later, the Yandruwandha themselves believe their ancestors may have been trying to communicate in sign language, which was used across Aboriginal Australia to bridge the gap between the different tribal dialects. Rather than trying to frighten the men away, the Yandruwandha might have been asking, 'What are you doing?', 'Why are you here?' or, most pertinent of all, 'How long are you going to stay?'

Groups like the Yandruwandha who lived in harsh environments were always anxious to conserve their food supplies, and they moved around so as not to exhaust a particular waterhole. Visitors who camped one or two nights could be tolerated, but what if they were to stay longer?

In fact the explorers were hardly a danger to the local food supplies. They did little more than take a few pot shots at ducks. Neither Burke nor Wills made any real effort to establish relations with the local people, despite the fact that the Yandruwandha showed no immediate aggression and often approached the explorers with offerings of fish or invitations to dances and ceremonies. All such advances were rejected. The rebuffs were sometimes delivered with a bullet in the air just to make sure the message was clear.

Burke may have had good reason to fear the Aboriginal people. Tales of their aggression and barbarism were common currency back in Melbourne and it was not unheard of for tribes to attack settlers and in some cases to kill them. He was also justified in worrying about the theft of his equipment, as much of it was highly desirable to the locals. The Aborigines were more inclined to share property than the Europeans, and they expected that their gifts of fish and nardoo would be reciprocated with objects such as knives and axes. These were particularly sought-after, since the Yandruwandha (in common with all Aboriginal people) had no metal of their own. But, although Burke tossed them a few trinkets, he ignored them as far as he could. Wills was equally dismissive, even cruel in his assessment of the indigenous people:

> A large tribe of blacks came pestering us to go to their camp and have a dance, which we declined. They were very troublesome and nothing but the threat to shoot will keep them away; they are, however, easily frightened, and although fine-looking men, decidedly not of a war-like disposition…from the little we saw of them, they appear to be mean-spirited and contemptible in every respect.

Apart from the fact that Wills' hostility was unfair, the explorers' behaviour also robbed them of vital information and squandered any possibility of hiring a local guide. Whilst their actions may make sense when viewed in the context of their age, an age when it was common to regard Aboriginal people as 'hostile savages' or 'ignorant blacks', Burke and Wills did not have the wit to realise that, whatever their cultural differences, local people were the best judges of their land and its resources. Unlike explorers such as Gregory and Leichhardt, they lacked the vision to see beyond their prejudices. They were in too much of a hurry even to plunder the Cooper's most precious resource—the wisdom of its indigenous people.

If Burke and Wills had shown even an ounce of friendliness, they might have begun to understand how to harvest the local food sources. If they had lingered long enough they could have realised how to communicate using smoke signals and message-sticks as the Aborigines did. Would they have learned lessons that changed the course of the expedition?

Eleven

A Sense of Perspective

'Some call it desert
But it is full of life
Pulsating life
If one knows where to find it
In the land I love.'
Jack Davis—Aboriginal poet

While Burke and Wills explored the comparative paradise of the Cooper, William Wright made his way back to Menindee. His instructions were to 'follow-up' the main party as fast as possible. Out in the desert, swollen with confidence and divorced from reality, this seemed like a good plan. But when he rode back into town on 5 November 1860, Wright realised he was in an impossible situation.

Burke had plundered the best of the expedition, leaving Hermann Beckler in charge of the ragtag remains. This party of five was now camped eleven kilometres along the Darling River from Menindee, at a shady spot near the junction with Pamamaroo Creek. Signs of the camp can still be found today.

Wright came back to find that Beckler had disappeared on a botanical expedition to the nearby Scrope's Ranges. Ludwig Becker was ensconced in his small furnace-like tent, sketching, writing and observing the local wildlife. Everyone else had lapsed into sullen indifference. Apart from taking the animals out to graze, they lounged around in the heat, swore at the flies and escaped to Thomas Paine's Hotel in search of inspiration at the bottom of a rum bottle.

Wright was supposedly third-in-command of the most prestigious expedition in Australia, yet he had no written orders,
dubious official status and little financial credibility. Solid but
uninspiring, he lacked the natural authority of the ruling class
and admitted later: 'I did not rightly know what to do.'
Returning to find 'a mere station manager' was now in charge,
Beckler refused to accept the appointment until it was confirmed
in writing from Melbourne. This placed Wright in an untenable
position. He was charged with carrying six tonnes of supplies a
distance of 600 kilometres over arid terrain in the middle of
summer using: a doctor who refused to accept his command in
Herman Beckler; a lame naturalist, Ludwig Becker; the second
blacksmith, Alexander MacPherson; a journalist, William
Hodgkinson; and Belooch, a dispirited sepoy. The animals were
even worse—ten mangy camels and seven feeble horses.

To mount a decent relief party, Wright calculated that he
needed at least ten more strong horses, ten packsaddles and four
bullocks for meat. The cost would top £400—more than three
years' wages for a station manager. Conscious that Burke's men
were dependent on him the embattled Wright struggled to
assemble a suitable party. Then on 10 November news came that
a horseman had ridden into town with urgent dispatches from
Melbourne. He was at Thomas Paine's pub demanding fresh
horses.

Trooper Lyons was nothing if not determined. He was a
police officer from Bendigo who had been told to deliver his
messages personally to Burke—and that was what he intended to
do. Wright objected, arguing it was madness to rush off into the
desert without proper preparation, but Lyons insisted he must be
allowed to catch up with the main party. The trooper carried
with him news of John McDouall Stuart's retreat from Attack
Creek in northern Australia, as well as letters from the
Exploration Committee urging Burke to make haste. The

dispatches were all unnecessary. Burke knew about Stuart from the newspapers on the *Moolgewanke* and he was already travelling as fast as he could towards the Gulf. As the argument continued, Wright felt himself at a disadvantage. His advice was sound—but to Lyons he was simply an unco-operative, illiterate sheep farmer who had no authority to flout the committee's orders.

Burke had apparently promised Wright that he would stop at least twice on his way to the Cooper to rest his animals, so in the end the station manager agreed that it might just be possible to catch him up. He arranged with Lyons that once the messages were delivered, the trooper would bring back the extra horses and camels Burke had mentioned to shuttle the rest of the supplies up to the Cooper. Wright instructed the blacksmith, Alexander MacPherson, to accompany the trooper, and he enlisted an Aboriginal tracker named Dick to show them the way. On 11 November, the trio set out towards Cooper Creek.

Burke was restless. Taunted by the unknown terrain to the north of the Cooper, he took off alone on an impromptu reconnaissance mission, but returned without finding water or a way forward. On 16 November Wills took up the challenge, beginning a series of solo journeys to explore the surrounding desert. He soon discovered that the land around the creek was divided into distinct types—none of them particularly appealing to an aspiring explorer.

In some areas he found huge tracts of sandhill country. It stretched before him like a giant ploughed field of fiery orange, furrowed with salt lakes and claypans that were dotted with small trees and shrubs. In other areas, the sand solidified into rock and Wills had to pick his way through the 'gibber plains' that had repulsed Charles Sturt. The surveyor stared out over this vast landscape, feeling the heat that made the air throb and the stones quiver in the sunlight. It was a land without scale. Perspective returned only when a few rocky outcrops appeared on the horizon; their distinctive flat tops offered reassurance and a land-mark to aim for. In such an immense intimidating space, they were the only affirmation of progress.

When the stones relented, open woodland took over. This unexpected feature is now sadly depleted by the loss of topsoil, loosened by the hooves of imported grazing animals and blown into oblivion by the desert winds. Before the cattle stations were set up, fine stands of mulga and gidgee trees were interspersed with patches of grassland around the creek beds and waterholes. Now there are only fences whose posts are suspended in mid-air, dangling in the breeze from rusted wires, as if searching for the soil that once anchored them to the plains.

Wills returned to the depot disappointed. The waterholes were shrinking fast and there was no obvious way north. Determined to try again, the surveyor decided to take McDonough on his next scouting trip—a journey that nearly proved fatal for both men. After setting out with three camels and travelling 130 kilometres, Wills and McDonough looked for water until they were exhausted. Thinking their camels were just as tired as they were, the two men turned them loose. While McDonough prepared supper, the surveyor settled down to con-duct his scientific observations. To their horror, the camels staged an immediate recovery and the explorers looked on in despair as the 'exhausted' animals trotted off into the distance. Wills remarked sardonically that they were 'not nearly so done up as they appeared to be'.

Losing the camels put the pair in a desperate position. They were stranded in the extreme heat with no pack animals and thirty-five litres of water in a leaking goatskin bag. Wills and McDonough were forced to abandon all their equipment and search for water on the return trip. Later, in a letter to his sister,

Wills admitted, 'it is dry work travelling in the middle of the day with the temperature varying from 90 degrees to 105 degrees in the shade and about 140 degrees in the sun...I can assure you there is nothing like a walk of this sort to make you appreciate the value of a drink of cold water.'

The two men trudged fifteen kilometres when, by chance, they found three stagnant pools to replenish their leaking water bag. Over the next two days they marched another 115 kilometres to the creek, stopping for just a few hours to rest when the sun was at its height, and sipping their limited supply of stinking black water. When the exhausted pair reached the Cooper, they had just half a litre of liquid left between them. McDonough conceded that without Wills' determination he would never have survived the journey. The camels fared rather better. After a year frolicking across the desert, two of the errant beasts were discovered near Adelaide—healthy, happy and, it appeared, none the worse for their experience.

At Wright's makeshift camp on the Darling, confusion reigned. In the unrelenting heat, the mood veered from morose lassitude to outright aggression. Petty disputes festered. Hodgkinson in particular seemed to antagonise everyone. Beckler lost patience first with him and then with Ludwig Becker, who was tired and grumpy after too much physical exertion and too little food.

No one bothered to go fishing or hunting, and with their credit exhausted at the local store, the men lived on flour, sugar, tea and small amounts of dried beef. Their vitamin-deficient diet was already affecting their health, making them vulnerable to further medical problems later on. Both Becker and Beckler wrote several times to the committee, outlining their plight and requesting more money and further instructions. Neither received any reply.

As no one knew what was happening, there was no reason to keep things in order. Stores lay scattered on the ground. To replace the rancid pemmican, Wright bought in four bullocks to stockpile extra supplies of dried meat. The flesh was cut into long strips and strung between the trees. The fat was salted, wrapped in the skin of the dead beasts, buried for five days and then dug up and hung out to dry. The smell of rotting meat hung around the camp, attracting clouds of flies and forcing the men to spend several hours each day inspecting the meat to remove the balls of maggots.

Wright took little interest in the camp, provoking widespread disapproval by retiring instead to the comfort of his homestead at Kinchega station. Locals whispered that 'it was folly of Mr Wright to stop and let the season pass' just because he was waiting for his appointment to be approved. Wright was unrepentant. He maintained that he had taken all possible steps to resolve the situation by sending a formal request for confirmation to the Exploration Committee, along with some dispatches from Burke and Wills, by the first post after he returned from Torowoto.

Wright's packet of letters arrived in Melbourne on 3 December 1860. Burke's glowing descriptions of his progress towards the Cooper through excellent grazing country hardly reflected the expedition's disarray, but they were enough to seduce the committee. Its members were so carried away by their enthusiasm that they overlooked the urgency of Wright's predicament. Despite further dispatches from Becker and Beckler dated 27 November they failed to reply—to confirm the station manager's appointment or issue any written orders.

Up at the Cooper, Burke and his men were overrun by a plague of native rats. They descended on the camp in swarms, devouring food supplies, boot leather and bedding. Soon the surrounding trees resembled washing lines as gear was suspended from the branches to protect it, but the rats still scuttled over the men as they slept, gnawing their hair and chewing their toenails. Brahe trapped and shot three hundred in a single night. Exasperated, and in danger of losing more precious supplies, Burke decided to move on.

A few kilometres along the creek, he established a new camp, which proved tolerably less popular with the local rodent population. It was dominated by a magnificent coolibah tree; a tree that had survived on the Cooper for nearly two centuries. Its massive trunk was encased by distinctive zigzag-patterned bark and its branches grew out in a great circle, casting a welcome shadow over the sunbaked earth. The men slept, ate and cooked beneath its canopy and the coolibah soon became the centre of camp life.

Depot Camp 65 lies just inside what is now the south-western corner of Queensland. Today the area looks much as it did then—luxuriant grasses and shrubs thrive under the shade of the giant gums and great flocks of budgerigars flit from branch to branch. It is an exuberant slice of park-like beauty that obliterates the desert beyond. But respite is brief. Just a few paces away from the water's edge, the temperature climbs. The earth is baked hard and then wrenched apart into a crinkled rusty jigsaw. The trees diminish in size until they become stunted skeletal replicas scattered across the plains. All that is left is the earth and the sky. Back at the water's edge the dishevelled landscape is shaped by drought and flood. Tree trunks are stained dark where water has lapped against them for weeks on end, branches are tangled with debris, ragged channels scar the earth and impenetrable bogs linger between the waterholes.

As Burke's men set up their new depot camp, their leader continued to fret. The arguments for staying at the Cooper until Wright arrived were overwhelming. Wills' recent experiences proved that the route north was already perilous and from now on, the weather would only get hotter and the waterholes less reliable. Burke had no way of knowing how long it might take Wright to catch up with the rest of the supplies. A prudent leader would spend the next few weeks securing a line of communication and supply back to Menindee. A prudent leader would not rush off into the desert while so much uncertainty surrounded his back-up party.

Explorers with greater experience, from Marco Polo to Robert Scott, have learned that the most frustrating part of any journey is doing nothing. After a winter stuck aboard the *Belgica*, stranded off Antarctica in 1898, explorer Frederick Cook wrote: 'We are as tired of each other's company as we are of the cold monotony of the black night and the unpalatable sameness of our food. Physically, mentally, and perhaps morally, then, we are depressed, and from my past experience I know this depression will increase.'

For Burke, the thought of descending into the somnolent rhythms of summer by the Cooper was more terrifying than the prospect of tackling the desert—whatever horrors it might have to offer. His blood was up and his honour depended on him reaching the Gulf before any other man. In any case, he reasoned, a delay would not necessarily be the safest option.

When Charles Sturt tried to penetrate the interior in January 1845, he became trapped and sheltered in a small canyon for five miserable months, waiting for cooler weather to release him. Instead, his thermometers exploded, the lead slipped from his pencils and his supplies rotted away. He and his men deteriorated in the grinding heat. Their hair stopped growing, their nails turned brittle and dropped out, and one man died in agony from scurvy.

When at last it rained, Sturt struggled forward but his debilitated party found it impossible to find a way through the fearsome dunes. He returned to Adelaide a broken man; strapped to his horse, almost blind, his gums bleeding and his legs black with scurvy. Burke was not keen to repeat Sturt's ordeal. He dreaded lingering through the height of summer, killing time, imagining the criticism of him back in Melbourne, tortured by visions of his beloved Julia Matthews and of Stuart reaching the north coast before him. Already, days by the Cooper were sliding into an inexorable recurring pattern of their own. The dawn brought with it a few brief hours of cool temperatures when the men could take the animals out to graze and attend to camp duties. But as the sun hit its stride, the day grew heavier and it became difficult to do anything at all. Even swatting flies or drawing water from the creek was such an effort that the men ended up cowering in the shade swathed in netting and wondering how such an infinite landscape could become so claustrophobic.

Around late afternoon, a soft glow swept over the creek, banishing the midday glare and recasting the colours with a tinge of gold. For a brief, beautiful hour tranquillity returned. Tempers were smoothed and minds roused from their languor. Around sunset, as the birds quarrelled above them, the men stoked up the campfire and prepared supper. Afterwards, when the stories and jokes were exhausted, there was little for them to do except crawl into their bedrolls and gaze skywards at the edge of universe.

Days and nights on the Cooper melted together. Time belonged to another life. But Burke was not seduced. Succumbing to the tide of inertia was unthinkable, and besides, life at the depot camp was not proving comfortable. The insects were unbearable. Tiny black bushflies crawled into the men's eyes, ears, noses and mouths, prompting even Wills to complain: 'One can do nothing without having a veil on; and whilst eating the only plan is to wear goggles.' Sunset heralded new tortures as the mosquitoes came out in search of blood. The men had two choices. They could sit in the choking smoke of the campfire or breathe freely and be bitten to death. Burke was losing patience. On 13 December, he wrote to the committee that 'the flies, mosquitoes and rats here render it a very disagreeable summer residence'. A rumble of thunder in the distance only added to the feeling of suffocation.

For several days lightning scampered along the horizon. The atmosphere became fretful, as if the whole landscape was waiting for release. Men and animals were restless. As Burke surveyed the dark clouds to the north, he contemplated the possibilities. Rain would fill the waterholes and make his crossing easier. Why wait any longer and use up more valuable supplies? His decision was inevitable. He would not wait for Wright. He would strike north for the Gulf at once.

In a dispatch to the committee, Burke justified his plan to leave the Cooper:

> I shall endeavour to explore the country to the north of it, in the direction of Carpentaria, and it is my intention to return here within three months at the latest. I did not intend to start so soon but we have had some severe thunderstorms lately with every appearance of heavy falls to the north; and as I have given the other route a fair trial, I do not wish to lose so favourable an opportunity.

The letter was disingenuous. Burke had never shown any real signs of wanting to consolidate his position on the Cooper, and if he had been genuinely expecting Wright to arrive, he could have sent Brahe south to help bring up the rest of his supplies.

Later that afternoon, Burke called Brahe to one side and suggested they go for a swim. As the two men floated in the cool waters of the creek, Burke revealed his plan to leave immediately with a flying party consisting of just three men: William Wills, soldier John King and sailor Charley Gray. Then he said, 'I want someone to stay here and take the party back to the Darling if we don't return. I will give you command if you stop. It will be a distinction.'

Brahe was not convinced. The proposal sounded more like a nightmare than a promotion, especially as he too dreamed of crossing the continent. The two men clambered ashore but Brahe refused to commit himself, and Burke was reluctant to force him. Wills had no such scruples. The next morning the surveyor called Brahc into his tent: 'We are in a fix,' he said. 'Someone must take charge here. You do it.'

Brahe remembered later that he 'hummed and hawed over the suggestion but just at that instant Burke came into the tent. Then Wills simply forced my hand. He said, "Brahe has offered

William Brahe was promoted to take charge of the depot camp. For many years after his return to Melbourne, he refused to discuss the Burke and Wills expedition in public.

to stay." "That's good," replied Burke, patting me on the shoulder, and so that settled it.' The German had already proved himself a capable member of the party, but he had never expected to take on such a great responsibility.

Apart from Brahe, three others would remain at the Cooper: Thomas McDonough (who was exhausted from his trip northwards and still in disgrace for losing the camels), William Patten, the blacksmith and, most surprisingly, Dost Mohomet. After thousands of pounds had been spent caring for the precious camels, the only skilled handler was to be left behind. With his plans now out in the open, Burke made preparations to get away as soon as possible. He ordered his men to slaughter two horses and jerk the meat. Burke retired to his tent, where he concluded his dispatch to the committee, full of enthusiasm:

> We are all in good health, and the conduct of the men has been admirable. Mr Wills co-operates cordially with me. He is a most zealous and efficient officer. I have promoted Mr Brahe to the rank of officer. The position he is now placed in rendered it absolutely necessary that I should do so. He is well qualified for the post, and I hope the Committee will confirm his appointment.

Burke reassured Brahe by telling him that Wright would have left Menindee on 15 November, and allowing around a month for the journey, he would therefore be due to arrive any day soon. John King confirmed this assertion, saying that Burke 'expected Mr. Write Daily'.

But clearly Burke had not thought the situation through. How could Wright possibly be expected to procure extra horses, camels and jerked meat, then assemble a new party by 15 November? Then, there was the journey time from the Darling to the Cooper. Burke had made spectacular progress, completing the 600-kilometre march in just twenty-three days. But with summer advancing and the waterholes disappearing, he grossly underestimated Wright's task in retracing his steps. Obsessed with reaching the Gulf first, Burke had no credible contingency plans in case Wright failed to arrive, or in case he himself was away longer than expected.

The Irishman continually confused his men with contradictory plans and off-the-cuff proposals. At one point he suggested that Brahe might head back to Menindee with more animals for Wright, or that the two could team up and survey a more convenient route between the Darling and the Cooper. Given the resources available, both these schemes were as unlikely as they were dangerous. Often Burke's baffling instructions were the result of his tendency to tell each man what he wanted to hear. The result was uncertainty and misunderstanding.

Despite his ignorance of the terrain ahead, Burke was certain that he would complete the journey to the Gulf and back in ninety days. According to Brahe, Burke asked him to wait for three months or until the supplies ran out. Thomas McDonough confirmed that Burke's instructions were to wait for 'three months and longer if he could'. Since northern Australia had already been mapped, Burke must have known that he faced a return journey of around 3000 kilometres. To complete the trip within ninety days, his party would have to average at least thirty kilometres a day or else run out of food. It was a momentous task.

Wills took a more realistic view. He made a point of asking Brahe to hang on for four months if he could. Nevertheless, the surveyor was still optimistic about the expedition's chances of success. As he prepared to leave the Cooper, he told his family he was in the very best of health, and even enjoying the rather limited diet of horseflesh, which he said was 'so delicious you would scarcely know it from beef'. With typical reserve he wrote to his sister that their 'travels so far had been very comfortable; in fact more like a picnic than a serious exploration'. He acknowledged there might be 'some little difficulties to contend with soon' but predicted that the expedition would be back in Melbourne by August at the latest. Wills had abandoned all hope of a scientific expedition; he was now resigned to a race for the Gulf.

It was now twelve weeks since the explorers had left Melbourne and the party was about to split into three, with its supplies scattered from Menindee to Cooper Creek over a distance of 600 kilometres. Burke may have been following orders by dividing the expedition, but by forming three parties he had backed himself into a tight corner. With only a small cache of supplies at the Cooper, he was limited in the amount of food he could take to the Gulf, especially as he had to leave enough behind to feed Brahe and his men. In the end he took 150 kilograms of flour, fifty-five kilograms of dried beef, forty-five kilograms of dried pork, approximately twenty-five kilograms of rice, twenty-five kilograms of sugar, fifteen kilograms of meat biscuit, six kilograms of tea, three kilograms of salt and a few tins of preserved vegetables and ghee. Using Augustus Gregory's formula for calculating the minimum necessary to nourish his men, these amounts were barely enough for four men for ninety days.

But Burke had made a more fundamental mistake when he assessed his rations. He assumed that the men would consume the same amount each day for three months. He made no allowances for delays or the fact that the men would need extra food towards the end of the trek. Here, he displayed an error of judgment that has afflicted even the most experienced explorers. Like Robert Scott many years later, Burke underestimated the demands of the return journey and left too little room for error. Both men were so focused on their goals that they forgot about the rigours of coming back in a debilitated state.

According to King, Burke proposed to enhance his rations by shooting wild pigs and buffalo further north but, in the light of the expedition's indifference to bush tucker so far, this seemed an unlikely option. His second strategy was rather more drastic. Burke had decided to eat his transport. Valuable horses and camels would be sacrificed for food whenever necessary, even if it reduced the expedition's carrying capacity. The exploring party had left Melbourne with enough livestock to start a small farm but there were now just twelve camels and thirteen horses left on the Cooper. Burke decided to take six camels and one horse to the Gulf and, since the animals might have to carry water as well, supplies and equipment were cut to a minimum. Apart from food, his party took just a few firearms, some spare clothing and a small number of scientific instruments. There was no room for luxuries. Even the tents were jettisoned, leaving the men just a bedroll and a blanket for shelter. By any standards they were under-resourced for the journey ahead.

On the evening of 15 December, Burke handed his new officer, William Brahe, a sealed packet of papers, with instructions that they should be tossed into the creek unread if he failed to return. Wills also left behind a number of personal papers and, in a last gallant gesture towards scientific endeavour, bequeathed his collection of barometers and thermometers to Brahe so he could keep meteorological records on the Cooper.

The next morning Burke lined up his men to say goodbye under the early-morning shade of the coolibah trees. However erratic his leadership might have been, the Irishman still inspired the loyalty of his men and the whole party was overcome by the occasion. William Patten the blacksmith burst into tears and sobbed as Burke embraced each of his men. Burke took him aside and reassured him that if he 'was not back in three months', then Patten 'might make his way to the Darling'.

Starting a brand new notebook, Wills wrote: 'Sunday Dec 16, 1860. The two horses having been shod and reports finished, we started at forty minutes past six am for Eyres Creek, the party consisting of Mr Burke, myself, King, and Charley, having with us six camels, one horse, and three months provisions.'

The Victorian Exploring Expedition had started with twenty tonnes of equipment. Now it was embarking on the most punishing section of the journey with only a fraction of these resources. With no spare animals, the 'best equipped explorers ever to try for the Gulf' would be walking the whole way.

Soon after leaving Cooper Creek, the explorers found themselves tackling 'ridges of loose sand' up to twenty metres high.

Twelve

Anticipation of Horrors

'If there is such a thing as darkness which can
be felt, then the Australian desert possesses a silence
which can be heard, so much does it oppress the
intruder into these solitudes.'
Ernest Favenc

Without William Wills, we would have almost no record of the first European crossing of Australia. To begin with, the surveyor maintained his diary scrupulously, leaving a detailed if somewhat clinical journal that bears all the hallmarks of his rationalist beliefs. Later, as the trek began to take its toll, dates become muddled and days get lost in the battle for survival. The original volumes survive to this day—they include a set of scientific records, consisting of up to fifteen meteorological readings a day, followed by pages of long-winded navigational calculations.

Overland navigation in 1860 was a laborious business. Sir Thomas Mitchell (or rather his servants) carried a sextant that weighed twenty-four kilograms. In addition, a typical surveyor needed compasses, a telescope, a chronometer, a theodolite, and special measuring chains the length of a cricket pitch known as 'Gunter chains'. Wills travelled light. His most useful tool was a prismatic compass. The surveyor set his course, then kept to it as far as the terrain allowed. Some areas were littered with rocky outcrops, rivers or boggy country, which meant detours and recalculations. Other patches of open desert were so devoid of reference points that the party stuck as best they could to a predetermined bearing for days on end with nothing to aim for except the dreamlike world of the mirages hovering above the horizon.

In order to compile a proper map, Wills also had to calculate the distance travelled each day. The most accurate methods were time-consuming. Some surveyors used a measuring wheel, others laid out their 20.1-metre Gunter chains end to end. Wills guessed his speed for a fixed distance and then extrapolated from that figure.

Latitude, the party's north–south position, was established by measuring the sun's altitude using a sextant and a pool of mercury enclosed in a vibration-proof box to create an artificial horizon. Wills looked through a system of lenses until he saw dual images of the sun reflected in a mirror. He then moved an index arm on the sextant until the two suns became superimposed and read off an angle from the instrument's scale. Several pairs of readings were necessary to make an accurate calculation and, despite years of practice, Wills found it a tricky process. 'In windy weather,' he complained, 'it is seldom possible to keep the mirror free from dust even for a few seconds and this so interferes with the readings of the spirit level that the altitudes taken with this horizon cannot be depended on within one minute of arc.' Once altitude readings had been obtained, Wills used a special set of tables known as a nautical almanac to calculate his latitude.

Longitude, the party's east–west position, was established by comparing the local time with the time at a fixed point such as the Greenwich meridian. Since the earth revolves fifteen degrees every hour, if Wills knew the difference between the two times, he could then calculate his longitude. In order to ascertain the local time, the surveyor used his sextant to determine when the sun reached its highest point. This method was dependent on the accuracy of his chronometers, and in the 1860s it was a tall order to expect a watch to function without error throughout the rigours of a desert expedition. Indeed, it was not uncommon for variations of several degrees to creep in over a number of months.

As Charles Sturt and John McDouall Stuart had discovered to their cost, taking sun sightings in the desert was a painful process that ruined their eyesight. For most of the journey Wills avoided the problem because he was also proficient at taking star sightings, and even seemed to prefer the nocturnal method. If the night sky was clear he would spend at least an hour and a half working out the altitude and position of selected stars. Then, using his astronomical tables, he could calculate his latitude and his longitude without having to 'shoot the sun'.

In contrast to Wills' meticulous records, Burke's entire 'diary' consists of no more than 850 words. Even the barely educated John King kept a better record than his leader. Burke's efforts are contained in a leather-bound pocketbook, which is still smudged with red earth. It contains an inscription on the first page: 'Think well before giving an answer, and never speak except from strong convictions.' The rest of the entries comprise little more than a scrappy list of dates and campsites scrawled in pencil on random pages throughout the book.

The first few notes read:

16th December Left depot 65, followed by the creek.
17th The same.
18th The same. 67
19th We made a small creek, supposed to be Otta Era (?), or in the immediate neighbourhood of it. Good water. Camp 69.
20th Made a creek where we found a great many natives; they presented us with fish, and offered us their women. Camp 70.
21st.—Made another creek: Camp 71. Splendid water; fine feed for the camels; would be a very good place for a station. Since we have left Cooper's Creek, we have travelled over a very fine sheep-grazing country, well-watered, and in every respect well suited for occupation.

22nd December 1860.—Camp 72. Encamped on the borders
of the desert.
23rd December 1860.—Travelled day and night, and
encamped in the night in the bed of a creek, as we supposed
were near water.

Burke had always disliked paperwork. Visitors to his Beechworth
home were shocked to discover the walls were plastered with
scraps of paper containing scribbled messages in English, French
and German. A sign read: 'You are requested not to read anything on these walls, I cannot keep any record in a systematic
manner, so I jot things down like this.'

By nineteenth-century standards, Burke's diary is particularly
disappointing. Sometimes expedition journals were works of literature in their own right commanding sizeable advances from
publishers. They were also of great commercial and political
interest with enormous consequences for investment, infrastruc-
ture and population growth. The Exploration Committee had
asked Burke to keep a detailed record of his journey, but in the
end impatience overruled obligation. Burke would sometimes
read Wills' journal and make suggestions but that was all. It is a
pity. He may have provided a livelier, more personal record than
his surveyor.

Once they left Depot Camp 65, Burke, Wills, Gray and King
found the first few days of the journey almost idyllic. Predictions
of desiccated wastelands and aggressive Aboriginal warriors came
to nothing as they led their camels through the shade of the gum
trees alongside the Cooper. Even when they turned north, away
from the benevolent influence of the creek, Wills was delighted
to find that between the sand dunes, the valleys were 'very
pretty...and covered with fresh plants, which made them look
beautifully green'. If anything the ground was too wet rather
than too dry, and the confusion of boggy gullies made setting a
course and walking in a straight line a luxury.

William Brahe accompanied the party for the first day. The next morning, 17 December, Burke reiterated his belief that William Wright would be 'up in a few days', even instructing his new officer to catch him up with any messages if his back-up arrived soon. With this reassurance ringing in his ears, Brahe turned his horse around and headed back to camp. His only function now was to survive and await his leader's return. Neither he nor Burke had any idea of the extraordinary events taking place in Menindee, a few hundred kilometres to the south.

On 19 December, Hermann Beckler was checking the supplies of dried meat at the camp on the Darling when a ragged emaciated figure stumbled into view. 'His face was sunken,' the doctor recalled, 'his tottering legs could hardly carry him, his feet were raw, his voice hoarse and whispering. He was a shadow of a man. He laid himself at my feet and looked at me wistfully and soulfully.'

It was Dick the Aboriginal tracker. He had left Trooper Lyons and Alexander MacPherson at Torowoto—home to the Wanjiwalku people. All the horses were lost or dead and the two white men were so weak they were unable to travel. Dick had walked alone for a week to save his companions. He had eaten just two birds and a couple of lizards during his 300-kilometre journey.

Contradicting Burke's accusation that he was too scared to leave the settled districts, Beckler offered to mount a rescue mission. Dick was in no condition to assist, so the doctor took Belooch and another Aboriginal guide named Peter. They set out with three camels and a horse, pushing themselves as hard as they could to reach Lyons and MacPherson. Despite the crisis, Beckler was effusive about the surreal beauty of Australia's desert country:

Nothing could disturb us from the sensual ecstasy of this day, neither the worry about the success of our journey north, the continually oppressive heat, nor even the extremely unpleasant behaviour of our animals...Parts of the chain of hills before us seemed to be reflected on expansive surfaces of water whose edges the eye could never determine. Here and there vertical lines cut through the wavelike contours of the chain of hills; once again everything seemed to blur into a blueish haze. To the east, the ghostly shapes of gigantic tree-tops, towering over sheets of water, appeared to form the entrance to a fairy land. What could be more natural than that

Providing the only permanent water for many kilometres, the rock pools at Mutawintji attract emus, kangaroos, euros and yellow-footed wallabies. Ludwig Becker was enchanted by them.

this unexpected mirage should intensify the magic of this land, a land we have never seen, that we entered as the first Europeans, a fata morgana, the gateway to terra incognita!

Guided by Peter, the doctor followed Burke's old track towards Mutawintji, where he delighted in the Aboriginal art he found around the cool rocky overhangs:

The walls and ceilings were covered with the impressions of outstretched human hands in the most varied colours, a decoration, which had something ghostly about it at first sight. These impressions were such that the hand with its extended fingers appeared in the natural grey or yellow grey of the rock, while their very sharp outline was formed by a halo of colour which gradually disappeared around the outside and which looked as though it had been sprayed on...Later I was informed by a native that the artist held a solution of colour in his mouth and sprayed it over his or another's hand, which was held spread out over the rock. These people paint with their mouths, and their oral cavity also forms their palette.

After a week of hard travelling, it was Beckler who spotted Alexander MacPherson: 'He raised himself laboriously from a stooped position in which he seemed to be gathering something from the ground. He staggered towards us. For several minutes he was completely speechless, but finally he cried out, "Oh Doctor!", and tears streamed from his eyes.' Lyons was not far away. He was in better shape physically but seemed resigned to his fate in the desert and 'had to be cheered up constantly by the others so that he did not despair completely'. Both men had lived for two weeks under an old horse blanket. They had scratched themselves raw from the mosquitoes.

MacPherson told Beckler they had suffered constantly from diarrhoea and vomiting as they tried to head north from Torowoto, and once their horses died, they had no choice but to retreat. Sometimes they were so thirsty they 'rinsed out their mouths with their own urine, and derived great relief from it'. It had taken all their strength to return to the waterholes, where Dick negotiated with the local Aborigines to bring them food, while he returned to Menindee to fetch help. For a few days they received birds, snakes and the odd goanna before the local hunters moved on and they were reduced to gathering the local nardoo plants to grind into flour.

It would have been sensible for Beckler's rescue party to head back to Menindee all together, but by this time the doctor was thoroughly carried away with his new role as an explorer. He decided to strike out for the nearby Goningberri Ranges with Peter, leaving the other three to walk back by themselves. The trio then argued over the choice of route and Belooch walked off by himself. Quite by chance, Beckler found him five days later wandering in circles, delirious and almost dead from thirst. It was another lesson (if one was needed) that dividing up parties in such treacherous country was not a good idea.

In all, the Lyons debacle had been nothing but a dangerous waste of time. Three men had nearly died, four horses were gone and Wright had lost more valuable time—it was now two and a half months since Burke had left Menindee.

After Brahe departed a new routine settled over Burke's party. Between 4 and 5 a.m., as the sun rose, the men would crawl from their bedrolls, shake the insects from their blankets and turn their boots upside down to check for scorpions. As Charley Gray began the packing, John King set out to retrieve the camels. He led them back to the camp, selected a soft level piece of ground, and ordered them to 'hush down'. The animals roared and groaned as they rocked backwards and forwards, then dropped down on their haunches into the sand.

The camel is not a creature designed for freight. The hump

means that cargo inevitably slides downhill and it is essential that the load is well distributed and securely anchored. An unbalanced pack results in saddle sores and abscesses, followed by flies, infections and maggot infestations. The average pack camel can carry around 200 kilograms for fifty kilometres a day. More weight means less distance. Pushing an animal too hard results in a severe deterioration in condition and ultimately, premature death.

In the cool morning air, King adjusted each pack before enlisting the others to help him hoist it aboard. Then he prepared the riding camels, fitting a bridle and an Indian-style saddle, which is placed on the back with the hump protruding through the middle. Stirrups could be fitted if necessary and there was plenty of room to suspend water bottles, rifles, oilskins, binoculars and other assorted paraphernalia.

When everything was ready, King joined the animals together via their nose-pegs (since camels chew cud continuously, they cannot be fitted with a bit and bridle like a horse) and then cajoled them into line ready for the day's work. Accompanied by another chorus of bellowing and cursing, the expedition moved off.

The party tried to cover as much ground as possible before the sun took hold, so breakfast was postponed until mid-morning. Burke or Wills marched ahead carrying the compass followed by Gray leading Billy, and King bringing up the rear. Camels walk best in a particular order. Just one intractable animal can cause havoc, tripping up the others and breaking their rhythm. King soon learnt which camels to put where, and they loped along comfortably, taking just one stride for every three human steps.

After marching for two or three hours the men stopped for a meal of salted meat, damper and tea. If they were lucky, they might find a scrubby tree or a bush to provide a metre or two of

John King's health problems made him an unlikely candidate to cross Australia, but his expertise in handling the camels won him a place in Burke's final party.

shade, though often they squatted down behind the camels to shelter from the sun. Sometimes the explorers pulled off their boots, inspected their blisters and settled down for a snooze, but they soon realised that the longer the break, the harder it was to get going again. After a few days, they confined themselves to just a few minutes' rest. Burke took all the major decisions regarding route and pace, but it was Wills who determined their course and plotted their position.

As the temperatures increased, the party would rest in the middle of the day and then travel late into the evening, continuing by moonlight if conditions allowed. Campsites were selected for their proximity to water, firewood, shade and good

Crossing the Terrick-Terrick Plains by Ludwig Becker. This stylised painting omits the expedition's bolting horses, recalcitrant camels and bogged wagons.

Border of Mud Desert near Desolation Camp by Ludwig Becker. In January 1861, choking in the 'hell-like air' and blinded by the 'sombre dusty haze', Wright's relief party struggled to reach Cooper Creek.

River Darling and the Mouth of Pamamaroo Creek by Ludwig Becker. At first Becker was entranced by this 'rich and poetical' scenery, but after three months the heat, the flies and the boredom became unbearable.

The First Day's Order of March by William Strutt. Furnished with twenty-one tonnes of supplies, the expedition formed an unruly procession more than half a kilometre long when it departed Melbourne on 20 August 1860.

Portrait of Dick by Ludwig Becker. This portrait was made after Dick's journey to rescue Lyons and MacPherson. Sustained by only a couple of lizards and birds, Dick had walked 300 kilometres to obtain help for his stricken companions.

Burke's 'fine intelligent eyes' and 'magnificent beard' gave him a 'daring, reckless look' that the ladies of Melbourne found irresistible. After his death, with John King by his side, he was hailed as Victoria's first hero, and inspired artists and writers.

feed for the animals. The camels nibbled at nearly anything but their favourite food was a succulent plant known as parakeelya and Wills mentions that they were often able to camp in areas with an abundant supply. After a hard day's work, the camel's favourite relaxation was to sink down for a roll in a patch of soft sand. Unlike Landells, King only released them in hobbles. After Wills' experience losing the animals near the Cooper, everyone was careful not to let the animals stray too far.

Without tents or tonnes of equipment, camps were quickly established. Within minutes of halting, King was tending the animals and Gray was collecting wood for the campfire. It was his job to prepare the evening meal and bake the damper for the next day's journey. Once these tasks were complete, there was always equipment to mend, packs to reorganise and sores to bathe—no one relaxed for very long. With darkness falling, the cicadas revved up for their evening performance. Their rasping calls throbbed through the campsite as the men fell upon their suppers with relish. Most nights, while supplies were plentiful, they ate a sort of stew made with salt beef, poured over rice and bread, and finished off with a cup of tea and sugar.

It is unclear how much Burke contributed to the running of the camp. As leader, he was not expected to perform menial jobs, but with such a reduced party it seems unlikely that he did nothing at all. Wills was always busy, taking meteorological observations, writing up his journal, and completing his scientific records. After supper, the bedrolls were laid out, the campfire was stoked up to ward off the mosquitoes and each man lapsed into his own thoughts.

With the flames flickering beneath the gum trees, the desert shrank. For a few brief hours the toil was over—a warm glow of security suffused the camp and shut out the vastness beyond. Only the eerie howl of the dingo reminded them of the world outside. Burke seemed unconcerned about the threat of attack by the local Aborigines. No one kept guard at night. Only Wills stayed awake. The surveyor moved away into the gloom to take star sightings and finish his navigational calculations. He was the only one of the party to go to bed at night with any idea where they were.

There was one important task that had to be completed each day. In order to tame the 'pathless wilds', the Exploration Committee had asked Burke to mark his route 'as permanently as possible, by leaving records, sowing seeds, building cairns at as many points as possible'. The expedition leader was careless about such obligations but, every evening, King took a knife and hacked away the bark of a tree to engrave the letter 'B', followed by the camp number. Once the tracks of the horses and camels were washed away, these small engravings became the only evidence of the first European journey across Australia.

Since 1860, many Burke and Wills enthusiasts have souvenired these carvings or marked trees of their own, leading to confusion about the precise position of authentic expedition camps. There are two ways to spot a 'fake' Burke and Wills tree. The explorers never carved 'BW' (it was Burke's expedition and Wills was only recognised later on) and they always inscribed the camp number in roman numerals because straight lines are easier to carve.

The dynamics of this small group were finely balanced. Each man was dependent on the skills of the others, so personal quirks and weaknesses stood out. In practical terms, Wills was a more capable leader than Burke, but the Irishman possessed a combination of dash and charisma that either infuriated or inspired. The two men were complete opposites in most respects, yet they developed a relationship of 'affectionate intimacy', with Burke habitually referring to his deputy as 'My dear boy'. As the days passed, the four men seemed to settle down well and the journey north was free of the hostility that had torn the expedition apart on the way to Menindee. In particular, twenty-two-year-old John

King was distinguishing himself as a versatile and capable member of the party. Small, quiet and shy, he was an unlikely explorer.

John King grew up during the years of the Great Famine in a thatched whitewashed cottage in the village of Moy, County Tyrone. To ensure he escaped a life of poverty his father (himself a soldier) enrolled him at the Royal Hibernian School, a military college in Dublin. At the age of fourteen King found himself a member of the British army. In his neat handwriting he wrote down his particulars in his regimental account book:

Height: 5 feet 1 inches
Hair: Brown
Complexion: Fresh
Eyes: Hazel
Next of kin: William and Samuel King (brothers, 70th regiment)
Date of birth: December 15th 1838

A year later King was posted to India, where he joined the military band and then took a posting as a teacher, attached to the 70th infantry regiment. In 1857, he was stationed in Peshawar at the height of the Indian Mutiny. A fellow soldier described one example of the brutality that occurred when groups of rebels were brought into the barracks:

The forty men condemned to death were brought out in batches of ten and were placed with their backs against the muzzles of field guns. No word of command was given by the officer of the artillery detachment, but the gunners knew that when he raised his sword arm they were to fire. This was done to save the men who were to be shot from hearing the word of command. I think this form of death was much more merciful than the alternative of either hanging or shooting, the charge of the blank powder in the gun instantaneously breaking the body into some four pieces. This process was repeated until the whole of the number had been executed.

King was among the lines of soldiers watching this grisly punishment and shuddered with revulsion each time the blast of the cannons shattered another body in front of him. Soon afterwards he went on leave for sixteen months after contracting 'fever of a bad type', a complaint that was probably exacerbated by the initial stages of consumption. King was convalescing in Karachi in 1859 when he met George Landells. The camel trader was impressed with the young man's ability to speak the various languages of the sepoy camel handlers, and it wasn't long before he suggested that King sign up for a grand expedition across Australia. It was the perfect excuse to leave the army. King purchased his discharge and joined Landells on the trek through India to take the camels back to Australia. By the time they reached Melbourne, Landells was more convinced than ever of King's worth and persuaded Burke to hire him at a salary of £120 per year.

During the power struggle that erupted on the way to Menindee, King might have been expected to sympathise with Landells, but there was never any hint of him taking sides or incurring Burke's wrath. Always calm and reserved, with a strong sense of duty, King melted into the background and got on with his job. His reward was a place in the forward party.

With King in charge of the camels, the rest of the camp work fell to ex-sailor Charley Gray. A tall bear-like man in his forties, his employer Thomas Dick described him as a 'stout and hearty' worker, who got drunk just once a month when he received his wages. With his cheerful grin and easy-going personality, Gray was a favourite at the pub in Swan Hill, where he worked as an ostler, and he seemed to get on well with everyone on the expedition. Now, with his sinewy arms covered in tattoos of mermaids and anchors, Gray was about to embark on the first overland crossing of Australia.

In the first week the expedition averaged around twenty-five kilometres a day. Wills was pleased to report on 23 December that so far, the journey had been relatively painless:

> We found the ground not nearly so bad for travelling on as that between Bulloo and Cooper's Creek; in fact, I do not know whether it arose from our exaggerated anticipation of

De Gruchy & Leigh, Lith

Charley Gray was well-liked and had proven bush skills. The controversy that later surrounded him led to intense scrutiny of Burke's behaviour.

horrors or not, but we thought it far from bad travelling ground and as to pasture, it is only the actually stony ground that is bare, and many a sheep run is in fact, worse grazing than that.

Burke and his men were doing well. As the terrain grew harsher, they displayed an uncanny ability to discover the most fertile strips of land, in areas where just a kilometre either way might make the difference between finding water or dying of thirst. Their first stroke of good fortune was to traverse an area 100 kilometres above the Cooper, known as Coongie Lakes.

These magical lagoons lie nestled amongst brick-red sand dunes. Nourished by an almost permanent supply of milky orange water, the lakes form one of the richest ecological sites in Australia, providing sanctuary to people, animals and plants. They are important to many Aboriginal groups but principally to the Yawarrawarrka people, who know the area as Kayityirru. When Burke and Wills stumbled across Coongie, it was in pristine condition—before the influx of rabbits and cattle ravaged the soil and dislocated the trees. They saw it before the wide dirt roads of the oil and gas prospectors crept ever closer and the thump of the seismic equipment echoed through the soil. Even now, with pipelines and mines sneaking through the dunes, Coongie retains its tranquillity and magnificence. It is a remote area, often cut off for months by floodwaters, but anyone persistent enough to come here is rewarded with the sense of entering into an enchanted kingdom, insulated from the rest of the world by a sea of rippling sand. Wills was delighted to find such fertile country:

At two miles further we came in sight of a large lagoon bearing N by W, and at three miles more we camped on what would seem the same creek as last night, near where it enters the lagoon. The latter is of great extent, and contains a large quantity of water, which swarms with wildfowl of every description. It is shallow, but is surrounded by the most pleasing woodland scenery, and everything in the vicinity looks fresh and green. The creek near its junction with the lagoon containing some good water-holes some five to six foot deep.

Coongie's Aboriginal inhabitants were astounded by the strangers who set up camp at their waterholes, but they expressed neither fear nor hostility. Wills found the local people to be remarkably welcoming:

> There was a large camp of not less than forty of fifty blacks near where we stopped. They brought us presents of fish, for which we gave them some beads and matches. These fish we found to be a most valuable addition to our rations. They were the same kind as we had found elsewhere, but finer, being nine to ten inches long, and two or three inches deep, and in such good condition that they might have been fried in their own fat.

Later, both Burke and Wills mention that the local tribesmen offered them women, according to their custom. These invitations were rejected in disgust.

So far Wills had proved to be somewhat condescending towards Aboriginal behaviour and traditions. Burke's attitude ranged from indifference to hostility. Now the journey was under way, he wanted to travel across the continent with as little interference as possible. Most of the time he did just that. Wills was often surprised that they didn't see more Aborigines, unaware that the party was being constantly monitored by a network of well-camouflaged messengers. The camels and Billy meant the expedition was never molested. Speed also helped. Since the party never lingered for more than a night at each campsite, it was not seen as a threat. Indeed, the local people often overcame their shyness to point out the best creeks and waterholes to the men as they passed through.

On several occasions Burke and Wills tried to persuade
Aboriginal men to guide them, although they did not resort
to the brutal tactics of later explorers such as David Carnegie.
He would often hunt and capture Aboriginal people, then tie
them to a tree until thirst forced them to point the way to the
nearest billabong. Wills offered beads and mirrors as enticements
but there was no time to win anyone's trust and his attempts
failed.

On Christmas Eve, nearly 200 kilometres from the Cooper,
they reached a campsite Wills described as their most beautiful
so far:

> We took a day of rest on Gray's Creek, to celebrate
> Christmas. This was doubly pleasant, as we had never in our
> most sanguine moments anticipated finding such a beautiful
> oasis in the desert. Our camp was really an agreeable place for
> we had all the advantages of food and water attending a posi-
> tion on a large creek or river, and were at the same time free
> of the annoyances of the numberless ants, flies and mosqui-
> toes that are invariably met with amongst timber or heavy
> scrub.

The men rested by the creek and indulged in extra rations.
Burke planned to catch up on his diary but perhaps his Christmas
feast got the better of him. He managed just forty-two words:
'We started from Cooper's Creek, Camp 66, with the intention
of going through to Eyre's Creek without water. Loaded with
800 pints of water, four riding camels 130 pints each, horse 150,
two pack camels 50 each, and five pints each man.' One can
easily imagine Burke asleep under a gum tree, his cabbage-tree
hat over his face to keep out the flies and his notebook lying in
the dirt beside him.

The party left Gray's Creek at 4 a.m. on Christmas Day, but
lethargy soon overtook them. Burke recorded: 'At two pm, Golah
Singh [a camel] gave some very decided hints about stopping and

lying down under the trees. Splendid prospect.' Every hour of rest was a luxury. The party was still travelling too slowly and using up too much food. The journey was degenerating into a test of endurance—as much a race against dwindling rations as against McDouall Stuart. Burke's diary declined further into a series of dates and times:

> December 30th—Started at seven o'clock; travelled 11 hours.
> 31st—Started 2.20; 16½ hours on the road. Travelled 13½ hours.
> 1st January 1861.—Water.
> 2nd January.—From Kings Creek; 11 hours on the road. Started at seven; travelled nine and a half hours. Desert.
> 3rd January.—Five started. Travelled 12 hours. No minutes.
> 4th.—Twelve hours on the road.

The terrain was unpredictable. There were stretches of easy walking across drying claypans and lightly timbered plains, but there were also large tracts of boggy ground and kilometres of monotonous red dunes. Even so, the horrors of Sturt's Stony Desert were never fully realised. The simmering rubble appeared only in patches, leaving Wills sceptical of their fearsome reputation: 'We camped at the foot of a sand-ridge jutting out on to the stony desert. I was disappointed although not altogether surprised that the latter was nothing more than the stony rises we had met with before, only on a larger scale and not quite as undulating.' The camels coped better on the rugged sections than expected. They possessed a surprising ability to pick their way through the stones, while the men were limited to stumbling along, never quite hitting their stride on the rock-strewn plains.

Twelve hours' march through the desert soon becomes a tiring and tedious experience. In the desiccated atmosphere, hair becomes brittle, skin burns and flakes, nails crack between scaly cuticles, hands and feet split open and cuts fester into ulcers that never heal. Streams of sweat mix with the sand and dust to produce a gritty paste that chafes like sandpaper in the elbows and groin. Constant wind and intense light leave eyes sore and throats scratchy, reducing voices to a whisper. Sleep is often interrupted by a raspy cough. Flies swarm around the face, provoking a constant swishing motion with the arms and an occasional outburst of total frustration.

The sun heats up the environment until the air, the sand and the rock radiate heat, putting the explorers under enormous physical strain. As their work rate increased, their core body temperatures rose from 37°C to around 39°C. They sweated profusely and their skins flushed as their blood vessels dilated and carried the heat to the surface. At the start of the journey, before they were acclimatised, the men would have been susceptible to salt depletion and cramps. If they worked too hard their heads began to pound and they felt dizzy. Disturbed vision and stomach cramps followed. The only solution to this was to slow down.

Sweating requires energy and large amounts of liquid. Dehydration was a constant danger, especially as it was easy to ignore. The body does not always send the right signals to the brain and many people do not feel thirsty even when they are seriously dehydrated. In severe conditions, when a person sweats up to two litres per hour, it becomes almost impossible for the gut to absorb enough water to keep up. The explorers compounded the problem by marching for many hours without drinking, then guzzling large amounts of liquid in one go once they had stopped. This was the worst way to rehydrate. Since their blood had been diverted away from the gut, their digestive systems couldn't cope and they felt bloated and sick.

Burke and his men carried about three and a half litres with them per day, yet they would have needed at least fifteen litres just to replenish the liquid they were sweating away. Although they always had sufficient water each evening, they must have been dangerously thirsty throughout most of the day's march. Dehydration also has a devastating effect on the body's physical performance. A 2 per cent deficiency in body liquid results in a 10 per cent reduction in endurance capacity. Many of the body's most important functions including the efficient digestion of food depend on a plentiful supply of water. In their dehydrated state, Burke, Wills, Gray and King were not even getting the full benefit of their limited diet. The explorers were pushing their bodies to the limit day after day. It was an extraordinary demonstration of stamina and determination but the cumulative effects were inescapable.

Mentally, such journeys are just as testing. When trekking hour after hour, it is the small things that irritate. Seeds from tangles of spinifex grass work their way inside socks and boots, irritating the skin until there is no alternative but to spend every rest-stop picking out the burrs and scratching the itchy red sores. Sweat stings, flies buzz, belts pinch, boots rub and water bottles jangle. Just the sound of someone humming a tune over and over or swishing a stick in the sand can be the final straw. Keeping a sense of perspective while marching becomes a conjuring trick of the mind and people have to find their own way of coping.

Burke and Wills were stoic about their physical circumstances. By now they were sometimes achieving sixty kilometres in a single march. If anything, the relative ease with which they coped during the early stages of the journey belied the magnitude of the task ahead. For now, luck was running in Burke's favour. It was Christmas, and the explorers were about to receive a geographical gift that would take them all the way to the Gulf of Carpentaria.

Thirteen

Never More Severely Taxed

'A live donkey is better than a dead lion isn't it?'
Ernest Shackleton to his wife, after turning back
ninety-seven miles from the South Pole in 1909.

The revelation occurred as Burke's party toiled through the sandhills. In the open sun, the men clawed their way up the ramparts as the grit slithered away beneath them. 'Each day,' John King scribbled wearily towards the end of December, 'we had to face the Desert again.' Even Wills was exhausted:

> We found the ground much worse to travel over than any we have yet met with. As the ridges were exceedingly abrupt and steep on their eastern side, and although sloping gradually towards the west, were so honeycombed in some places by the burrows of rats, that the camels were continually in danger of falling.

They tried to keep to the meshes of vegetation that anchored the sand—but marching through the clumps of spinifex was like striding through a forest of razor blades and their trousers hung in rags around their bloody ankles. Every dune was the same and every summit revealed another confusing mass of orange laid out like a giant rumpled tablecloth. Marching parallel to the hills, down in the claypans, was easier. Sometimes it was possible to follow the shelter of a valley for hours, unaware of anything but the strip of greenery stretched out ahead. The danger was that by sticking to the low-lying ground, the explorers might miss creeks or lagoons just one sandhill to the left or right. It would be easy to die just a few hundred feet from a water source hidden by a wall of sand.

This area of western Queensland is now known as the channel country. Flying is the best way to appreciate the arid landscape and the fragility of the river system that feeds it. Watching the carpet of ochre pass beneath, hour after hour, imagining what it would be like to cross it on foot, is an awe-inspiring experience. Only a few tiny capillaries of green, spread out like a network of blood vessels, give any clue that life is being pumped through isolated corridors of land. In a fertile year, latching on to one of these creeks is like connecting with the slenderest branches of a tree. Following it will lead to larger and larger branches until the trunk is reached and, with any luck, it will be rooted to the coastline.

Without a map, grasping one of these elusive lifelines is a lottery. A party could wander for weeks, as Sturt's did, and find nothing, but Burke and Wills hit the jackpot on 27 December, just south of the present-day town of Birdsville. They climbed yet another dune, unaware of the stunning view that awaited them. Moments later they were gazing down over a floodplain, lined with rich vegetation and dotted with snowy white cockatoos. There were birds everywhere. 'We saw plenty of turkies,' wrote King in delight as he watched the plump Australian bustards taking off from their hideaways in the spinifex.

Today the sight of the lime-green ribbon draped between the orange dunes is still as unexpected as it is striking. Burke and Wills had found a branch of the Diamantina River. If they had veered any further to the west, they would have found themselves entangled in the world's largest parallel dune system: the Simpson Desert.

The Simpson is like a giant sand maze covering 150,000 square kilometres. Some of the dunes reach forty metres in height. In fertile seasons the desert is a patchwork of purple, white, yellow and red wildflowers but there is not a drop of permanent water in the whole area. Without rain it is reduced to bare expanses of sand sparsely covered with the spiky remains of spinifex, hakea and acacia plants.

Every expedition deserves its share of good luck and Burke and Wills had just received theirs. Finding the Diamantina was the key to reaching the Gulf of Carpentaria. It would lead them towards the Georgina River system, and from there almost directly north to the coast. From now on, finding water would not be a problem. It seemed Burke's gamble was paying off.

The explorers were not the only people taking advantage of the river. Many tribes, including the Wangkamana, the Yarluyandi, the Wangkangurru, the Mithaka and the Karuwali, lived in the area. John King was amazed to find that some were not only brave enough to approach but generous enough to point out the best billabongs as well: 'they saw our fire & were making to the spot when they saw us they kept going away & point(ing) to where the water was.'

Over the next few days Wills noticed further evidence of Aboriginal occupation:

Jan 5th.—We came to a creek with a long broad, shallow waterhole. The well worn path, the recent tracks of natives, and the heaps of shells, on the contents of which the latter had feasted, showed at once that this creek must be connected with some creek of considerable importance.

It was now nearly three weeks since the party had left Depot Camp 65. Despite the plentiful grass Wills realised that the camels were 'greatly in need of rest'. It was a worrying sign, especially as they had at least 1200 kilometres to go to reach the north coast.

Camels are uniquely adapted to cope with the desert. They can alter their body temperature over a range of seven degrees, allowing them to operate in a wide range of conditions. Their long eyelashes and small fur-lined ears protect them from the sand and their fat-rich humps and ability to recycle their urine insulate them from dehydration. But camels are not as 'invincible' as the newspapers of the 1860s had believed. While they can travel enormous distances (up to 100 kilometres in a day), they cannot sustain this for long periods without sufficient time to recuperate. 'A common fault with European officers,' wrote one camel expert, Arnold Leese, 'is to be in too much of a hurry.' Burke insisted on marching for twelve hours a day and hobbling the beasts at night. His camels were not getting enough to eat.

In Burke's defence, he had probably been taken in by the extravagant claims Landells had made to impress the committee. Inspired by false confidence and oblivious to the first signs of the camels' distress, Burke surged on, taking no rest days and still managing to average thirty to forty kilometres a day. A rare diary entry for 5 January 1861 reveals that the pace was beginning to tell on him as well as his animals:

> Water at Wills' or King's Creek. It is impossible to say the time were up, for we had to load the camels, to pack and feed them, to watch them and the horse, and to look for water, but I am satisfied that the frame of man never was more severely taxed.

As the explorers trekked towards the Georgina River system they found that the country was improving 'by the yard'. The grass was abundant and the riverbanks were smothered with yellow and white 'poached egg daisies'. Travelling was easy and they soon reached an area near the present-day outpost of Boulia, a town deriving its name from the Pitta-Pitta Aboriginal phrase *bulla-bulla* meaning large waterhole. The journey was progressing smoothly until on 7 January, one of the pack camels decided to roll, slightly damaging some of Wills' instruments. He worried that the accident might affect the accuracy of his navigational calculations.

As they followed a large creek, now known as the Burke River, the explorers noticed the vegetation was changing; the dark gnarled coolibahs were giving way to smooth silver ghost gums, magnificent trees whose trunks glowed in the moonlight like skeletons. Wills noted that flocks of pelicans were reappearing along the waterways and, as the camels swept through the long grass, the occasional kangaroo or wallaby hopped away in fright. Kookaburras with azure blue wings surveyed them knowingly from the trees and giant anthills began to litter the countryside like tombstones in a graveyard. The worst of the desert was behind them and the tropics were close at hand.

Until the failure of Trooper Lyons' mission, William Wright clung to the idea that Burke would send back extra pack animals to help him carry the stores to the Cooper. But when Dick returned alone, he realised it was not to be. Exasperated by the delay, the journalist William Hodgkinson took matters into his own hands. On 22 December, he wrote out a dispatch dictated by Wright and set off for Melbourne. Showing remarkable speed, he completed the journey in nine days, arriving on John Macadam's doorstep on New Year's Eve.

It is impossible to tell how much Hodgkinson influenced the content of Wright's dispatch but the message raised the fear that Burke might have pushed on without waiting for his extra supplies. According to Wright, there was now 'the most serious apprehensions to the safety of himself and his party'. Macadam responded by convening an emergency meeting at which the committee expressed surprise that Wright was still in Menindee and not on his way to the Cooper. It confirmed the station manager's appointment as third-in-command and authorised him to spend £400 buying extra horses and saddles. Business complete, the members retired to their new year festivities satisfied they had done everything necessary for the expedition. Hodgkinson left the next morning and by 9 January he was back in Menindee.

While Burke and Wills followed creek after creek towards the Gulf and Wright battled to organise his relief party, another expedition was also preparing to head north. It was Burke's rival—John McDouall Stuart.

As Burke had discovered back in Menindee, Stuart's first attempt to cross Australia had ended in failure. Nevertheless, he had travelled more than three-quarters of the way, well and truly lifting the 'veil' on Australia's mysterious centre. There was no inland sea and there were no lost cities or giant mountains—but nor was there just an empty desert wasteland. The truth was somewhere in between. Stuart's journey revealed 'barren tracts and dismal ranges' but also stretches of the 'finest pastoral country'. To the delight of Adelaide's business community, the explorer had dispelled the myth of the 'ghastly blank': 'We are not, after all,' cried the *Register*, 'the occupants of a mere strip of country, shut in by the sea on one hand and the impassable desert on the other. There opens before us a new world, with new fields for our enterprise and new outlets for our industry.'

This optimistic interpretation ignored the fact that Stuart had conclusively proved that the 'empty interior' was in fact full of indigenous people with established cultural and social networks. The news was not what the land-hungry sheep farmers and prospectors wanted to hear. They continued to maintain that unsettled Australia was 'terra nullius'—a land owned by no one.

Stuart's discoveries reignited South Australia's hopes of running a telegraph line from Asia down through central Australia, but they still needed to establish a suitable port to bring the line ashore. They knew they would have to move fast to secure an advantage. Victoria, smug in the knowledge that its party was well on the way to the coast, had already dismissed Stuart's first attempt as a fake. Furious, the South Australians suggested that perhaps Stuart had been 'lying concealed in a cellar in Adelaide' during his 'supposed journey'. The row culminated in the Melbourne Lands Department sending a rather impertinent request for 'any authentic information you may possess as to Mr Stuart's recent journey', adding that it would be 'happy to reciprocate when opportunity presents'. A two-line telegram followed containing Stuart's final co-ordinates and a promise that, 'as soon as the map and journal are published information will be available'. In other words—go and buy the book like anyone else! Infuriated by Victoria's response, the South Australian parliament voted to provide Stuart with another £2500—enough money for him to try again with a much larger party.

The Scotsman was not in the best of health to mount a renewed attack on the Australian interior. He had returned with advanced scurvy, which turned his legs black and inflicted such pain that he admitted he 'almost wished death would come and release me from my torture'. Taking sun sightings had destroyed his eyesight and left him with periods of double vision and blindness. Yet, with the personal carelessness that afflicts an explorer denied his goals, he volunteered to try again. As Burke had predicted, Stuart began to assemble a new expedition at once.

The Chambers brothers again assisted with horses and supplies, but it took three frustrating months to gather a staff of nine men and a string of forty horses. As usual, rations and equipment were kept to a minimum. Food was limited to dried beef, flour, sugar, tea and whatever the party could gather en route. Only the leader had a tent to work in; the rest of the men slept in swags.

Each horse carried around fifty-five kilograms, with the heaviest items such as ammunition and spare horseshoes being split up amongst the strongest animals. Liquor of any sort was banned—Stuart had not lost his love of spirits, but not even the lure of a whisky bottle could compromise his ruthless style of packing. The only luxury was tobacco. Each man was allowed four ounces (115 grams) a week.

Stuart ran a very different style of expedition from Burke. He travelled hard each day but rested every Sunday to observe the Sabbath. The Scotsman selected his staff based on personal knowledge and previous experience. Discipline was harsh but, judging from the loyalty of his men, it was also fair. Later on, Stuart compiled a written set of rules, which governed all his subsequent expeditions:

> All orders are to proceed from the leader, and during his absence, from the second-in-command, who will be in full charge of the party, and whose orders must be obeyed as if they came from me.
>
> No horses are to be abused, kicked or struck about the head. Sore backs etc are to be attended to after unsaddling. No horse to be put out of a walk except of necessity.
>
> When anything is used it must be packed up in the same manner as found and returned to the place whence it came.
>
> Breakfast to be ready at the same time, for which half an hour will be allowed. Immediately after the horses will be brought in and unhobbled. The riding-horses will be first unsaddled, and everything belonging to them placed on the saddles.
>
> No one is to leave the line of march without my knowledge or that of the officer in charge. When leaving camp no one must go without arms and ammunition.
>
> No one is to fire on the natives without orders unless in self-defence.
>
> When on the march no water to be used from the canteens without permission of the leader.
>
> No swearing or improper language shall be allowed.
>
> Each man must sleep with his arms at his side, and in case of attack from the natives a half-circle to be formed three feet apart.

This strict routine meant each expedition ran like clockwork. The horses and their packsaddles were numbered and divided into groups. Each animal learned its place and lined up automatically every morning and evening in the correct order so the foreman could always locate whatever equipment was needed. One of Stuart's men, Pat Auld, remembered that the party was always ready to leave within half an hour of waking:

> When every horse was packed we would mount. Stuart would light his pipe—he was very fond of his pipe—take a bearing with his prismatic compass, replace it in the case, and start. Then Turpin, the bob-tailed cob, would follow close behind and the others would come on, one behind the other, like ducks.

Unlike Burke, Stuart never divided his party unless absolutely necessary and he fretted about anyone separated from the main group. He relied heavily on his two most trusted officers, Francis Thring and William Kekwick. In particular, Thring and his beloved horse Gloag possessed an uncanny ability to find water and the pair saved the party in many desperate situations.

On Friday 11 January 1861, after several weeks' preparation 'in the broiling sun', Stuart's party set out from the outpost of Mount Margaret Station, north of the Flinders Ranges. Perched on top of the leading horse was the expedition's pet dog Toby, who had latched onto the party and now refused to stay behind. Even by the usual outback standards, conditions at the beginning of the journey were severe. It was mid-summer and many of the best waterholes had dried out, resulting in several forced marches of many kilometres without water.

'Poor little Toby' was the first casualty, upsetting even Stuart, who recorded that his death was 'regretted by us all, for he had already become a great favourite'. The men battled on against constant thirst, sunburn, chapped lips, sore throats and stinging eyes. The intense glare tortured Stuart in particular and as the party continued north towards the MacDonnell Ranges, there were periods when he could hardly see at all.

On 11 January, Burke's party rose as usual at dawn, but the daylight seemed sluggish in arriving. An eerie gloom enveloped the camp, unsettling the camels and mystifying the explorers. It was Wills who realised what was happening:

> Started at 5 am and in the excitement of exploring fine well-watered country, forgot all about the eclipse of the sun, until the reduced temperature and peculiarly gloomy appearance of the sky drew our attention to the matter. It was then too late to remedy the deficiency, so we made good the day's journey, the moderation of the mid-day heat, which was only about 86 deg., greatly assisting us.

Even when the eclipse had passed, the conditions remained favourable. Flocks of colourful zebra finches zigzagged across the sky and the silence was punctuated by the peculiar door-creaking cry of the crested pigeons as they flew up from the long grass. The pleasant temperatures and excellent countryside made an agreeable change from the sun-scorched rocky desert: 'The country traversed has the most verdant and cheerful aspect,' wrote Wills, there is an 'abundance of feed and water everywhere'.

Wills' diary is usually an excellent indicator of the expedition's morale. When the going was good, his entries contain enthusiastic descriptions of the surrounding landscape. When it was tough, he lapses into silence, often for days at a time. The party had enjoyed several days of good country and fine weather, but on Sunday 13 January, a ragged line began to tear at the horizon. Small but vicious outcrops of sharp stone started to replace the lush grasslands, forcing the explorers to stop and try to protect the camel's feet: 'We did not leave camp until half-past seven, having delayed for the purpose of getting the camels shoes on—a

Approaching the Selwyn Ranges, the explorers were watched by hostile Kalkadoon warriors. The mountains left the men exhausted and the camels 'sweating with fear'.

matter in which we were eminently unsuccessful.'

It was Wills' last entry for six days.

It was the Standish and Selwyn ranges that caused the sharp break in Wills diary. In 1977, two experienced bushmen, Tom Bergin and Paddy McHugh, set out with a couple of Aboriginal friends to recreate the Burke and Wills journey using camels. Tom later described the land around the Selwyns as 'the cruellest ground I have ever dragged an animal over'.

From a distance the Selwyn Ranges are magnificent—jagged russet-red walls glinting in the sunlight, intersected by valleys of parched yellow Mitchell grass and stunted white gum trees. But the bewildering labyrinth of gorges is crisscrossed with sharp slaty ridges and steep slopes of loose scree. Wills' map shows that the men tried to scrabble their way westwards through the range, but were forced to turn back and try a route further to the east. For once it was Burke who described their ordeal:

18th January. Still on the ranges, the camels sweating profusely from fear.

20th January. I determined today to go straight at the ranges, and so far the experiment has succeeded well. The poor camels sweating and groaning, but we gave them a hot bath in Turner's Creek, which seemed to relieve them very much. At last through—the camels bleeding, sweating and groaning.

It wasn't just the terrain that was dangerous. Burke and Wills were deep inside the territory of the Kalkadoons—one of the fiercest Aboriginal tribes in Australia. In later years, these warriors resisted European settlement by mounting successful guerrilla-style campaigns against miners, pastoralists and policemen.

The men soon realised that the Kalkadoons were watching them from lookouts high up in the mountains. 'We found here numerous indications of blacks been here,' remarked Wills, 'but we didn't see them.' Twenty years after the Burke and Wills expedition, a miner out prospecting for copper got to know some of the Kalkadoon tribal elders. They told him that the younger men had been determined to attack and kill the explorers and had prepared themselves by feasting on kangaroo meat, holding ceremonies and painting their chests with ochre and chalk. But when the time came for the ambush, the warriors realised that the men were accompanied by giant roaring beasts, which they assumed must be supernatural. They retreated and watched the party from a safe distance high up in the cliffs.

Ignorant of the drama taking place around them, the explorers slowed dramatically, making just eight or ten kilometres a day. Wills had little time for writing. His diary does not resume in earnest until 27 January when he noted with relief that the party had now crossed the Selwyn Ranges.

As the terrain began to flatten out, the expedition skirted the site of the present-day town of Cloncurry (named after Burke's cousin Lady Cloncurry) and headed north-west. Several falsely marked trees and vandalised campsites mean there is now confusion about whether the party followed the Cloncurry or the Corella rivers, but Wills' diary suggests that the Corella is more likely. This route led them north until the end of January. Then, the party crossed Augustus Gregory's 1856 east–west track along the Top End of Australia, approximately 200 kilometres from the coast.

According to Burke's instructions, the expedition had fulfilled its official responsibility to explore the country between the Cooper and Gregory's track. Burke could have turned back with honour. Even more importantly, the party had reached what modern explorers refer to as 'Drop Dead Day' or the 'PNR' (point of no return). On 30 January Burke should have abandoned the expedition, turned south and headed for home. In terms of time, he was halfway through his allotted schedule of ninety days. In terms of food, the party was using up its supplies faster than anticipated. Every day spent travelling further north diminished the rations available for the return journey and decreased the odds of survival. If Burke was aware of these facts, he chose to ignore them. He once declared he would reach the Gulf even if he got there without the shirt on his back. Now it seemed he was prepared to make the trip without enough food to feed his men.

Did the more circumspect Wills ever raise the subject of retreat? He knew how far they still had to go, and he must have been aware that rations were running short. Did King or Gray ever realise they were in danger or petition their leader to turn back? If such discussions took place, they are not recorded.

Burke thought of his reputation. He thought of Julia waiting for him in Melbourne. He thought of his triumphant return. There was never any doubt that he would press on past the point of no return.

Fourteen

Beneath the Veil

'Haste ye, Stuart, do not sleep: in
Settled districts never lurk.
Onward! Or you're surely beaten
By the great O'Hara Burke.'
Melbourne *Punch*

Beyond the Corella River, the land stretched out into a dreary two-tone vista of swaying yellow grasses under gloomy grey skies. Crossing the Selwyn Ranges had banished the dry heat of the desert and plunged the countryside into the oppressive heat of the tropics. Somehow the sky is lower here. The leaden ceiling pushes down, compressing the steamy atmosphere until it squeezes behind the eyes. People have been known to 'go troppo' in the unrelenting heat; everything from bar-room brawls to murders are blamed on the pressure-cooker environment of Australia's Top End.

The expedition was in what is now known as the Gulf country, an area of flat terrain governed by a tropical climate of two seasons: the 'dry' between May and November and the 'wet' between December and April.

Burke and Wills hit the Gulf country at the worst possible time of year. The monsoon was late, so they were travelling in what is known as the 'build-up'. This is a period of a few weeks just before the rainy season, when the humidity climbs and the air thickens until it is almost difficult to breathe. With the atmosphere at bursting point, spectacular electrical storms dance along the horizon and everyone prays for rain.

The dry air down by the Cooper had sucked liquid from the explorers' bodies, allowing them to perspire freely and perform relatively well despite the very high temperatures. Now the air was at saturation point. They continued to sweat, but the liquid didn't evaporate to keep them cool. It poured from their bodies, running into their eyes and carving salty trails through the grime on their skin. The men suffered from lethargy, headaches and irritability. Even sleeping was difficult. The temperature no longer fell at night and they lay on their bedrolls, tossing and turning under their damp, woollen blankets, used in a vain attempt to ward off the mosquitoes. In the muggy atmosphere, food rotted and the leather harnesses grew furry with mould. The camels were fretful and listless. Struggling over the ranges had taken its toll, Burke was pushing the animals too hard and, at the beginning of February, disaster struck.

Camels have large feet like soup plates with horny pads. These are designed to provide grip in sandy terrain but they are hopeless in boggy country because they are so difficult to extract from the mud. Riverbanks presented a particular hazard, sometimes forcing them to make long detours to find an easy approach to the water. On this occasion Golah, a large bull, clambered down into a creek but couldn't get back out. After pushing the exhausted beast for five kilometres along the creek bed without success, the explorers were forced to abandon him.

Burke, Wills and King had no choice but to redistribute the loads and continue with their remaining five camels. Soon afterwards they found a new waterway heading north. It was the beginnings of the Flinders River. The silty sluggish waters were broken every now and then by turtles poking their heads through the algae and occasionally by a crocodile floating just under the surface.

There are two species of crocodile in Australia—the saltwater and the freshwater. 'Freshies' are smaller with narrower snouts;

they do not normally attack humans. 'Salties' are a different matter. They grow up to seven metres long and, with one twist of their powerful torso, they can propel themselves right out of the water and take down a fully-grown cow. These primeval creatures are aggressive, territorial and numerous throughout the Gulf country. It is difficult to know whether the explorers realised the danger they were in camping alongside these rivers and each day going down to the crocodile's favourite hunting ground along the water's edge. It seems, however, that they were lucky enough to pass unmolested through crocodile country.

After Golah's accident, Wills diary is once again silent until 9 February. Since leaving Melbourne, Burke, Wills, Gray and King had marched in tough conditions for more than five months with hardly a rest day. They had endured a journey of more than 2500 kilometres through bogs, deserts and mountain ranges in frost, hail, rain, windstorms, sandstorms, heat and overpowering humidity. Now, as they followed the Flinders River, their goal was close.

It is tempting to imagine the explorers scenting the salt in the air, climbing a small rise and seeing a white sandy beach falling away into the sparkling ocean. How quickly their hardships would have melted away as they shouted with delight and flung themselves into the waves. How overwhelming their sense of achievement would have been as they sat on the northern edge of Australia under the Union Jack, celebrating with three cheers, a double serving of bread and sugar and an extra cup of tea. The reality was so different.

As Burke and Wills neared the north coast, the countryside seemed to close in around them. The thickets of small trees grew so dense it was difficult to force a way through. As the ground became wetter, the depressing reality dawned—the camels could go no further. The men unloaded their gear and made camp at a small waterhole on the junction of the Bynoe and Flinders rivers.

Camp 119 is still there today. It is a mournful, drab clearing, surrounded by spindly box trees and infested with clouds of mosquitoes. The cloying atmosphere is made worse by the scrub, which clutches at your clothes and rips at your hair. The air is filled with the rotten smell of festering mud. The water from the creek is cloudy and unpleasantly warm. It is also salty.

It is not recorded who first noticed the bitter saline taste or realised that twice a day, the murky liquid rose and fell a few centimetres, but these clues confirmed that Burke's party had just about reached its objective. They were camped on the upper tidal reaches of an estuary and the ocean could not be far away. By this stage, not even Wills knew exactly where they were. He had plotted their route towards the Albert River, which was actually 100 kilometres away to the west and he had no idea they were, in fact, camped on the Flinders River.

This dank muddy campsite was as far as Gray and King ever reached. Leaving them to care for the camels, Burke and Wills set off together into the territory of the Yappar Aboriginal people to see if they could find the ocean. Perhaps rejuvenated by the discovery that they were so close to the coast, Wills wrote a full account:

> After breakfast we accordingly started, taking with us the horse, and three days provisions. Our first difficulty was in crossing Billy's Creek, which we had to do where it enters the river, a few hundred yards below the camp. In getting the horse in here, he got bogged in a quicksand so deeply as to be unable to stir, and we only succeeded in extricating him by undermining on the creek's side and then lunging him into the water. Having got all the things in safety, we continued down the river bank, which bent about from east to west, but kept a general north course. A great deal of the land was so soft and rotten, a horse, with only a saddle and about twenty-five pounds on his back, could scarcely walk over it. At a distance of about five miles we again had him bogged in crossing

Camp 119—Burke's dismal, most northern camp—lies next to a waterhole at the junction of the Bynoe and Flinders rivers on the edge of the mangrove swamps.

a small creek, after which he seemed so weak that we had great doubts about getting him on. We, however, found some better ground close to the water's edge, where the sandstone rock runs out, and we have stuck to it as far as possible. Finding that the river was bending about so much that we were making very little progress in a northerly direction, we struck off due north, and soon came on some table-land, where the soil is shallow and gravely, and clothed with box and swamp gums…

After floundering through this for several miles, we came to a path formed by the blacks, and there were distinct signs of a recent migration in a southerly direction. By making use of this path, we got on much better, for the ground was well trodden and hard. At rather more than a mile, the path entered a forest through which flowed a nice watercourse, and we had not gone far when we found places where the blacks had been camping. The forest was intersected by little pebbly rises, on which they had made their fires, and in the sandy ground adjoining some of the former had been digging yams, which seemed to be so numerous they could afford to leave lots of them about, probably having only selected the very best. We were not so particular but ate many of those they had rejected, and found them very good.

About half a mile further we came across a blackfellow, who was coiling by a campfire whilst his gin and his picaninny were yabbering alongside. We stopped for a short time to take out some of the pistols that were on the horse, and that they might see us before we were so near as to frighten them. Just after we stopped, the black got up to stretch his limbs, and after a few seconds looked in our direction. It was very amusing to see the way in which he stared, standing for some time as if he thought he must be dreaming, and then, having signalled to the others, they dropped on their haunches and shuffled off in the quietest manner possible.

Near their fire was a fine hut, the best I have ever seen, built on much the same principle as those at Cooper's Creek, but much larger and more complete. I should say a dozen blacks might comfortably coil in it together. It is situated at the end of the forest, towards the north, and it looks out on an extensive marsh, which is at times flooded by seawater.

Hundreds of wild geese, plover and pelicans were enjoying themselves in the watercourses on the marsh, all the water on which was too brackish to be drinkable, except some holes that are filled by the stream that flows through the forest. The encampment is one of the prettiest we have seen during the journey. Proceeding on our course across the marsh, we came to a channel through which the sea water enters. Here we passed three blacks, who, as is universally their custom, pointed out to us, unasked, the best part down. This assisted us greatly, for the ground we were taking was very boggy. We moved slowly down, about three miles and then camped for the night; the horse, Billy, being completely baked. We started the next morning, leaving the horse Billy short hobbled.

Burke and Wills managed only a few kilometres more. The ground disintegrated into a tangle of impassable mangrove swamps and they had neither the energy nor the resources to look for another way through. The journey north was over. They did not see the ocean.

Burke wrote later in his notebook: 'At the conclusion of the report, it would be well to say that we reached the sea, but we could not obtain a view of the open ocean although we made every endeavour to do so.' Wills made no diary entry at all.

The explorers had made it to within twenty kilometres of the coast. It must have been deeply disappointing to turn around without looking north across the waves towards Asia. Charles Sturt knew what it was like to be denied by the fickle nature of the Australian landscape:

To that man who is really earnest in the performance of his duty to the last, and who has set his heart on the accomplishment of a great object, the attainment of which would place his name high up in the roll of fame; to him who had well nigh reached the top most step of the ladder, and whose hand has all but grasped the pinnacle, the necessity must be great, and the struggle of feeling severe, that forces him to bear back, and abandon his task.

Burke and Wills left no monument to mark their historic crossing. There was no moment of exhilaration, no time to sit and contemplate victory. Instead, exhausted and demoralised, they turned and waded back through swampy water towards Camp 119. Back in the small clearing, King and Gray had kept themselves busy catching a few fish and keeping watch over the camp. King spent several hours marking a circle of trees with the letter B. It was the only evidence that the expedition had ever reached this far north.

Burke reassured himself that the committee would be 'quite satisfied' that he had completed his mission 'as far as it was necessary'. And he could take some comfort in knowing that he had beaten John McDouall Stuart across the continent, even if the culmination of the journey had yielded little useful information about the north coast. Now he must face the unpleasant prospect of retracing his steps to the depot on the banks of the Cooper, 1500 kilometres to the south.

As the men contemplated their return, the weather deteriorated. So far the monsoon had been light but now the rain fell in torrents. The mood was grim. Even Gray and King must have realised the expedition was in a desperate situation. It had taken nearly two months to reach the Gulf from the depot camp, yet Burke had told William Brahe to wait just three months before considering them 'perished', or 'on their way to Queensland'. Wills must have been remembering his whispered entreaty to Brahe to hang on for four months if he could. Suddenly the expedition was no longer a race for glory. It was a fight for survival.

At Menindee, William Wright was busy trying to break in ten horses. After receiving his money from Melbourne he set about purchasing pack animals and saddles, but knowing he was desperate, the station owners asked vastly inflated prices. Training the horses was a mammoth task and the expedition was delayed for a further two weeks as Wright struggled to knock his disorderly mob into shape. In the end it was more than three months after Burke's departure from Menindee before the back-up party was ready to leave. It was 26 January 1861 when William Wright and his men finally set out.

In the meantime, William Brahe and his men had been stranded in the middle of the continent, sitting in the shade of the large coolibah tree on the banks of Cooper Creek. The men were finding it difficult to cope with the insidious effects of boredom and inactivity. Arctic adventurers like William Edward Parry, trapped in the ice for months on end, devised a fixed daily schedule of exercise, maintenance, even cross-dressing theatre performances to stave off the harmful effects of doing nothing. Ernest Shackleton hid books, games and spare tobacco for times when morale was low.

Brahe and his three companions, Patten, McDonough and Dost Mohomet, had no such diversions. The first few weeks after Burke left were reasonably busy. They built a stockade next to the old coolibah to store their equipment and ammunition. They pitched their tents around a central cooking area and established a routine to take care of the animals. Each day, one man would take out the horses to graze, while another watched over the camels. It was a wearisome business, tramping as much as ten or fifteen kilometres up and down the creek looking for the best fodder, and then having to retrieve any optimistic beast that still entertained thoughts of home far away to the south.

The other two men stayed behind, one on guard and the other gathering firewood, collecting water and baking endless loaves of damper. Apart from their periodic encounters with the local people, each day was crushingly similar to the last—a dislocation from reality—trapped on the creek cut off on all sides by a desert that shimmered in the raging heat.

The Aboriginal tribes were fascinated but perplexed by their new neighbours. They attempted to make contact by bringing presents of fish and nets but they also had a tendency to take whatever they could find lying around the camp. Their ability to appear from nowhere and steal everything from tin cans to saddles made Brahe jumpy. Outnumbered, in hostile territory, he couldn't afford to take risks. Under such stress, the cultural divide between the parties was just too great. No meaningful communication was ever established and relations swung between tolerance and hostility.

One day in January, frustrated by the constant pilfering, Brahe drew a circle in the dirt and indicated that no one should cross the line. The warriors retreated but returned later with spears, body paint and vigorous displays of anger. Brahe fired over their heads to reinforce his point. They scattered, running through the herd of horses and yelling until they caused a stampede. Brahe rode into the melee firing his gun into the air and once again the young men retreated. It was nightfall before the horses were recaptured.

The Aborigines could not understand why these unfriendly strangers wanted to stay so long at one of their best waterholes. A few braver souls from the tribe continued to approach the camp with gifts. Brahe continued to refuse them. These confrontations had a paralysing effect on Dost Mohomet. He had been the major supplier of ducks and fish from the creek, but he became so scared that he refused to go out hunting at all.

When Brahe wasn't checking over his shoulder, he was scanning the horizon looking for William Wright. He remained convinced that the relief party would appear at any moment. But the sun rose and fell each day, and still no one came. Brahe was perplexed. By March, his thoughts began to turn north instead of south. He knew that Burke would go 'all out' for the coast, but he also knew that the party only had rations for three months. When April arrived, Brahe began to ride to the top of the surrounding hills each day to look out for any signs of Burke's return. There was nothing.

The four castaways lapsed into a lethargic mechanical routine. Their food supplies were dwindling and as the days dragged by, fear began to penetrate the monotony. Patten was complaining that his gums were sore and that his legs ached. The fear turned to panic. Brahe's party did not possess detailed knowledge of scurvy but they were familiar with 'barcoo rot', a scurvy-like disease that afflicted stockmen on an inadequate diet. They also knew that without fresh food barcoo rot could result in an agonising death.

All around them the sun melted the horizons and the ground throbbed in the heat. They huddled under the shade of the giant coolibah—and waited.

Fifteen

The Awful Truth

'Now for the run home and a desperate struggle.
I wonder if we can make it.'
Captain Robert Scott

Up at Camp 119 there was mud everywhere. When it rained, which was often, the glutinous slime clung to their boots, blankets, camel harnesses and cooking pots. When the sun came out, it set like concrete. The monsoon turned the camp into a quagmire reminiscent of those on the journey towards Menindee. The only difference was the temperature. The warm fetid air hung about the small clearing, increasing the sense of confinement. Without tents Burke, Wills, Gray and King slept huddled under scraps of damp canvas, sweating and cursing in the darkness as the mosquitoes whined around them.

All four were in a pitiable condition. Their bodies were thin; their hair and beards were ragged mats plastered around their gaunt features; their clothes were rotten and their boots battered and torn. The animals were little better. Billy was exhausted after his recent ordeal in the swamps. The camels were scrawny and 'leg weary'. Would anyone finding this wretched group recognise the men from the 'finest expedition ever assembled in Australia'?

The oppressive heat and constant drizzle conspired to make every small chore into a herculean task. There was a strong temptation to let go and do nothing at all. The journey to the Gulf had been a great achievement—far in excess of anything Burke's critics had predicted. But the triumph had been achieved at great cost. An audit of the remaining supplies on 12 February 1861 revealed the four men had used up nearly three-quarters of their rations. For the 1500-kilometre march back to the Cooper, they would now have to live on thirty-eight kilograms of flour, sixteen kilograms of deteriorating dried beef, two kilograms of pork, five kilograms of meat biscuits, five kilograms of rice and four kilograms of sugar. It seemed unlikely that they would have the time or the energy to supplement their food with bush tucker so Burke ordered that each man's daily ration should be cut in half.

As the fatigue set in, it was King who took charge of the camp. On the morning of 13 February 1861, he 'hushed down' the five remaining camels into the mud and packed the last of the supplies. To cut loads to a minimum, Wills sacrificed more of his instruments and 'a considerable number of books'. They were buried with a note under a box tree and have never been recovered. The four men turned south.

On the outward leg of an expedition, enthusiasm, obsession or sheer bloody-mindedness can bury logic and caution so deeply that the potential costs of the journey are irrelevant. Even the most level-headed explorer is susceptible to the thrill of victory or the fear of failure. In the excitement of the quest, minds and bodies are pushed further than ever anticipated and the consequences are inevitably played out on the journey home.

For Burke, Wills, Gray and King, conditions were miserable from the start. It continued to rain. Progress became a matter of cajoling, threatening and beating the camels, as they sank into the mud. Each step was marked by a loud slurp as the beasts struggled to pull their huge round feet from the slimy morass. During the first week of the return journey, they managed just six or seven kilometres a day. As they plodded south, daily thunderstorms tore open the skies, surprising even Wills with their ferocity:

> The flashes of lightning were so vivid and incessant as to keep up a continual light for short intervals, overpowering even the

moonlight. Heavy rain and strong squalls continued for more than an hour, when the storm moved off W.N.W; the sky remained more or less overcast for the rest of the night, and the following morning was both sultry and oppressive with the ground so boggy as to be almost impassable.

For the most part, navigation was easy. They simply retraced their steps from camp to camp. On Saturday 2 March, after battling south for two and a half weeks, they found Golah waiting for them near a creek. The unfortunate animal had worn a path along the bank, walking up and down looking for his companions. The effort reduced him to a virtual skeleton but he began to eat as soon as the others arrived. The temperature continued to hover around 38°C. Combined with the humidity it sapped their energy so much that even Wills' customary optimism deserted him:

> The evening was most oppressively hot and sultry—so much so that the slightest exertion made one feel as if he were in a state of suffocation. The dampness of the atmosphere prevented any evaporation, and gave one a helpless feeling of lassitude that I have never experienced to such an extent. All the party complained of the same sensations, and the horses, showed distinctly the effect of the evening trip, short as it was.

Day and night ceased to matter. The routines of the outward journey degenerated into a makeshift schedule that depended on the weather, the state of the ground and the grinding necessity of making as much progress as possible before the food ran out. They started at 2 a.m. or 2 p.m., or whenever they could muster the energy to carry on.

One ritual dominated each day's proceedings. Morning and evening, the explorers would line up with their backs to Burke, waving away the flies until he told them to call out a number. One by one the men turned around to claim their designated plate and remove the handkerchief that covered it. Underneath they found a measure of flour or a few sticks of rotting meat. This pitiful process was all they had to look forward to each day.

With supplies running low, food was not just important—it was an obsession. Gastronomic fantasies during times of hardship are a recurring theme in expedition literature. Hours of marching have been filled with imagining the ideal menu or the perfect meal. During Sir John Franklin's ill-fated journey through the Canadian Arctic in 1819, the expedition's naturalist Dr John Richardson wrote, 'we are scarcely able to converse on any other subject than the pleasures of eating'. Once desperation sets in, anything appears edible. Franklin became notorious as 'the man who ate his boots'. Others in his party took a more direct approach. They ignored the boots and carved up the men wearing them instead.

Burke's party must have suffered from similar culinary cravings. Despite traversing far more fertile country than Franklin's men, they still made little effort to utilise the natural foods that thrived all around them. During his time as a shepherd at Deniliquin, Wills proved he was quite capable of filling the cooking pot with ducks and wallabies, but now he was too tired to hunt for long. King reported seeing 'kangaroos, emues, and any quantity of ducks and pelicans', but Wills only managed to shoot one pheasant-like bird, which proved to be 'all feathers and claws'.

The only living food source they exploited was portulac, a fleshy plant that covered the riverbanks throughout the channel country. Once boiled, it tasted like spinach and soon became a staple part of their diet. Wills declared it an 'excellent vegetable'. He was right. Packed with vitamins A and C, it was all that stood between them and scurvy.

On 3 March, for the first (and only) time on their journey, they tried a more exotic form of bush food when Charley Gray rode over a large snake. Wills wrote later:

He did not touch him, and we thought it was a log until he struck it with the stirrup iron. We then saw that it was an immense snake, larger than any that I have ever before seen in a wild state. It measured eight feet four inches in length, and seven inches in girth around the belly. It was nearly the same thickness from the head to within twenty inches of the tail, it then tapered rapidly. The weight was eleven pounds and a half.

That night they dined on python steaks. Wills seemed satisfied with his meal, christening that night's stopover 'Feasting Camp' but he spoke to soon—the reptile had a disastrous effect on the intestines of Burke and Gray:

Started at 2 am on a S.S.W. course, but had soon to turn in on the creek, as Mr Burke felt very unwell, having been attacked by dysentery since eating the snake. He now felt giddy, and unable to keep his seat. At 6 am, Mr Burke feeling better, we started again, following along the creek...

The next day things improved. After several painful and undignified hours, Burke and Gray seemed to be regaining their strength, the weather lightened and the humidity dropped bringing 'a beneficial effect to all'. Relief came too late for Golah. He had never recovered from his time alone on the creek and, even without a load, he could no longer keep up. Inexplicably, Burke and Wills didn't shoot the ailing beast for meat but abandoned him once more in the bush.

As the hardships of the journey took their toll, it was inevitable that tensions should begin to appear within the party. The problems began with the decline of Charley Gray. His jovial personality was disappearing, and he began to lag behind in silence.

The largest, most robust men often fail first on an expedition, probably because of their greater calorific needs. Gray had grumbled about headaches on the journey north and, now the rations had been reduced, he complained of leg and back pains as well.

After eating the snake, he began to weaken rapidly. 'Mr Burke almost recovered,' Wills wrote impatiently on 7 March, 'but Charley is again very unwell, and unfit to do anything; he caught cold last night through carelessness in covering himself.'

Wills' attitude towards a companion in distress seems callous—but perhaps it was a sign that, in order to survive, each man was lapsing into his own constricted world. The journey was draining their reserves of compassion as cruelly as it wasted their muscles. A sick man, incapable of carrying out his duties, was a huge burden on such a small party and with the Selwyn

Near the Selwyn Ranges, Wills noted 'a single conical peak' and a series of 'fine valleys'. The explorers tried unsuccessfully to fit the camels with special shoes to protect them from the sharp stones hidden beneath the grass.

Ranges looming once more on the horizon, Wills in particular began to feel resentment towards the listless Gray.

Second time around, they were lucky with the mountains. Wills found a better route and the party were soon 'safely over the most dangerous part of our journey'. On 13 March, they established themselves 'near the head of the gap in a flat about three kilometres below our former camp', a site that is now known as O'Hara's Gap. That evening it rained heavily and floods forced them to take shelter in a cave. The next day they set off to find their old track to the south of the ranges but swollen creeks and waterlogged ground forced endless detours and slowed them even further.

Wills makes no special mention of 15 March 1861 in his diary but he must have known the significance of the date. It was three months since they had left the Cooper. Their time was up. According to Burke's instructions, Brahe was now authorised to return to Menindee if he chose. Yet Burke, Wills, Gray and King were still 1100 kilometres from the depot camp. Would Brahe wait any longer? Would he hang on for four months as Wills had implored him to just before leaving?

To speed things up, Burke reduced their rations once more and rummaged through the packs for superfluous equipment. Men who had expected to dine at oak tables and bathe in a brass tub were now reduced to dumping their spare trousers or their extra water bottle. The cast-offs were gathered together into a bundle (reckoned by Wills to weigh twenty-eight kilograms) and suspended from a tree nearby.

As the days dragged past, and Wills found it harder to maintain his diary, it was often the camp names that told the story of their journey. 'Humid Camp' was 21 March, followed by 'Muddy Camp', and 'Mosquito Camp'. Each night the four men struggled to build a small fire with their damp wood and soggy matches. Wills described their efforts to cook a few small loaves of damper:

We halted on a large billibong at noon, and were favoured during dinner by a thunderstorm, the heavier portion of which missed us, some passing north and some south, which was fortunate as it would otherwise have spoiled our baking process, a matter of some importance just now.

After crossing the Selwyn Ranges, Burke and King began to complain of leg and back pains, but it was still Gray who was causing the most concern. On Monday 25 March, the grim unity that had sustained the party for nearly six weeks since they left the Gulf evaporated. That evening, Wills wrote:

After breakfast took some time altitudes, and was about to go back to the last Camp for some things that had been left, when I found Gray behind a tree eating skilligolee. He explained that he was suffering from dysentery, and had taken the flour without leave. Sent him to report to Mr Burke, and went on. He, having got King to tell Mr Burke for him, was called up and received a good thrashing. There is no knowing to what extent he has been robbing us. Many things have been found to run unaccountably short.

King remembered the incident differently. He said that Gray was terrified of admitting his crime to Burke. The sailor begged him to report the incident on his behalf. King agreed and then stood to one side as Burke lost his temper:

Mr Burke called him, and asked him what he meant by stealing the stores, and asked him if he did not receive an equal share which of course, he could not deny; Mr Burke then gave him several boxes on the ear with his open hand, and not a sound thrashing, as Mr Wills states; Mr Wills was at the other camp at the time, and it was all over when he returned. Mr Burke may have given him six or seven slaps on the ear.

Under normal circumstances, Gray's crime was trivial. To four starving men in the middle of the outback, it was a major offence. Trust had disappeared. From that moment on, Gray was not allowed near the packs without supervision and King was placed in charge of the stores. Charley—the easy-going, gentle giant—had betrayed them all.

Wills was furious. He found Gray's weakness deplorable. Another man might have lashed out, but Wills, a model of self-discipline, followed the rules and let Burke administer justice. After further questioning, the sailor admitted that he had helped himself to extra rations 'several times' without permission. Wills was so incensed he even went to the trouble of examining Gray's stools, suspecting that 'dysentery' was just an excuse for his crime. There were no more friendly mentions of 'Charley' in Wills' diary. From now on he was only ever referred to as Gray.

It must have been a difficult atmosphere as the men loaded up the remaining supplies the next morning. The weather provided the only relief. As they moved further south, the monsoon began to lose its influence and the lush tropical vegetation gave way once more to spinifex and mulga scrub. Wills noticed how areas that had been 'so fresh and green' were now 'very much dried up'. For long stretches at a time, there were 'no signs of water anywhere'.

The terrain was now so changeable that the men did not know what trial they might face next. As the stone country reappeared, the glittering tangles of rock tore at their tattered boots. Out on the open plains, the sense of space, so exhilarating on the way north, was now a terrible reminder of how far they had to go. On 25 March a strong breeze blew up, 'which conveyed much of the characteristic feeling of a hot wind', but by five that evening the temperature plummeted so far that the men had to 'throw on' their oilskin ponchos during the night. A few hours later, it was back up to 35°C and they found themselves being blasted by a raging dust storm. Without tents, they had no protection and by morning they had to dig themselves out of the sand.

Rations were critically low. Burke had always intended to shoot his camels for food if he had to. (It is safe to conclude that this was a plan he never revealed to the gentlemen of the Royal Society, who had signed the cheques for these expensive beasts.) Since it was now a toss-up as to who would collapse first—the men or the animals—Burke decided it was time to sacrifice the weakest camel. On 30 March, Boocha was led away from the rest of the herd and shot. His throat was cut, his skin peeled away and strips of meat were carved from the carcass to be dried. Wills was satisfied that 'a considerable portion of the meat was completely jerked by sunset'.

All four men were suffering from chronic exhaustion. Their diet was lacking in Vitamin B and the pains in their legs and backs were almost certainly symptoms of beri-beri or Vitamin B deficiency. A constant supply of portulac, however, boosted their intake of Vitamin C and none complained of the symptoms of scurvy. Their biggest problem was an overall lack of food. The men were not consuming enough calories to sustain their work-load and their bodies were gradually beginning to digest themselves.

It is more difficult to assess their mental state. If only Burke had been a writer. His emotions surged so much nearer the surface than those of his deputy that he might have revealed more than just temperatures and plant names. Other explorers in similar situations have provided insights into the types of stress that Burke's party was suffering.

In 1972, Geoffrey Moorhouse set out to cross the notorious 'Empty Quarter' of the Sahara Desert. Towards the end of his journey, tired, hungry and thirsty, he discovered how the mind and body react as they reach the limits of their endurance:

> There was a stiffness in my body that came not from the cold nor yet from long exertions, but seemed to issue now from the deepest fibres of my being in a translated protest of the soul at

the very thought of movement. I felt as though I were inhabiting a spent and useless contraption of tissue and bone which no longer had any relevance to me and what I really was…Under the dreadful, drilling heat of this appalling sun I had become an automaton who marched. I was scarcely recognisable as a human being, with the responses that alone distinguished us from the animals. I wondered whether I had forfeited a little of my soul to the desert—maybe the greater part of it.

Gray was deteriorating fastest. He now did little but complain of pains and weakness in his legs and back. Wills had little sympathy. On 8 April, as the party retraced their steps near the Diamantina River, he wrote: 'Halted fifteen minutes to send for Gray who gammoned he couldn't walk.' Soon afterwards the sailor collapsed. From now on he was another encumbrance to be carried by his weakened companions. In a brief moment of lucidity, as he was lifted onto a camel and strapped into place, he asked Wills to give his small cache of personal belongings to Police Superintendent Foster at Bendigo.

Only Billy was in worse condition. The next day, the horse's legs buckled and he sank into the sand. Given Burke's sentimental streak, it must have been difficult to shoot an animal that had struggled so gallantly across the continent. Wills on the other hand was practical. 'As we were running short of food of every description ourselves,' he noted, 'we thought it best to secure his flesh at once. We found it healthy and tender, but without the slightest trace of fat in any portion of the body.'

The meat was a welcome relief, but no amount of Billy-stew seemed to be enough to reinvigorate them. Gray was becoming a heavier burden. The rest of the men searched their consciences, just as Captain Scott's party would have to in the Antarctic with the dying Lawrence (Titus) Oates half a century later. How should they deal with a man whose death was inevitable, but whose lingering life was now endangering them as well? Robert Scott gave only the briefest of hints that he was frustrated by Oates' slow decline: 'Titus Oates is very near the end one feels. What we or he will do, God only knows. We discussed the matter after breakfast; he is a brave fine fellow and understands the situation, but he practically asked for advice.' Scott seems to imply that Oates should take the initiative himself, which in the end he did, by walking out into the blizzard to his death. How terrible the pressure must be on a dying man who knows that his companions are waiting for him to expire.

Nearing Coongie Lakes, with 150 kilometres to go to the Cooper, the sailor's condition continued to worsen. Wills became convinced that Gray's problems were his own fault. He declared that 'the man's constitution was gone through drink, as he had lived in a public house at Swan Hill, and I have heard since that he drunk very heavily there'. King reported that Wills 'did not understand Gray complaining so soon, as the other three of us did not seem to suffer, except from weakness'.

On 17 April, nine days after Wills had accused Gray of shamming, the sailor proved him wrong. Wills' diary entry is terse: 'This morning, about sunrise, Gray died. He had not spoken a word distinctly since his first attack, which was just as we were about to start.' According to King, Gray's pain had grown worse until he became delirious and unable to speak. He spent his last few days strapped semi-comatose to a camel.

It was Burke who gave the order to halt and give Gray a decent burial. Fighting his own exhaustion, King took a shovel and worked under the burning sun, scraping out a hole in the dirt. Despite Gray's emaciated state, it was all his companions could do to carry the body to the grave. There was no burial service. Charley Gray the sailor ended his days about as far from the sea as it was possible to be.

The digging took up an entire day. Was it guilt or respect that led the three survivors to spend so many valuable hours scratching out a last resting place for their comrade? It was certainly the honourable thing to do—proof that they were still human.

The next morning everything except the absolute essentials was discarded. Camel pads, pots, even a rifle were all left behind. The only food they carried was a few pounds of dried horsemeat. The situation was still desperate, but without Gray they might make better progress. Provided their strength held out, relief was not far away. A surge of optimism returned and they even talked of coming back in a few days to pick up the things they had abandoned. The depot was close enough to allow thoughts of a victorious homecoming to sustain them during the final hours of the journey.

The first sign of safety would be that abrupt shift in the landscape as the Cooper's benevolent influence carved its way through the desert. There would be a smudge of green, perhaps even a wisp of smoke in the haze. The noise would come next, the squawking of the cockatoos or the rush of wings as a flock of budgerigars swirled past heading for water. The trees would thicken into a comforting canopy of the river gums and the smell of the campfire would waft through the dry desert air. There would be meat roasting in the camp oven, tea boiling in the billy.

Surely William Brahe had hung on even though they had been away four months rather than three? Backed up by Wright's party and its fresh supplies the depot on the Cooper would be substantial; perhaps even Ludwig Becker had made the journey and was sitting in his tent sketching as usual?

How surprised Brahe and his companions would be to see this ragged trio stumble in from the unknown. The dishevelled explorers could almost hear the shouts of welcome and disbelief, feel the joyous embraces as they announced they had become the first men to cross Australia. There would be food—thick crusty damper saturated with the butter and sugar they craved, endless brews of tea, perhaps even a nip of rum...then rest, fresh blankets and sleep. Their nights would be peaceful, their days free of the dreadful unceasing marches. Gradually the pains that had wracked their bodies would subside and they would prepare to return victorious to Melbourne.

They would be the most famous men in Australia. When the welcome banquets and civic receptions were over, Wills would publish the expedition's diaries and take up the scientific career of his choice. King, who had proved his loyalty and resilience, was assured of a secure future in any trade he desired. But it was Burke who had the most to gain. He was on the brink of accomplishing the status and respect he had always dreamed of. He had blazed a trail for the telegraph lines and the traders, he had crossed the largest island on earth. There was so much to look forward to—a hero's welcome, a grand reputation, £2000 in prize money and above all his beloved Julia Matthews. After such a triumphant return, surely even Julia would not be able to refuse him now?

Such was their confidence that on 20 April, the trio devoured the last of Billy. Wills knew the depot was not far away and they would need all the strength they could muster for one last effort. According to King they were still 'very weak' and the camels were so exhausted that 'they were scarcely able to get along', but that day they made it to within fifty kilometres of the depot. One way or another, tomorrow's march would be the last.

As the sun rose on 21 April 1861, all three men knew that surviving the day's ordeal would be a matter of willpower. To begin with they tried to save the camels but, in the final desperate hours, they found they could stagger no further and resorted to riding the two strongest animals. Burke sat astride one, Wills and

King clung to the other. It was early evening as they neared Cooper Creek. Wills had navigated for nearly 1500 kilometres since leaving the coast and he had returned them to the exact same waterhole they had left just over four months earlier.

Burke rode on ahead. The sun had set and dusk was settling around the waterholes. Several times, he yelled out in excitement to the others. There were tents ahead—he was sure of it. Exhilaration surged through the heavy mantle of tiredness and he began to shout out greetings to Brahe, McDonough and Patten. When they failed to answer, Burke mustered his last reserves of strength and bellowed a mighty 'coo-ee' into the bush.

There was no reply. Wills and King caught up and the trio rode into Depot Camp 65. Desperate now, they looked for the comforting glow of the campfire. There was none.

The three men stared in disbelief at the remaining timbers of the stockade, the ashes of the old campfires and the few bits of abandoned equipment. Undaunted, they reasoned that the base camp must have shifted further down the creek. Brahe would have needed fresh food for his horses and camels—of course, that was it—he must have moved. Exhausted, they prepared to tramp the last few kilometres to find their companions.

It was Wills who saw the carving on the coolibah tree:

DIG
UNDER
3 FT NW

There was a date engraved on a low branch next to the message: April 21st 1861. King bent down to feel the ashes of the campfires. They were still warm. The men of the depot party were gone. They had left that day.

Sixteen

Dig

'Before my highest mountain—stand I,
And before my longest journeys,
Therefore must I descend deeper
than I have ever ascended.'
Zarathustra

As Burke, Wills and King stared at the word 'DIG' engraved on the tree, the terrible reality began to permeate their disbelief. Burke collapsed in the dirt. He couldn't move. It was Wills and King who fell on their knees and scratched away the earth beneath the tree. They found an old camel trunk with a bottle and a note inside:

> Depot, Cooper's Creek, 21 April 1861
>
> The depot party of the VEE leaves this camp today to return to the Darling. I intend to go SE from Camp LX, to get to our old track near Bulloo. Two of my companions and myself are quite well; the third—Patten—has been unable to walk for the last eighteen days, as his leg has been severely hurt when thrown by one of the horses. No person has been up here from the Darling. We have six camels and twelve horses in good working condition.
> William Brahe.

Underneath the note, there was flour, sugar, tea and some dried meat. Instinct took over. It was all they could do to crawl to the creek and collect a billy of water, but somehow King mustered the strength to prepare a meal. As they devoured spoonfuls of porridge and sugar, a trickle of energy returned and the three men began to contemplate their predicament.

Their renewed clarity brought with it an even greater sense of anguish. They had fulfilled their mission in 127 days. According to the message and the warm ashes of the fire, they had missed Brahe by eight or nine hours—about the same time they had lingered to bury Charley Gray. So many questions welled up through the despair. Why hadn't Wright been up from the Darling? Why had Brahe abandoned them? How far away was he now?

Later that evening Wills wrote:

Our disappointment at finding the depot deserted may easily be imagined—returning in an exhausted state, after four months of the severest travelling and privation, our legs almost paralyzed, so that each of us found it a most trying task only to walk a few yards. Such a leg-bound feeling I never before experienced, and hope I never shall again. The exertion required to get up a slight piece of rising ground, even without a load, induces an indescribable sensation of pain and helplessness, and the general lassitude makes one unfit for anything.

This acknowledgment of physical hardship provoked a rare display of sympathy from Wills. With a shudder of remorse, he realised how Charley Gray must have felt before he died:

Poor Gray must have suffered very much many times when we thought him shamming. It is most fortunate for us that these symptoms, which so early affected him, did not come on us until we were reduced to an exclusively animal diet of such an inferior description as that offered by the flesh of a worn out and exhausted horse.

After eating, Burke recovered himself and began the discussions about what to do next. The obvious move was to catch up with Brahe, but did they have the strength to continue? They read the note again and again. It stated that all the horses and camels were in good condition—how could they possibly hope to overtake a fresh party? Both Wills and King agreed that it was impossible to go any further that night.

As the moonlight shone between the branches of the old coolibah, and the cicadas hummed in the background, the three men sat in the dirt staring at the campfire. Perhaps the cool morning air would bring inspiration. They unrolled what was left of their bedding and slept.

Twenty-two kilometres to the south, William Brahe and his men were also settling down for the night, oblivious to the fact that their companions had returned. They were in a far worse state than the note in the camel trunk suggested. Patten was incapable of walking, several of the camels were suffering from advanced mange and the horses were footsore. It would be a slow journey to Menindee.

For Brahe, the decision to leave Depot Camp 65 was a release. For weeks he had fought a running battle with his conscience, each day riding to the top of the hill beyond the creek, scanning the horizon and reworking the possibilities in his mind. In the end, physical deterioration made the decision for him. Each morning as he crawled from his bedroll, his ankles were a little more swollen, as he ate his breakfast his mouth was slightly more tender, and every time he tried to mount his horse, his muscles were a fraction weaker. Everyone except Dost Mohomet was starting to suffer from scurvy—without fresh food, decline and death were inevitable.

Burke had promised to be back in three months. Perhaps thinking of Wills, Brahe had waited four months and one week. On 18 April 1861 he wrote:

> There is no probability of Mr Burke returning this way.
> Patten is in a deplorable state and desirous of being removed

to the Darling to obtain medical assistance and our provision will soon be reduced to a quantity insufficient to take us back to the Darling, if the journey should turn out difficult and tedious. Being also sure that I and McDonough would not much longer escape scurvy, I, after most seriously considering all the circumstances, made up my mind to start for the Darling on Sunday next, the 21st.

Brahe ordered William Patten to shoe the horses at once. He was just in time. The blacksmith collapsed soon afterwards and was unable to work again. On the eve of their departure, Brahe called McDonough as a witness and burnt the packet of letters that Burke had entrusted to him before he left for the Gulf. As the fragments of ash floated skywards, it seemed like the final acknowledgment that Burke was never coming back.

On 20 April, Patten was unable to move at all. The other two men packed up their gear and tidied the camp. Afterwards Brahe buried the camel chest full of supplies then took out his knife and began to carve a message in the old coolibah tree. He stripped away the thick wavy grooves of bark to reach the smooth inner surface of the trunk. Opposite the original camp number, in roughly hewn letters, he chiselled out the command 'DIG'. Then, on a lower bough, he inscribed his arrival and departure dates. The coolibah that had protected them for so many months was now a giant living message-stick. It was all that was left for Burke to return to.

At 10.30 a.m. on 21 April 1861, Brahe, McDonough, Patten and Dost Mahomet took one last look around Depot Camp 65. They mounted their horses and camels and headed for home.

The man everyone had been expecting, William Wright, was battling to keep his own party alive, let alone bring relief to anyone else. After leaving Menindee on 26 January 1861, it became clear that his outfit was hopelessly inadequate for the journey to Cooper Creek.

Hermann Beckler kept a detailed record of the trip. Inspired by his rescue of Trooper Lyons, the doctor had decided to accompany Wright. Beckler declared that, although the station manager had an illiterate's tendency to use 'hideous words', he was also 'an excellent bushman' who possessed 'a certain natural equanimity, to my mind an excellent quality in an explorer'. This assessment was an implicit criticism of Burke, whom Beckler had regarded as dangerously impetuous.

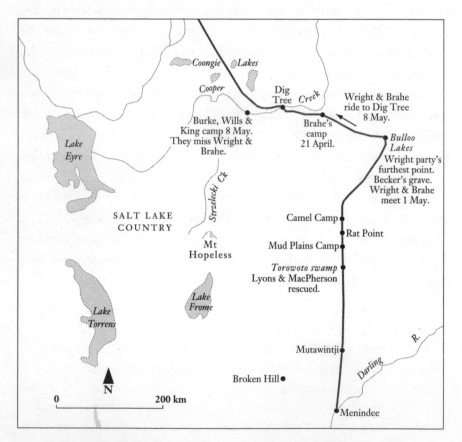

On 21 April, Burke, Wills and King returned to the depot camp; Brahe was just twenty-two kilometres away. They missed rescue a second time when Brahe and Wright rode to the Dig Tree on 8 May.

The rest of Wright's party consisted of Becker, Stone, Hodgkinson, Purcell, Cook, Smith, Dick and Belooch. They took with them thirteen horses and ten camels loaded with as much food as they could carry. The new horses proved unruly from the beginning. They pranced from side to side, throwing their loads and forcing their handlers to chase after them in the blinding heat. By the end of the first day Beckler found that 'a carefully packed and lined basket of medicaments, which I had sent on ahead with the horses, was now largely filled with broken bottles'.

Dick, the Aboriginal guide who had rescued Trooper Lyons, soon realised that tragedy was inevitable. On the first night, he availed himself of a nice clean shirt and slipped away into the darkness.

Wright was dismayed to find that the waterholes that sustained Burke's party on his journey north had now shrunk to an undrinkable sludge. As a result, he adopted a policy of splitting up his convoy and sending men on ahead with camels to deposit waterbags along the route. These could then be used by the horses following on behind. With such an inexperienced party, it was a disastrous strategy. The splinter groups wasted time and energy as they traipsed backwards and forwards looking for one another. By the third day, Beckler found the horses were in a 'shocking condition':

> The sheen on their coats had vanished, their previously rounded forms were angular and hollowed, their eyes lay fixed and lustreless in their sunken sockets. Their heads hung down almost to the ground as they were incapable of holding them upright, and they made no attempt to eat...The anuses of the poor animals lay deep between the surrounding soft parts and stood wide open. Through the opening one could see into a much larger, dark cavity whose mucous membranes were completely dried out and resembled dark red velvet. All of

this was of course the result of a complete absorption of water from the tissue.

In the end the horses became so thirst-crazed that they burnt their lips trying to sift through the embers of the fire looking for water. Each night they tried to bolt for home. One evening, as he set out to recover them, Beckler gazed at the vast landscape—but the desert that had so inspired him on his journey to rescue Lyons now gave him little comfort: 'I remember this scene as the saddest of our journey; a waterless land and a quiet, cloudless night in a region where all native life seemed to have died out.'

Beckler was only half-right. Life had disappeared in a drought-defying strategy that was millions of years old. The spinifex had thrust its roots deep into the soil and shrivelled its razor-sharp stems to prevent evaporation. The gum trees had dropped many of their giant limbs to concentrate their nutrients and the acacias began to use water stored in a special taproot. The kangaroos halted reproduction, leaving their embryos in a state of suspended animation to await more favourable conditions. Smaller marsupials like the fat-tailed dunnarts retreated under-ground in a state of biological torpor, lowering their body temperatures and living off food reserves stored in their tails. Others like the mulgara stayed alive by concentrating their urine and excreting dust for droppings. Frogs took the opposite approach; before the water had disappeared they had filled their giant bladders with excessively diluted urine, and prepared to reabsorb it during the dry season.

Wright's party had no such survival techniques. Heat, exhaustion and thirst took their toll physically and mentally. Beckler and Hodgkinson renewed their hostilities, with the doctor branding the young reporter 'a gnawing worm we carried with us'. In early February the party followed Burke's track out through Mutawintji and towards Torowoto—but Wright's general disorganisation hampered its progress. He was incapable of

establishing a routine. Packing, camp duties and animal hus-
bandry never progressed much beyond improvised chaos. The
camels contributed to the disorder by bolting, bucking, kicking
and biting during the day—then vanishing every night. Burke
reached Torowoto in eleven days. Wright took seventeen. He
arrived on 12 February 1861, just when Burke was about to turn
south from Camp 119.

Wright's appearance at the waterholes was greeted with exuberant ceremony by the Wanjiwalku people, the same tribe who
had looked after Lyons and MacPherson. They were rewarded
with tomahawks and 'scotch twill' shirts, prompting a night of
dancing and singing in celebration. Beckler was in no state to
join in. He described the local tribes as 'ugly wretched creatures...nearly all daubed with clay...they seemed to be astonished
at us and our animals and were very friendly and talkative'. The
next morning, two young men were persuaded to accompany the
party as far as the next waterholes at Bulloo Lakes, 150 kilometres south of the Cooper.

This arrangement broke down almost at once when the guides
indicated that the water along Burke's route had now dried up.
They pointed insistently in another direction, but Wright was
reluctant to depart from the track. He needed to maximise his
chances of meeting anyone heading south and was also terrified
of getting lost. Without a surveyor, he could never be sure where
he was or how far he had to go. The Aboriginal guides refused to
follow Wright and returned to their tribes.

Beyond Torowoto the springy green pastures that Burke had
described as 'fit to mow' had atrophied into brittle yellow wastelands. Beckler choked in the 'hell-like air' and stared through the
'sombre dusty haze' towards 'small, sterile hills, desolate in
appearance'. Now and then 'an eerie impetuous wind' flung
handfuls of sand into their sunburnt faces and, high above, the
sun was relentless in the blue sky.

Wright tried digging wells, then ferrying water up from Torowoto but it was such a tremendous waste of energy that he soon abandoned the scheme. Thirst dominated every hour and Beckler began to savour every drop of liquid he could scavenge:

> In these circumstances one treats this precious fluid in a quite different manner from when there is enough of it...I usually took a desert-spoon full of water every hour, some of which I usually poured back into the container. In the evening, just before going to bed, I drank about 4 ounces through a straw with great ecstasy.

A few kilometres further north, a new camp was established on 19 February and christened Rat Point. As its name suggested, it was crawling with vermin and flies. While most of the men searched for water, Becker and Purcell were left cowering under mouldy tarpaulins to guard the stores in temperatures that hovered around 38°C. In conditions of utter degradation, Becker still completed seven fine paintings, including one generous depiction of the long-haired rats that chewed at his feet as he tried to sleep.

With no obvious water up ahead, the party remained at Rat Point for twenty days. Sickness was inevitable. No one had bothered to boil the water they found along the way, and soon Wright, Smith, Belooch and Hodgkinson were all suffering from various forms of 'dysentery'. The entire party was losing weight with alarming speed. Becker, Purcell and Stone were also showing signs of beri-beri, scurvy and barcoo rot. Research now suggests that the vomiting and diarrhoea associated with the latter can be traced to the bacteria found in stagnant water. But Beckler, ignorant of this fact, continued to treat his patients with antiscorbutics. Stone had other problems. Unbeknown to anyone but Beckler, he had been suffering from advanced syphilis for some time. Now his legs swelled and pustules broke out over his body.

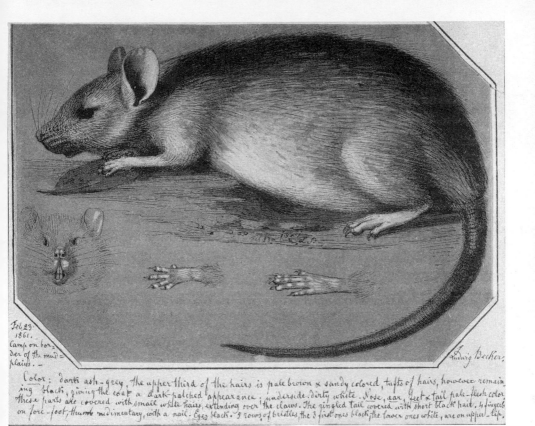

Color: dark ash-grey, the upper third of the hairs is pale brown & sandy colored, tufts of hairs, however remaining black, giving the coat a dark patched appearance; underside dirty white. Nose, ear, feet & tail pale flesh color these parts are covered with small white hairs, extending over the claws. The ringled tail covered with short black hair. 4 fingers on fore-foot, thumb rudimentary, with a nail. Eyes black. 5 rows of bristles, the 3 first ones black, the lower ones white, are on upper-lip.

Feb 23 1861. Camp on border of the mud-plains.

Ludwig Becker.

With hundreds of native rats scampering over him as he slept, Becker had no trouble obtaining specimens. The rodent plague indicates the expedition was travelling in a particularly fertile season.

The dogged Wright decided to continue north on 12 March. Sensing more work, the camels scarpered into the sandhills, forcing Beckler and Belooch to walk more than eighty kilometres to retrieve them. Soon after the party left Rat Point, Becker's horse keeled over and died, and many of the men complained they were too 'knocked up' to travel any further. But stopping in the middle of the desert was not an option. They kept walking because they had to.

The next camp at Poria Creek also degenerated into a pestilent hole. Beckler ran from one fetid tent to the other, examining his patients' stools and administering what treatment he could. Ludwig Becker was housed with Purcell, who had descended into a delirious stupor punctuated by streams of curses and recriminations. Both men had only the vaguest control over their bowels and often lay for hours in their soiled blankets. Yet Becker continued to paint. Propping up his bloated body on some old camel bags, he sought to 'make himself independent of all external influences by studying, writing and sketching'. Despite the 'great ravages' of the rats and the flies who 'sucked the colours and inks from his quills and brushes, and threw themselves recklessly onto every damp spot on the painting', he completed one more picture. Becker feared it would be his last. He described his state of mind as one of 'utter misery'.

Still Wright decided he must press on. On 26 March those men who could walk staggered towards Koorliatto Creek. The rest were propped on any animal still strong enough to carry them. Three days later, rain fell for the first time in weeks, filling the air with the astringent odour peculiar to deserts that have not felt water in months. It should have been a relief but the damp atmosphere and the drop in temperature only seemed to chill the men and make them sicker than before.

The party arrived at Koorliatto on 30 March. Leaving Beckler behind in charge of the invalids, Wright set out again and found reasonable water up ahead at Bulloo Lakes. On 12 April, he sent Hodgkinson back to bring up the others, but Beckler refused, saying that Becker and Purcell could not travel. The next day, after Hodgkinson had left to return to Bulloo, Beckler realised that a sizeable group of Aborigines had gathered and seemed intent on enticing him away from the camp with what he described as 'a visit to a black beauty'. Believing that being 'struck dead' was also part of the deal the doctor declined the invitation.

Later that evening the tribesmen returned, 'all decorated, freshly painted, shining with fat smeared over the whole body and armed with shields and boomerangs, some with spears'.

Becker was suffering terribly by the time he completed his last sketches.
While Wright took the stronger men to look for water, the rest stayed
behind in their squalid, basic camp.

They began a menacing cacophony of yelling and shouting until
an elder came forward and explained with gestures that the tribe
would leave now but return in four days by which time they
wanted the strangers gone.

Peace lasted only a few hours. The tribe came back early and
resumed another threatening vigil around the camp. Beckler
tried to placate them with presents of sugar and flour but it was
obvious that in such dry conditions they resented the Europeans
camping at their best waterholes. The doctor retreated to his
tent and sat wondering if sickness or a spear would get him first.

Beckler endured Koorliatto for three weeks. In filth and
squalor, he tended the invalids, stubbornly refusing to move lest

he should endanger their lives any further. On 21 April, when it became clear that his patients were not likely to improve, Beckler agreed to join Wright. Becker and Purcell survived the journey but only just. By the time they reached Bulloo, Purcell was hurling obscenities at anyone who approached him, Stone was defecating blood and 'had such pains in both his knee joints that he screamed aloud', Becker was fainting with every movement, Belooch was covered in sores, Hodgkinson had toothache and even Beckler had 'a catarrhal eye infection'. They didn't stand a chance of reaching the Cooper. In three months since leaving Menindee, they had covered 450 kilometres.

One hundred and fifty kilometres north of this disaster, on the banks of the Cooper, Burke, Wills and King woke on 22 April 1861 to the chatter of birdsong in their abandoned depot. Daylight brought with it clearer recognition of their predicament. They were still trapped 600 kilometres from Menindee, cut off by a lethal tract of waterless country with only two weakened camels and a small cache of supplies.

As they continued to gorge themselves on porridge and tea, Wills and King pleaded with Burke to follow their old track back down to the Darling River. If rescue came, they argued, it would surely arrive from that direction. But Burke had another idea. He wanted to try for Mount Hopeless, the South Australian police outpost 250 kilometres away, used by Augustus Gregory on his 1858 journey from the Cooper back to Adelaide. Burke was adamant that his party could retreat the same way. He overlooked the fact that Gregory made the journey with eight men, a string of forty horses and plenty of supplies. Even then he had struggled in the barren salt-lake country.

To tackle such a large area of unknown terrain in the middle of the dry season was madness. Burke, however, was so insistent that Wills and King gave in. It is difficult to say just how Burke managed to make such a disastrous decision at this point in the expedition. Vitamin deficiency, malnutrition, stress and exhaustion can all impair mental clarity and Burke was at the end of his physical tether. Logic was never his strong point. Now it had deserted him completely.

The preparations began. An examination of the camel trunk revealed that Brahe had left behind what Wills called 'ample supplies'. There were twenty-three kilograms of flour, nine kilograms of rice, twenty-seven kilograms of oatmeal, twenty-seven kilograms of sugar and seven kilograms of dried meat and a few other 'odds and ends'. Their main deficiency was clothing. The flannel shirts and trousers they had worn to the Gulf were reduced to shredded stinking rags. The men had no choice but to patch them with old horse blankets.

The night before they left the depot, Burke wrote a sad, courageous note, the nearest thing to an account of their amazing journey he would ever write:

Cooper's Creek Camp 65

The return party from Carpentaria, consisting of myself, Wills, and King (Gray dead), arrived here last night and found that the depot party had only started on the same day. We proceed on, to-morrow, slowly down the creek towards Adelaide by Mount Hopeless, and shall endeavour to follow Gregory's track; but we are very weak. The two camels are done up, and we shall not be able to travel faster than four or five miles a day. Gray died on the road from exhaustion, and fatigue. We have all suffered much from hunger. The provisions left here will, I think, restore our strength. We have discovered a practicable route to Carpentaria, the chief position of which lies in the 140° of East longitude. There is some good country between this and the Stony Desert. From thence to the tropics the land is dry and stony. Between the Carpentaria a considerable portion is rangy, but well watered

and richly grassed. We reached the shores of Carpentaria on the 11th of February, 1861. Greatly disappointed at finding the party here gone.
Robert O'Hara Burke
April 22, 1861
P.S. The camels cannot travel, and we cannot walk, or we should follow the other party. We shall move slowly down the creek.

Next morning, John King took the old shovel and reburied the trunk. Carefully he raked over the ground, and scattered the cache with horse dung so as not to arouse the suspicions of the local Aborigines. Then, he leaned the rake against a tree and with a broken bottle, cut out a piece of leather from the door of the stockade to repair some equipment. When he finished, he placed the bottle on the edge of the stockade.

Just as they were ready to leave, King asked if he should carve out a new message on the tree. 'No,' replied Burke, 'the word DIG serves our purpose as much as it served theirs.' And so the three explorers left the old coolibah just as it was and started down the creek. To the casual observer, there was no sign that anyone had been there at all.

As Burke's party struck west for Mount Hopeless, the deaths had begun at Wright's Bulloo camp. Stone succumbed first on 22 April. He devoted his last hours to waving his revolver and abusing the Aborigines. Purcell departed the next morning. He had been fainting for several days and after experiencing difficulty in breathing, he let out a large groan and expired.

As preparations were made for a burial service, the Aboriginal tribes returned. They laughed, threw sticks and seemed to indicate that Wright's men would soon be following their companions to an early grave. Beckler deflected the threats by showing them a box of matches and teaching them to light fires.

This worked until nightfall, when a series of shouts pierced the darkness, convincing Beckler that the Aborigines were still intent on scaring them away with their 'wild noise'.

Using his limited knowledge of the local Aboriginal dialects, Wright ordered the warriors to leave the camp. Most retreated, but one young man came forward and made many attempts to communicate. Wright gave him some clothes and nicknamed him 'Mr Shirt'. He soon became a sort of ambassador running between the native and European camps conveying messages and carrying presents—but the atmosphere of foreboding continued to grow. More warriors gathered, some with 'reddish dogs tails bound around their heads', giving them 'a singularly savage appearance'. Several ran into the camp removing cooking utensils and tools 'with unspeakable haste'. After the robbery Mr Shirt reappeared. It seemed to Beckler that he wanted to negotiate:

> Shirt was a born diplomat and it was one of the most inter-
> esting experiences of our journey to see an Australian savage
> display the same characteristics and the same behaviour that we
> would normally associate with the concept of a diplomat...he
> was serious, friendly, extremely calm, with no trace of passion,
> and definite and stubborn in his demands...The area belonged
> to his tribe. Soon they were coming here to celebrate a feast.
> We were not to be too venturesome; neighbouring tribes were
> already coming to drive us away.

It was a reasonable request. Shirt repeated his demands but Wright, determined not to show weakness, picked him up by the neck and promptly threw him out of the camp. The stand-off continued.

Overwhelmed by disease, invaded by rats and surrounded by warriors, the men crept around the camp. Wright ordered them to stack up tree branches to provide crude fortifications, then occupied himself by shooting rats. Only Ludwig Becker was

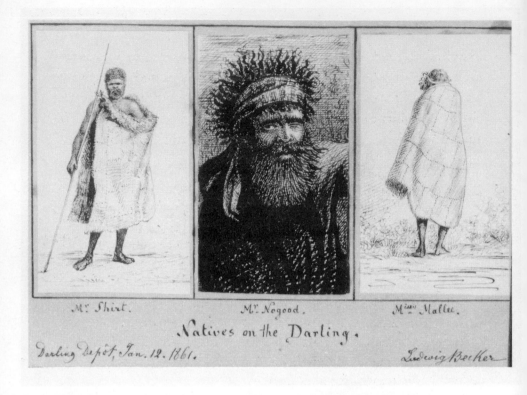

Mr Shirt.   Mr Nogood.   Miss Mallee.

Natives on the Darling.

Darling Depôt, Jan. 12. 1861.   Ludwig Becker

Becker spent many hours gaining the trust of the indigenous people. Included here is a depiction of 'Mr Shirt', the courageous Aboriginal ambassador who tried to prevent bloodshed at Bulloo Lakes.

oblivious to the danger. He grew weaker by the hour but still infuriated Beckler with his constant demands for attention:

> He was suffering continually from very frequent diarrhoea. He was dependent of me in every respect and a major part of the day and night was spent exclusively in tending him. My nightly rest was interrupted so much by this that I slept only very little, and hence all the more heavily as soon as I had peace, hearing neither Becker's quiet calling nor his little bell. Nothing remained but to tie a string around my arm. This ran under the wall of the tent to his bed; by pulling it he could call me to him at any time.

On 27 April, as Becker slipped into unconsciousness, the Aboriginal tribes returned with reinforcements. About one hundred men had divided into two groups and were moving forwards in a pincer movement along the creek. Beckler reached for his gun while Wright stood and shouted, warning them not to come any closer. Mr Shirt gestured that there was nothing more he could do and the warriors rushed forward brandishing their spears:

> At twenty paces Wright ordered us to fire. A few fell, several apparently from fright. Shirt fell right before us…He alone was severely wounded…He was a hero from head to toe. Slowly, and with difficulty, he raised himself from the ground and hurled upon us what we assumed was the curse of his tribe. It was to our advantage that it was he, the leader, who alone fell, but we all felt sorry for this noble leader and representative of his tribe. Hobbling slowly, and pressing his dirty shirt carefully to his abdomen, he staggered down to the water and disappeared into the scrub, accompanied by sinister, incoherent curses which did not, however, raise his calm to a visible excitement for a moment.

Wright fired again sending up showers of sand. The rest of the tribe scattered into the bush. No one knows whether Mr Shirt survived the encounter but the sorrowful wails that drifted through that night air would seem to indicate that he did not. The Aboriginal ambassador was no match for rifles and revolvers.

After the showdown, the situation reverted to an uneasy calm. The men trod warily around the camp, always with their revolvers at their side. Sleep came in restless bursts.

As Burke, Wills and King walked towards Mount Hopeless, Wills felt a new surge of optimism: 'We only went about five miles, and camped at half past eleven on a billibong, where the feed was pretty good. We find the change of diet already making a great improvement in our spirits and strength. The weather is delightful, the days warm, but the nights are very chilly.' The

Yandruwandha seemed pleased their visitors were on the move. As they followed the explorers offering gifts and laughing, Wills' harsh views about the local tribes began to soften:

> We had scarcely finished breakfast when our friends the blacks, from whom we obtained the fish, made their appearance with a few more, and seemed inclined to go with us and keep up the supply. We gave them some sugar, with which they were greatly pleased. They are by far the most well-behaved blacks we have seen on Cooper's Creek.

This constant bartering improved the explorers' diet, banishing their 'leg-tied feeling' and allowing such good progress during the next week that the incorrigible Wills began to lament the loss of his scientific instruments. Then, on 28 April, as they walked by moonlight alongside the Cooper, his mood changed.

Linda, a perversely named bull camel, slipped down the muddy bank and became bogged in 'bottomless quicksand'. Wills was furious. 'Being of a sluggish stupid nature,' he wrote, Linda 'could never be got to make sufficiently strenuous efforts towards extricating himself.' The unfortunate creature moaned and roared, then lay there, 'as if he quite enjoyed his position'. Covered in mud and exhausted by their efforts to free him, the three men had no choice but to stop and camp. At dawn, they tried again, but it was no use. King shot the camel and the trio spent an unpleasant morning wading into the swamp and hacking off as much flesh as they could from the carcass.

It was a bitter blow. 'A man must shape himself to a new mark,' Ernest Shackleton once said, 'directly the old one goes to ground.' But as Burke's situation changed and his resources diminished, there is no evidence that he sat down to reassess his predicament and make a new plan. The three men set off once again towards Mount Hopeless, dragging their one remaining camel behind them.

That evening, on 29 April 1861, Wright and Beckler were asleep in their tents. It was two days since Mr Shirt had been shot. In the small hours of the morning they were woken by the tinkling of horse bells away to the north. Someone was approaching the camp. Bewildered, they ran outside. Could it be Burke returning?

In the darkness they could just make out the shapes of several horses grazing and, as morning broke, they got close enough to see the animals had government brand marks on them. Hodgkinson rode out to see where they had come from, when another horseman appeared on the horizon. It was William Brahe. Quite by chance, the two back-up parties had found one another in the middle of the desert.

There was a lot of catching up to do. Brahe was appalled to find Wright's party in such a wretched condition but he was also relieved that someone else was in charge. For his part, Wright was quietly thankful to learn that Burke had disappeared northwards without waiting for more supplies. Since he had failed to return to the depot, and was now probably dead or on his way to Queensland, Wright reasoned that his own failure to reach the Cooper was immaterial. There was no harm done.

Wright and Brahe debated what to do next. The combined party may have been larger but it also contained more invalids. No one considered making another attempt to take supplies up to the depot in case Burke returned. In fact, according to Beckler, only 'one single tenuous thread' stopped them from turning back to the Darling immediately. Poor Ludwig Becker still clung to life in a malodorous tent on the edge of the camp. He was delirious and unable to recognise Brahe, but still turned to Beckler for comfort. 'I want your neck,' he moaned as he embraced the doctor for the last time. A few hours later, he died alone in his tent. He was buried on the morning of 30 April.

The rest of the men were deteriorating fast. Smith, Patten and

Belooch had advanced scurvy and beri-beri. McDonough had been kicked by a horse and was all but crippled. 'Nonetheless,' wrote Beckler, 'I was not yet very worried. I hoped that we would now leave Bulloo quickly and soon arrive at the Darling.'

With Becker dead, and Burke presumed dead, there seemed little else to do but retreat. But something continued to nag at Brahe's conscience. What if Burke had not gone to Queensland or perished in the desert? What if he had returned to the depot camp? The German suggested that he and Wright should make a dash back up to the Cooper, just to be sure. Both men thought it unlikely that they would find anything but they were aware that, by returning to Menindee for good, they were in effect abandoning their posts. The two men saddled the best of the horses and set out for Brahe's Dig Tree 150 kilometres away at Depot Camp 65.

As Brahe and Wright galloped north to the Cooper, Burke, Wills and King were still trudging south-west towards Mount Hopeless. Their meagre supplies made them more and more dependent on the hospitality of the local people. The tribesmen followed them like shadows, always ready with gifts of fish and nardoo, which the explorers swapped for one of their few remaining survival tools—fishhooks.

Four days after Linda's accident, Rajah began to show signs of being 'done up'. A few hours later he was trembling and sweating and, despite repeated attempts to lighten his load, he collapsed on 6 May. With the last of the camels gone, Burke should have realised that the journey to Mount Hopeless was as futile as the name suggested. But in an amazing display of denial the trio continued on, clutching just a small bundle of supplies each. As the Cooper splintered into hundreds of tiny rivulets, it is impossible to tell from Wills' diary exactly where they wandered, but it is probable that they veered away from the main stream down a side branch now known as the Strzelecki Creek. The surveyor was in despair as he found that every channel they tried to follow headed 'the wrong way'.

In an attempt to forge an escape route, Wills embarked on several solo reconnaissance missions but he was constantly confronted by 'high sand ridges, running nearly parallel with the one on which I was standing'. It was 'a dreary prospect offering me no encouragement to proceed'. Back at camp, the surveyor reflected ruefully, 'I suppose this will end in our having to live like the blacks for a few months.' One afternoon, he and Burke stumbled across several men catching fish:

> On our arrival at the camp, they led us to a spot to camp on, and soon afterwards brought a lot of fish and bread, which they call nardoo. The lighting a fire with matches delights them, but they do not care about having them. In the evening, various members of the tribe came down with lumps of nardoo, and handfuls of fish until we were positively unable to eat any more. They also gave us some stuff they call bedgery, or pedgery. It has a highly intoxicating effect, when chewed even in small quantities. It appears to be the dried stems and leaves of some shrub.

On 8 May, Wills left Burke and King behind and set out once again to look for 'the main channel' of the Cooper. It was useless. On his way back he found that 'my friends the blacks' had made him a place to sleep in one of their gunyahs, and prepared a supper of fish, nardoo and 'a couple of nice fat rats', which Wills enjoyed, 'baked in their skins'. As he lay down that night, exhausted from the day's exertions, Wills finally acknowledged that the journey to Mount Hopeless was impossible. They were stranded. The last two and a half weeks struggling down the creek had been a futile waste of resources.

That same day, thirty or forty kilometres to the east, Brahe and Wright reached the Dig Tree. They had already convinced themselves that they would find nothing and when they rode into the old camp, each officer gazed about him with the eyes of men who cannot wait to be vindicated. They took it for granted that the cache was just as Brahe left it. They attributed the mass of footprints and the remains of the campfires to the Aborigines. They didn't notice the broken bottle on the top of the stockade, the rake leaning against the tree or the piece of leather cut out of the stockade door. Everything looked exactly as they had left it. There were no new carvings on the tree. The two men felt relief. No one had been back. Their consciences were clear. Brahe and Wright stayed for just fifteen minutes before remounting and heading south to Bulloo.

Seventeen

This Extraordinary Continent

'Optimism is needed for survival, and realism
must be its worst enemy.'
Dr Mike Stroud

When Wills returned from his final reconnaissance mission
on 10 May, he found Burke and King still up to their
elbows in camel flesh. Rajah had been cut into strips, and laid out
in the sun to dry. A mood of stoic persistence still prevailed. No
one was ready to give up yet, but Wills was determined to con-
vince his leader that they must abandon their efforts to reach
Mount Hopeless. He still found it hard to believe he was reduced
to 'having to hang about Cooper's Creek, living with the blacks',
but his interactions with the Yandruwandha had precipitated a
profound change in his opinions. He realised that the men and
women he had despised for their 'primitive existence' were now
his only chance of salvation. He was especially interested in
nardoo, the seed he had observed the Yandruwandha grind into
flour, but since he had never seen them collect it, Wills didn't
realise it grew on the ground. The next morning the hapless
Burke and King conducted a futile search of the nearby trees.

Wills' reassessment was too little, too late. He, Burke and King
tried to copy the Yandruwandha but living off the land was not as
easy as they had imagined. Without fishhooks they couldn't fish
and without nets they couldn't trap birds. Worst of all their 'new
friends', the Yandruwandha, had moved off down the creek and
disappeared.

Despite the overwhelming arguments for abandoning the

journey to Mount Hopeless, Burke still refused to give in. He
knew the outpost existed and he was determined to reach it. Why
did he persist with such an absurd plan? A passage from explorer
Ludwig Leichhardt's diary, written during the last stages of his
struggle to reach Port Essington, provides a clue. Leichhardt
found that he had become obsessed with finishing his journey:

> At this time we were all sadly distressed with boils and with a
> prickly heat; early lancing of the former saved much pain.
> The cuts and sores of the hands festered quickly, but this
> depended much more on the want of cleanliness than any-
> thing else. A most dangerous enemy grew up amongst us in
> the irresistible impatience to come to the end of our journey;
> and I cannot help considering it a great blessing that we did
> not meet with natives who knew the settlement of Port
> Essington at an earlier part of our journey, or I am afraid we
> should have been exposed to the greatest misery, if not
> destruction, by an inconsiderate, thoughtless desire of
> pushing onwards.

Burke was still convinced that the remnants of his once
mighty expedition could escape via Gregory's route to Adelaide.
On 15 May 1861, he ordered his two men to bury the last of
their belongings and set off once more down the Cooper. Each
man was reduced to carrying just one blanket, some dried meat, a
little flour and a billycan of water.

After their brief examination of Depot Camp 65, Wright and
Brahe rejoined their companions at Koorliatto Creek on 13 May.
In retreat, the party looked more like an ambulance train than a
relief expedition. Men limped or rode home while the invalids
clung to their horses and camels. William Patten wailed in agony
as he was lashed to a makeshift stretcher on the side of a camel.
Every few minutes he demanded to be lifted down to relieve

himself, cursing his companions and accusing them of torture. Thomas McDonough spent most of the time unconscious and Belooch declared himself incapable of travelling. Even Beckler sunk into despondency: 'It is well nigh impossible to describe to the reader the deeply depressing effect of this futile struggling; the yearning to be delivered on one hand and our helplessness on the other.'

The doctor was mystified. Despite the administration of anti-scurvy medicines and a broth of a local plant (Mesembryanthemum), his patients continued to deteriorate until each night the camp-sites echoed with despair:

> Keeping watch in our camp each night was now pure misery. Wild dogs fought close by over the last remains of one of our horses, which had perished there previously. But the wild howling of these beasts was not half as unpleasant to the ear as the moaning and groaning of our invalids...

They still had nearly 400 kilometres to go to reach Menindee.

Burke, Wills and King found the creek was still fickle and difficult to follow but their spirits were lifted on 17 May, when King spotted a large patch of nardoo on the ground. According to Wills, the discovery 'caused somewhat of a revolution in our feelings, for we considered that with the knowledge of this plant we were in a position to support ourselves, even if we were destined to remain on the creek'. That evening the men realised it was Queen Victoria's birthday and Wills reported that they celebrated by collecting an extra large supply!

Within a week, nardoo had become 'the staff of life'. Each morning they toiled for several hours in the blistering sun, collecting enough seeds to pound into flour. It was an exhausting process that took up so much time and energy the men found it almost impossible to travel any further. Wills does not record the exact date when Burke at last gave up the idea of reaching Mount Hopeless, but by 27 May, a month after leaving the Dig Tree, they had travelled approximately sixty-four kilometres from the depot camp only to find the creek had shrivelled to a series of dusty channels leading nowhere. Without water, they were forced to retreat.

As usual it was Wills who assessed the situation in practical terms. He knew their chances of survival were diminishing and announced in his diary that he had decided to return to the Dig Tree alone to deposit his journals, 'in case of accident'. On his way back, he was reunited with his Aboriginal friends. Not only did they feed and shelter him each evening, but some even insisted on carrying his shovel and his swag 'in such a friendly manner that I could not refuse them'. Wills was becoming fond of these gentle people and he spent his evenings amusing them with any small trinkets he had left. But his nights were wracked with agony. The new diet of nardoo and fish may have been plentiful but it didn't suit his digestion. He suffered from stomach cramps, constipation and 'exceedingly painful stools'.

On 30 May, three days after leaving Burke and King, Wills arrived back at the Dig Tree. Seeing the deserted depot for the second time seemed to harden Wills' attitude to his plight. Originally the surveyor had shown little inclination to blame Brahe for leaving his post, even crediting him with leaving 'ample provisions to take us to the bounds of civilisation'. Now, after six frustrating weeks trying to escape the clutches of the desert, he buried his journals with a note that revealed a growing sense of bitterness:

> We have been unable to leave the creek. Both camels are dead, and our provisions are exhausted. Mr Burke and King are down the lower part of the creek. I am about to return to them, when we shall probably not come up this way. We are trying to live the best way we can, like the blacks, but find it

work. Our clothes are going to pieces fast. Send provisions
and clothes as soon as possible.
WJ Wills
PS The depot party having left, contrary to instructions have
put us in this fix. I have deposited some of my journals here
for fear of accident.

Wills found the cache just as before. He walked away from the
old coolibah to rejoin his companions, unaware that Brahe and
Wright had visited the Dig Tree three weeks earlier. They had
failed to leave a message of any sort and the tragic pattern continued unchecked.

Now Wills was weakening. On several occasions he was
forced to camp early 'from sheer fatigue'. Too feeble to gather
nardoo or hunt for game, he was reduced to scavenging through
the native camps, picking through the fishbones for scraps. One
particular Aboriginal man, nicknamed Pitchery (probably a
derivation of his totem group Pitjidi) seemed anxious to assist
him. He guided Wills to a camp and fed him until he was 'unable
to eat anymore'. These kind actions convinced Wills that with
the generosity of the local Aboriginal people, they stood some
chance of surviving. But when he arrived back at Burke's camp on
6 June, a catastrophic scene awaited him.

Burke and King were sitting in front of a burnt-out gunyah.
Their possessions, including the last of their bedding and
clothing, lay in charred tatters around them and the native camp
nearby was eerily silent. Wills discovered that while he had been
away, Burke and King had continued to barter for food, but when
a young Yandruwandha man tried to steal a worthless scrap of
oilcloth, Burke lost his temper and fired his revolver over the
man's head. A few minutes later another warrior crept up behind
King, laid a boomerang on his shoulder and, in sign language,
threatened to kill him if he called out. It was a warning. The
tribe had had enough. The Yandruwandha could not understand

Burke's animosity. Every day they brought gifts of food, yet when they wanted something in return, even a snippet of cloth, they were fired upon. That night the tribesmen tried yet again to restore relations by bringing gifts of fish and nets, but Burke was still angry and defensive. He knocked the nets out of their hands and again fired over their heads. King later reported his leader was afraid of 'getting too friendly with the blacks'.

Later, Burke was cooking when a pan full of fat caught fire. He panicked as a strong breeze fanned the flames setting the gunyah alight. All the explorers' possessions were ruined. Wills was distraught. Burke had destroyed their last remaining life-lines. The Yandruwandha melted away into the bush and all donations of food ceased. The incident was a sour end to the first contact between black and white at Cooper Creek, and placed Burke, Wills and King in an impossible position. They had no spare clothing, no bedding, no rations and no food supply except for the nardoo they could gather.

Several years later the first cattlemen working in the Cooper Creek area were told by the Yandruwandha that there had been a violent quarrel between Burke and Wills over the incident. Burke struck his deputy several times, knocking him to the ground, and the two men did not talk for some time afterwards. No official record of the incident was ever made but it is not hard to imagine it happening. The men were reaching their physical and emotional limits.

Wills left on the morning of 7 June to repair relations with the Yandruwandha. He stayed at their camp to 'test the practicability of living with them, and to see what I could learn as to their way and manners'. After a little persuasion, the tribe seemed to forgive the white men and even resumed their deliveries of food to Burke and King, but the atmosphere around the camp was uneasy. Two days later, the Yandruwandha indicated to Wills that they would be moving off up the creek. The explorers tried to follow but Wills found he 'could scarcely get along, although carrying the lightest swag'. With their rations exhausted, they took it in turns to look for nardoo, or stay at camp grinding and pounding the seeds.

According to accounts handed down through the generations, the Yandruwandha harvested the seeds from small fern-like nardoo plants with a special broom made from canegrass. Back at their camps, they had installed permanent grinding areas on the rocks to turn the seeds into flour. These rocks had channels carved into them so that, as the seeds were ground down, they were washed with water at the same time. Once it was reduced to paste, the nardoo was then cooked on the open fire. The result is an unpalatable, gritty cake, with a slightly nutty aftertaste that sticks in the back of the throat. It is even more unpleasant eaten raw, like a bitter version of gruel.

Without the proper tools or traditional knowledge, the three explorers prepared their nardoo incorrectly. They ground it without sluicing it with water and they also consumed it raw. The more they ate, the sicker they felt. By 15 June, Wills sensed that it was something in the nardoo that was to blame:

> Mr Burke and I pounding and cleaning. He finds himself getting very weak, and I am not a bit stronger. I have determined on beginning to chew tobacco and eat less nardoo, in hopes that it may induce some change in the system. I have never yet recovered from the effects of the constipation, and the passage of the stools is always exceedingly painful.

By 20 June, Burke's legs were so weak that he could walk only with great difficulty. His deputy was worse, which left King to gather food for all three. Wills could not fathom why the nardoo was having such a detrimental effect:

> I cannot understand this nardoo at all—it certainly will not agree with me in any form: we are now reduced to it alone,

Nardoo (*marsilea drummondii*) grows in swampy country. As the water dries out, it is harvested by the Aboriginal people and then ground to yield flour that is high in starch.

and we manage to consume four to five pounds per day between us; it appears to be quite indigestible, and cannot possibly be sufficiently nutritious to sustain life itself.

Why did the explorers suffer so much when the indigenous people ate nardoo regularly with no ill effects? There are several possible explanations. By the time the explorers began to rely on the nardoo, they were already malnourished and almost certainly suffering from Vitamin B deficiency, or beri-beri. Research done on nardoo shows that it is rich in the enzyme thiaminase, which blocks absorption of Vitamin B. The Yandruwandha destroyed the thiaminase by washing and cooking their nardoo. By failing to duplicate this process, it is possible that the men were, in fact, reducing their ability to absorb Vitamin B, which worsened their beri-beri. They had also been eating freshwater mussels, another food with high levels of thiaminase.

The term beri-beri came from Ceylon. It means 'I cannot, I cannot'. Typical symptoms include anorexia, sensitivity to the cold, an ill-defined lassitude associated with heaviness and weakness of the legs, and difficulties in walking. There may be tenderness of the calf muscles, pins and needles and numbness. The pulse is usually full and fast. In one form of the deficiency, known as 'wet' beri-beri, there is swelling throughout the body and limbs, but the essential feature of 'dry' beri-beri is muscle wasting, particularly of the legs.

Wills' description of his physical decline might suggest that the explorers poisoned themselves by eating nardoo, and that they were suffering from acute beri-beri. But he does not provide enough information to support this theory without question. Some of the specific indicators he mentions, such as his low, shallow pulse, are inconsistent with Vitamin B deficiency. An alternative explanation may be that the explorers were poisoned by a specific neurotoxin contained in nardoo that is neutralised by leaching or by heating. It is also possible that Wills' symptoms can be accounted for by plain malnutrition.

An average adult male needs 2000–3000 calories a day to stay healthy, but this increases to nearer 4500 during periods of intense physical activity. For many weeks, the explorers' daily calorific intake had been in the hundreds rather than the thousands, and by the time they abandoned their trek to Mount Hopeless, the trio were severely malnourished.

When the human body is receiving too little food, it burns fat and then protein. The muscles begin to waste, the metabolism decreases, the heart slows, blood pressure falls and wounds take longer to heal. Other symptoms include constipation, dizziness, faintness, apathy and depression. A loss of 35 per cent of total body weight is enough to prove fatal. A person who eats nothing at all and expends little or no energy will die after about eight weeks, but the intake of even very small amounts of food can keep a person alive for many months.

As their malnourishment grew worse on the Cooper, the explorers suffered weight loss, lethargy, constipation and muscle weakness. Any physical effort was onerous and their movements became sluggish. At night, they would have found it hard to sleep despite feeling tired during the day.

During the last stages of starvation, a loss of appetite may set in. After losing so many essential nutrients, the body is incapable of processing normal quantities of fat, protein and carbohydrate, so anorexia forms a defence against a fatal bout of overeating, should food become available.

These general symptoms are broadly compatible with Wills' and, although it is probable that beri-beri was partly responsible for his deterioration, exhaustion and malnutrition also played their part. One other detail rules out beri-beri as the sole culprit. Although starvation affects mood and memory, it does not usually produce an overall impairment of mental performance until just before death. Vitamin B deficiency, on the other hand, often results in paranoia and severe mental deterioration. It is clear from Wills' measured diary entries and letters that he remained lucid and articulate even as his body wasted away.

On 21 June, Wills acknowledged for the first time that death was a possibility and, for a few brief sentences, his usual reserve failed him:

> I feel much weaker than ever, and can scarcely crawl out of the mia-mia. Unless relief comes in some form or other, I cannot possibly last more than a fortnight. It is a great conso-lation, at least, in this position of ours to know that we have done all we could, and that our deaths will rather be the result of the mismanagement of others than any rash acts of our

own. Had we come to grief elsewhere, we could only have blamed ourselves; but here we are, returned to Cooper's Creek, where we had every reason to look for provisions and clothing; and yet we have to die of starvation, in spite of the explicit instructions given by Mr Burke, that the depot party should await our return, and the strong recommendation to the committee that we should be followed up by a party from Menindie.

While Burke, Wills and King clung to life on the Cooper, Wright's party was shuffling south, tormented by thirst, lost animals and the strain of caring for the dying. One by one the camels either expired or disappeared into the wilderness. As Belooch put it, the poor beasts had little to look forward to: 'Here no more camel...much walk, much carry, little eat.' William Patten had continued to deteriorate, lapsing into unconsciousness in his stretcher and dying on 5 June. His departure was a relief for the rest of the men, who could now make better progress.

The party made it back to Menindee on 19 June. One observer thought the men showed 'symptoms of great suffering, particularly about the eyes'. The whole journey had been a waste of time. Four men had died and not a single box of supplies had been delivered to the Cooper.

Wright disbanded the remaining men and left town on the next steamer to follow his family down to Adelaide. Beckler and the other survivors hung about recovering their strength. It fell to William Brahe to ride on ahead with news of Burke's disappearance and the expedition's disintegration. He set out at once for Melbourne.

As Brahe rode south on 22 June, the surviving explorers were camped by a waterhole the Yandruwandha named Tilka. Wills found he could hardly stand even to sponge himself down. He was confined to lying in an old gunyah on two small camel pads and some pieces of rag he had salvaged from the fire. His clothing consisted of a wide-awake hat, a merino shirt, a regatta shirt without sleeves, the remains of a pair of flannel trousers, two pairs of socks in rags, and a waistcoat. As winter set in, the cold became his enemy. The torture began as soon as the sun dipped below the horizon:

> June 24th—A fearful night. At about an hour before sunset, a southerly gale blew up and continued throughout the greater portion of the night; the cold was intense, and it seemed as if one would be shrivelled up. Towards morning, it fortunately lulled a little…King went out for nardoo, in spite of the wind, and came in with a good load, but he himself is terribly cut up. He says that he can no longer keep up the work, and as he and Mr Burke are both getting rapidly weaker, we have but a slight chance of anything but starvation, unless we can get hold of some blacks.

Wills knew that he was fading fastest of all. On 26 June, he decided the only honourable thing to do was to sacrifice himself to save his companions. 'Without some change,' he wrote, 'I see little chance for any of us.' He suggested that Burke and King should follow the Aborigines up the creek to try and procure more food. This upset Burke. He insisted he could not leave his 'dear boy' behind, but Wills was adamant. He made a point of recording in his diary that the stronger men 'have both shown great hesitation and reluctance with regard to leaving me, and have repeatedly desired my candid opinion in the matter'.

Burke and King spent the rest of the day collecting a stockpile of nardoo for Wills. It was a harrowing time. Scribbled in Burke's notebook was an entry for that day which reveals his bitterness about their situation: 'I hope that we shall be done justice to. We have fulfilled our task, but we have been aban—. We have not been followed up as we expected, and the depot party abandoned their post.'

The next morning Wills refused to change his mind about being left alone. He maintained that his plan was designed to save the entire party, but he knew he would probably die while the others were away. As Burke and King prepared to leave, he propped himself up on his camel pads and wrote a last letter to his father:

My dear Father,
These are probably the last lines you will ever get from me. We are on the point of starvation, not so much from absolute want of food, but from the want of nutriment we can get.

Our position, although more provoking, is probably not near so disagreeable as that of poor Harry and his companions.* We have had very good luck, and made a most successful trip to Carpentaria and back, to where we had every right to consider ourselves safe, having left a depot here consisting of four men, twelve horses, and six camels. They had provisions enough to have lasted them twelve months with proper economy. We had every right to expect that we should have been immediately followed up from Menindie, by another party with additional provisions and every necessary for forming a permanent depot at Cooper's Creek. The party we left here had special instructions not to leave until our return, unless from absolute necessity. We left the creek nominally with three months' supply, but they were reckoned at little over the rate of half rations. We calculated on having to eat some of the camels. By the greatest good luck at every turn, we crossed to the gulf through a good deal of fine country, almost in a straight line from here. On the other side the camels suffered considerably from the wet; we had to kill and jerk one soon after starting back. We had now been out a little more than two months, and found it necessary to reduce the rations considerably; and this began to tell on all hands, but I felt it far less than any of the others. The great scarcity and shyness of game, and our forced

---

* Wills' cousin Harry died on Sir John Franklin's Arctic expedition.

Cooper's Creek June 27th 1861

My dear Father

These are probably the last
lines you will ever get from me, We are
on the point of starvation not so much from
absolute want of food but from the want
of nutriment in what we can get.
Our position although more provoking is
probably not near so disagreeable as that of poor
Harry & his companions; We have had
every good luck and made a most
successful trip to Carpentaria and
back to where we had every right to
consider ourselves safe. having left
a Depôt here consisting of four men
twelve horses and six camels, they
had sufficient provisions to have lasted
them for twelve months with proper
economy. We had also every right to

Wills' last letter, written as he lay dying on the banks of the Cooper, is a
model of discipline and restraint. It is perfectly spelt and punctuated
throughout, without a trace of self-pity.

marches, prevented our supplying the deficiency from external sources to any great extent; but we never could have held out but for the crows and hawks, and the portulac. The latter is an excellent vegetable, and I believe secured our return to this place. We got back here in four months and four days, and found the party had left the Creek the same day, and we were not in a fit state to follow them.

I find I must close this that it may be planted, but I will write some more, although it has not so good a chance of reaching you as this. You have great claim on the committee for their neglect. I leave you in sole charge of what is coming to me. The whole of my money I desire to leave to my sisters; other matters I will leave for the present. Adieu, my dear father. Love to Tom.

WJ Wills

I think to live about four or five days. My spirits are excellent. My religious beliefs are not in the least bit changed and I have not the least fear of their being so. My spirits are excellent.

Wills read the letter aloud to Burke and King to reassure them that he had written nothing detrimental about them. He handed over his papers and his pocket watch with instructions that they should be given to his father.

By now the ailing surveyor was mixed up about dates. His last diary entry is attributed to 29 June but was probably written earlier. Despite the confusion, his last words appear in his usual meticulous handwriting:

…I am weaker than ever although I have a good appetite, and relish the nardoo much, but it seems to give us no nutriment, and the birds here are so shy as not to be got at. Even if we could get a good supply of fish, I doubt whether we could do much work on them and the nardoo alone. Nothing now but the greatest good luck can save any of us; and as for myself I may live four or five days if the weather continues warm. My pulse is at forty-eight, and very weak, and my legs and arms are nearly skin and bone. I can only look out, like Mr Micawber 'for something to turn up'; but starvation on nardoo is by no means very unpleasant, but for the weakness one feels, and the utter inability to move oneself, for as far as appetite is concerned, it gives me the greatest satisfaction. Certainly fat and sugar would be more to one's taste; in fact those seem to me to be the great stand-by for one in this extraordinary continent; not that I mean to deprecate the farinaceous food; but the want of sugar and fat in all substances

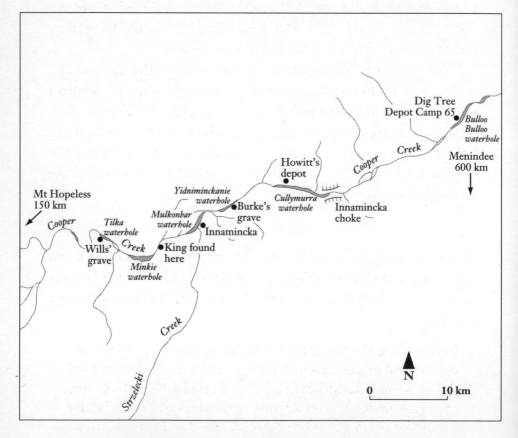

Burke, Wills and King scoured the Cooper and the Strzelecki for a possible route to Mount Hopeless before their need for water forced them back to the main channel.

obtainable here is so great that they become almost valueless to us as articles of food, without the addition of something else.

Later that day Burke and King left Wills a billycan of water, a supply of nardoo and some wood for a fire. Wills watched them disappear around the bend in the river. He was alone in the middle of his 'extraordinary continent'.

It is not known exactly when Wills died. It is likely that he found himself sleeping more and more, drifting in and out of consciousness and drawing himself into a foetal position as his organs began to fail. His heartbeat and pulse would have continued to drop until sleep deepened into death.

The site of his small gunyah on the banks of the Cooper can still be found fifteen kilometres west of the present-day outpost of Innamincka. It is on a rather desolate stretch of the creek, near a chain of dusty claypans that glow yellow in the soft evening light. Did he gaze at the pelicans and the parrots patrolling the waters of the creek as he slipped away, or did he look out on the vastness of the desert beyond?

Burke and King set off up the creek with nothing but a pistol and a few scraps of blanket. Walking was difficult and it soon became clear to John King that his leader did not have the strength to go very far:

In travelling the first day, Mr Burke seemed very weak, and complained of great pain in his legs and back. On the second day he seemed to be better, and said that he thought he was getting stronger, but on starting, did not go two miles before he said he could go no further. I persisted in his trying to go on, and managed to get him along several times, until I saw that he was almost knocked up, when he said he could not carry his swag, and threw all he had away.

There was no alternative but to camp for the night. King settled Burke down under a shady coolibah tree next to a waterhole known as Yidninckanie and then shot a crow for supper. Burke managed to eat a little but he knew he had few hours left. He took out his notebook and wrote: 'King has behaved nobly. I hope that he will be properly cared for. He comes up the creek in accordance with my request.' Then he composed a last message to his sister Hessie, revoking his will to Julia Matthews:

> Goodbye, my dearest Hessie; when leaving Melbourne, I foolishly made over what I left behind to a young lady with whom I have only a slight acquaintance. I hope you will not take it ill of me. I was wrong and I only meant and mean the bequest to apply to the few monies accruing to me in Melbourne and not to anything derived from home…I hereby cancel the bequest or will I left in Melbourne, and I leave all I possess to my sister Hessie Burke but I wish her to make over any money derived from my Salary or the sale of my things in Melbourne to Miss Julia Matthews…King has behaved nobly, and I hope if he lives that he will be properly rewarded…King staid with me till the last. He has left me at my request, unburied, and with my pistol in my hand. Good-bye again, dearest Hessie, my heart is with you.

As he confronted his own death Burke seems to have recognised the foolishness of his relationship with an actress half his age. Instead of returning a conquering hero to sweep Julia off her feet, he realised that his infatuation would make him a laughing stock in Melbourne society. The last of his dreams was shattered.

Burke handed his notebook and pocket watch to King with instructions that they should be delivered to Sir William Stawell and no one else. He asked King for his pistol and then whispered: 'I hope you will remain with me until I am quite dead—it is a comfort to know that some one is by; but, when I am dead, it is my wish that you leave me unburied as I lie.'

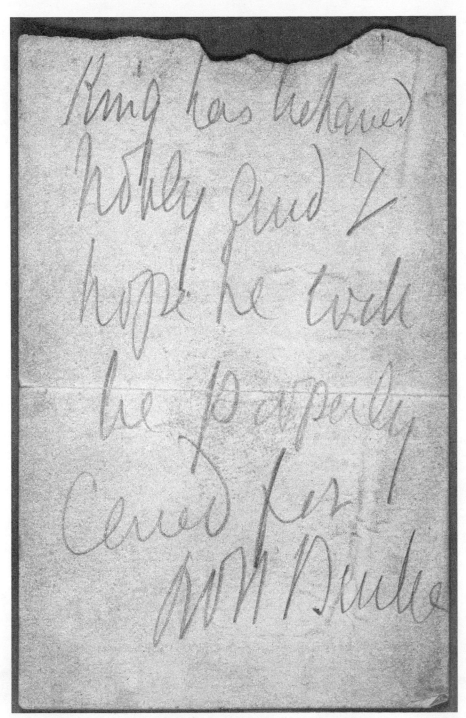

A testament to Burke's honourable death, the leader's last thoughts are for the safety of his remaining companion.

They were Burke's last coherent words. King stayed with his leader throughout the night. By the morning the Irishman was speechless. At around eight o'clock, he fell into unconsciousness and expired. He was still clutching his revolver in his right hand. Robert O'Hara Burke had died an honourable death. It was the end he had looked for all his life.

For several hours John King sat by Burke's body and wept. Clothed in rags, without proper food or shelter, he was suffering from beri-beri, scurvy, malnutrition and exhaustion. He was surrounded by desert on all sides and trapped more than 600 kilometres from European civilisation.

At last, he got up. With a last glance at his leader's corpse, now stiffening in the heat, John King set off along the creek to look for the Yandruwandha. 'I was very lonely,' he wrote, 'and at night usually slept in deserted wurleys belonging to the natives.' They were now his only hope.

Eighteen

From Inertia to Overkill

'The Aboriginals, within the limits set by
their particular terms of inquiry, use and explanation,
knew it all. We, in our quite different terms, can
never finally know it.'
Ray Ericksen

By March 1861, nothing had been heard from Burke since his departure from Menindee five months earlier. In official circles, there was little concern. The Royal Society was still confident in its belief that the expedition was a self-sufficient enterprise, furnished with every conceivable luxury. In fact, having given Wright the money to purchase extra horses, the committee didn't bother to meet at all in January of 1861. The members stirred themselves twice in February to audit their finances but otherwise they sat back and waited to hear of Burke's victory over Stuart. It was a conquest they all saw as inevitable.

The press too seemed unperturbed. After the ructions in Menindee and Landells' resignation, many journalists expected the expedition to break up completely. Some thought that crossing the continent 'might as well be left to Stuart' and the *Argus* ominously declared: 'Unless a light serviceable party is formed out of the present unwieldy expedition, we shall see them in Melbourne shortly; or, perhaps, not at all.' So reports that Burke had pushed on towards the Cooper with a lighter party were interpreted as good news. The papers assumed the intrepid Irishman was now too far north to send any further dispatches back to Melbourne.

But not everyone was so convinced of Burke's safety. In March,

William Wills' father started calling for a rescue party to be sent out. Most people regarded Dr Wills senior as a meddling nuisance but his cause was taken up by William Lockhart-Morton, an amateur explorer who had been passed over for leadership of the expedition. Morton attacked the Royal Society remorselessly for its inactivity. In a letter to the *Argus*, he demanded to know: 'What has become of the expedition? Surely the committee are not alive to the necessity of sending some one up? Burke has by this time crossed the continent, or is lost. What has become of Wright? What is he doing?'

Whispers began to circulate throughout Melbourne society that Julia Matthews (who continued to beguile Melbourne with her seductive theatre performances) had approached several newspaper editors to lobby for Burke's rescue. The *Argus* responded in April by joining the call for a relief party, adding that the public was losing confidence in a Royal Society 'yet to earn a name for skill in the management of its own or other affairs'. Georg Neumayer jumped to the Society's defence. He admitted it was 'rather strange' that no one had heard from Burke, but he insisted that there was no need to send a rescue boat to the north coast.

In an age of mobile phones, satellite tracking and twenty-four-hour news bulletins, it is difficult to imagine just how remote the expedition was, but it might as well have been in another galaxy. No one in Melbourne could have known that the continent had been crossed at such a heavy price. As rumours and recriminations rumbled around Melbourne, Burke, Wills and King were drifting helplessly along the Cooper, wondering why no one had turned up to save them. It was June 1861 before the Royal Society took any action.

Of course nothing could happen before the establishment of a sub-committee. Just to be on the safe side, the Exploration Committee set up two—the first to organise an overland party, the second to investigate sending a vessel to the north coast. Another undignified squabble ensued about who should lead the relief expeditions. For the overland mission, some factions favoured Neumayer, while others resurrected the name of George Landells. The camel-trader was now 'loafing about' in Melbourne, 'shunned by everyone', but anxious as ever to claim the moral high ground by charging to Burke's rescue. The wrangling continued for several days and then produced a surprising result—a highly suitable candidate.

Alfred Howitt had spent several years surveying and prospecting for gold as far afield as Lake Eyre, without ever losing a man. He was experienced, calm, practical, determined and, to the committee's delight, he was also a Victorian and a gentleman. He was so well qualified that many people lamented the fact that he had not been around to lead the original expedition. The committee instructed Howitt to make his way to the Cooper to see if he could find any trace of the lost explorers. It hoped his journey would be 'characterised by prudence, caution and energy'.

Howitt made meticulous preparations. 'As to the difficulties and dangers,' he wrote, 'I feel so thoroughly up to my work and I have so carefully chosen and examined the quality—even the smallest article of our outfit…that I have my mind easy on that score.' The public was fascinated with the rescue operation. Offers of help flooded in. One man suggested that he might supply a large tank mounted on a tower next to the Darling so water could be fed down a long hose out into the desert; another wanted to dispatch a hot air balloon to survey the land ahead. Howitt ignored these flights of fancy but he did avail himself of a less ambitious innovation. Amongst his supplies, a small basket of carrier pigeons settled themselves down for the journey to the Cooper.

There was no time to lose. 'My last week had been occupied from morning to night,' Howitt scribbled, 'running about pushing on arrangements—from saddlers to ironmongers—from tinsmiths to tentmakers etc etc...' In an astonishing feat of organisation, he left Melbourne on 26 June 1861, a week after the committee appointed him. There were no marching bands, no cheering crowds, no cavorting camels or prancing packhorses. Howitt caught a train at Spencer Street station, bound for Bendigo. From there he would take the coach to Swan Hill, where he would pick up horses and supplies.

Howitt took just three men: Edwin Welch, his surveyor, and two old hands from previous journeys, Alexander Aitken and William Vinning. They carried with them a satchel of letters for Burke. Most were official dispatches from the Exploration Committee, but one was more personal:

> Dear Sir,
> It is with fear I now address you but I hope my fears will soon be allayed by hearing of you safe and sound. Everything in Melbourne is very dull at present (except the parliament) which is all afire. The crisis has arrived. There is no ministry and Parliament is dissolved. Hoping my dear Sir that you and all your party are safe, that you met with a pleasant journey & good feed which is a great thing in travelling, my dear sir I dare say you almost forget me but if you scrape your various reminiscences of the past, you will recollect the laughing joyous &c.
> Cupid
> PS My sincere regards to you; all the citizens in Melbourne join in love to you, bless your little heart. C.

In this awkward letter, Julia Matthews attempted to send some comfort to her lover. He would never know that she had not forgotten him.

Three days after leaving Melbourne, Alfred Howitt stopped for refreshment at a coaching inn called the Durham Ox on the

The unflappable Howitt, an accomplished bushman, had often joked before the expedition, 'I'll have to rescue Burke yet.'

Loddon River. A few minutes later, a weatherbeaten young man entered the bar, looking for him. It was William Brahe.

He poured out the saga of Burke's dash north into the desert, his own retreat from the Dig Tree and Wright's disastrous attempts to provide relief. Burke and his three companions were missing, presumed dead. Howitt was horrified. He abandoned his journey north and prepared to return to Melbourne.

A telegraph from Howitt forewarning the Royal Society of Brahe's news reached John Macadam late on Saturday 29 June. For the rest of the weekend, reports of the expedition's demise swept through the city. The press speculated on the 'wildest rumours of death and disaster', predicting that Burke's entire party had been 'dissipated out of being, like dewdrops before the sun'. Forced into crisis management, the Exploration Committee convened an emergency meeting on Sunday 30 June, after which it insisted that all was not lost. Sir William Stawell declared publicly that Burke's disappearance could be 'accounted for on many grounds...His men might be knocked up with scurvy, or he might be in some place which it was not advisable to leave until the rainy season set in.'

In the light of this optimistic assessment, it seemed sensible for Howitt to resume his rescue mission immediately, but yet again the Royal Society choked itself with unnecessary complications. As Wills lay dying on the Cooper waiting 'like Mr Micawber for something to turn up', the Exploration Committee was doing a fair impersonation of the Circumlocution Office down in Melbourne. Matters were referred up and down through committees and sub-committees. All the time, Howitt sat helpless while the days slid past. It was 4 July before he was authorised to rejoin his men in Swan Hill.

Recognising that so far their expeditions tended to return far smaller than they set out, the Exploration Committee ordered Howitt to take plenty of men in case of scurvy or attack by the

Aborigines. Once more, Landells felt 'honour bound' to volunteer, 'out of deep solicitude for the lost party'. Despite promising (or threatening) that he was the only man who could restore all the camels to full health, his offers were rebuffed. 'If Mr Landells was the only man who could manage the camels,' Sir William Stawell declared, 'it was a singular thing…that he should leave Mr Burke to be sacrificed in the manner he had done.'

Once Howitt was on his way, attention returned to the ocean-going rescue mission. Neumayer stood by his promise and offered to sail to the Albert River at once. At first his proposal was welcomed. Politicians like William Stawell and Thomas Embling realised the voyage would also provide a crafty opportunity to survey a site for a northern port, thus strengthening Victoria's claim to the land to the west of Queensland.

Aware of these ulterior motives, the Queensland government became unusually enthusiastic about looking for Victoria's lost explorers. It was no coincidence that its candidate to lead a rescue mission was Frederick Walker, a bushman of renowned ruthlessness who, amid campaigns against the local Aboriginal population and drinking bouts of legendary proportions, had opened up huge areas of central Queensland for pastoralists. Neumayer was incensed at being sidelined and renewed his campaign to lead the rescue.

In a surprise intervention, it was Ferdinand Mueller who helped to sway the decision in Walker's favour. The government botanist had ignored many of the fiascos of the past few months, attending just one committee meeting since the expedition had left Melbourne. Now he re-entered the fray 'solely from a sense of duty' and split the committee down the middle. The Victorian government was forced to intervene to break the deadlock. The politicians chose Walker—it was a curious move given their territorial ambitions but they probably wanted to save money more than anything else.

The Exploration Committee compounded its ineptitude by handing complete control of Walker's expedition to the Queensland government. Realising that this was tantamount to giving 'a bunch of sheep farmers' a foothold in one of the most valuable portions of northern Australia, Sir William Stawell exploded. If the Exploration Committee 'were not fit for the responsibilities of their position', he thundered, 'they should retire from that position at once'. With this one careless gesture, Victoria threw away its chance to secure a northern port and change the political map of Australia forever. After such a huge investment in the expedition, it was squandering its hard-won advantage in order to save money in the short term. Only Sir William Stawell seemed to recognise the magnitude of the mistake.

Seizing the chance to consolidate its territory, Queensland appointed not one but two parties. Walker would travel overland from Rockhampton towards the Gulf of Carpentaria. Pastoralist William Landsborough would sail north aboard the *Victoria* (supplied from Melbourne), then land in the Albert River region and travel south.

As the colonial governments clamoured to assist, the South Australians couldn't contain their glee. They announced that £1200 would be made available for a rescue mission from Adelaide, with the *Register* adding that 'where life was at stake, they felt obliged to do all in their power to relieve those who stood in need of help'. Nothing had been heard from their man, John McDouall Stuart, since he had left the Flinders Ranges in January 1861, but the South Australians were confident he would be nearing the north coast by now. In Stuart's absence, they turned to another Scotsman to lead their rescue party. John McKinlay was a giant of a man with twenty years' experience in the bush and an uncanny talent for self-preservation. He was given as his deputy William Hodgkinson, the journalist and former member of Burke's party, along with five other men, twenty-four horses, four camels, several bullock carts and a flock of sheep. McKinlay was to travel to the east of Lake Eyre up to Cooper Creek and beyond, if circumstances permitted. He left from Gawler to the north of Adelaide on 16 August 1861 after a pigeon-shooting competition and a champagne lunch at the local pub.

After months of apathy, everyone was striving to outdo one another in the humanitarian stakes. There were now four rescue parties heading in Burke's direction from all points of the compass. But the rampant incompetency and petty squabbling that had preceded their organisation left the public and the press disillusioned. The *Leader* concluded that the Royal Society 'sheltered under the name of a learned society' and yet it was 'utterly incapable of managing the details of a foot-race in Richmond Paddock' let alone an expedition to explore the interior.

As Howitt rode north to the Cooper to look for Burke in July 1861, John McDouall Stuart was six months into his second attempt to cross the continent. So far it had proved a difficult journey. After the loss of Toby the expedition dog from heat exhaustion in January, the weather continued unusually dry and hot. North of the MacDonnell Ranges, he found himself battling 'very poor country indeed', which forced him to abandon his usual 'flying' tactics. Instead he resorted to setting up base camps while scouting parties searched for water up ahead.

By the middle of May, Stuart had passed his previous northernmost point near Attack Creek but found himself entangled in bullwaddie and lancewood scrub, a nasty combination that has been described as nature's attempt to grow a barbed wire fence. It was vicious terrain. Men and animals were cut to ribbons as they tried to find a way through. Stuart rode for hours at a time, until his horse tottered with thirst and he could barely keep his seat. On 20 May, just as the Scotsman began to think his journey was a 'hopeless case', he stumbled across a series of waterholes that he christened Newcastle Waters. Now at least, he had a base from which to explore further.

Each night, no matter how tired or sick he was, Stuart retired to his tent with his precious pipe to work on his charts and sketches. The overland telegraph was never far from his thoughts, and the discovery of Newcastle Waters convinced him that it was feasible to construct a line via the MacDonnell Ranges and through the waterless scrub towards the north coast. 'For a telegraphic communication,' he wrote, 'I should think that three or four wells would overcome this difficulty.' Later, R. R. Knuckey, a government surveyor who used Stuart's maps, commented:

> He was simply a marvel for horseback traverse. His map was so correct that we used simply to put a protractor and scale on it, get the bearings and distance and ride on with the same confidence as one would ride from Gawler to Adelaide. If we did not find the old JMDS tree we never thought Stuart was out but that we had made the mistake, and we always found it.

These meticulous efforts demonstrated just how different Stuart's relationship to the land was from Burke's. The Irishman relied on someone else to interpret and record his new environment for him and therefore he could never know it in any depth. Most of its danger and its potential passed him by.

In the lush oasis of Newcastle Waters, with ducks boiling in the pot and fish baking on the coals, Stuart's men began to perk up. The respite was short. Further investigations revealed that beyond the waterholes, the scrub closed in once again. In five months, Stuart had travelled only 250 kilometres further than on his last journey north and he was loath to give up now. He made at least ten desperate forays to the north but, by early July 1861, he knew he must turn for home:

I must give up all hope of reaching the Victoria, and am unwillingly forced to return, my horses being nearly worn out...We have now run out of everything for that purpose, and are obliged to make all sorts of shifts. We are all nearly naked, the scrub has been so severe on our clothes; one can scarcely tell the original colour of a single garment, everything is so patched. Our boots are also gone.

In the midst of such adversity the race to the north coast seemed frivolous and parochial. On 5 July, a week after Burke's death, Stuart named a small watercourse Burke's Creek 'after my brother explorer'.

Fifteen hundred kilometres away from Stuart's party, on the banks of the Cooper, Robert O'Hara Burke's body lay rotting in the sun. As requested, John King had left it unburied and set off down the creek in search of salvation. His survival hinged on small things, a patch of nardoo, a piece of fish or a place to shelter on a cold night. For two days, King lay in an abandoned gunyah recovering his strength and pondering his fate. As he did so, one thought kept surfacing through the despair. Was it possible that Wills had managed to cling on for just a few more days? King took his rifle and shot two crows. Perhaps some fresh meat might revive his dying companion?

On 1 July, King walked back to Tilka waterhole in trepidation. He arrived to find his friend:

lying dead in his gunyah...the natives had been there and had taken away some of his clothes. I buried the corpse with sand, and remained there some days but finding my supply of nardoo was running short...I tracked the natives who had been to the camp by their footprints in the sand.

Later that day, when John King stumbled into the Yandruwandha camp, the Aborigines seemed pleased to see their 'old friend'. They cooked him some fish and pointed out a place in one of their own gunyahs for him to sleep. Several of the men indicated in sign language that they knew Wills was dead, but they kept asking where the third man was? When King signalled that he too was gone, several of the tribe began to cry. That night they brought extra food for the stricken survivor.

The Yandruwandha were bemused by their new visitor. Most of the time they kept him supplied with fish and nardoo but, every now and then, they grew frustrated and gestured that he should return south. Some of the tribe grew so angry that they threatened to kill King, but others felt sorry for him. One woman named Carrawaw took particular care of him, building him a shelter and preparing his meals. One day he found a way of repaying her generosity:

> One of the women, to whom I had given part of a crow, came and gave me a ball of nardoo, saying that she would give me more only she had such a sore arm that she was unable to pound. She showed me a sore on her arm and the thought struck me that I would boil some water in the billy and wash her arm with a sponge. During the operation, the whole tribe sat round and were muttering to one another. Her husband sat down by her side, and she was crying all the time. After I had washed it, I touched it with some nitrate of silver, when she began to yell, and ran out crying, 'Mokow! Mokow!' (Fire! Fire!) From this time, she and her husband used to give me a small quantity of nardoo both night and morning, and whenever the tribe was about to go on a fishing expedition he used to give me notice to go with them. They also used to assist me in making a wurley or breakwind whenever they shifted camp...Every four or five days the tribe would surround me and ask whether I intended going up or down the creek; at last I made them understand that if they went up I should go up the creek, and if they went down I should also go down; and from this time they seemed to look upon me as one of themselves.

Carrawaw became King's particular *ngumbu* or friend. Arran Patterson, who traces his ancestry back to Carrawaw's family, believes that the woman was telling King she was *Karrawa*, which means she was from the eaglehawk totem group. Stories passed down through the generations tell of the Yandruwandha's compassion for King's predicament, stranded alone in the desert. Arran's ancestors have told him that the tribe had always preferred him to the other men, especially Burke, who was hostile and arrogant. Sometimes they joked that King was more like a woman than an explorer because he did most of the work around the camp and because the others were always telling him what to do.

Skin groups, family names and totems are important in Aboriginal culture because they dictate so many aspects of life: a person's custodial duty towards the land, their position in the tribe, their responsibilities towards others and their choice of 'marriage' partners. Any outsider must be given an identity by the elders in order to be integrated into daily life. Since King was with the Yandruwandha for more than a few days, it is likely that he too was assigned a 'name' and identity. In effect this meant he became part of a specific family, who then had a special responsibility to look after him. In theory it also gave him the right to consort with a certain woman in the tribe.

The Yandruwandha seemed anxious to know where Burke was, so King decided to show them. At the waterhole, he was touched by their grief and their respect for Burke's body:

> On seeing his remains, the whole party wept bitterly, and covered them with bushes. After this they were much kinder to me than before, and I always told them that the white men would be here before two moons; and in the evening when they came with nardoo and fish they used to talk about the 'whitefellows' coming, at the same time pointing to the moon.

But the moon waxed and waned and still no one came. King continued to deteriorate physically and mentally. As the weeks passed, he trudged up and down the creek, following his hosts and clinging to the hope of rescue.

Accompanied by William Brahe, Alfred Howitt collected the bulk of his party from Swan Hill and marched straight to Menindee on 30 July 1861. The whole enterprise was a model of efficiency. There were no stray animals, no splinter groups, no transport problems and no dissension in the ranks.

Menindee had changed even in the months since Burke had passed through. Speculators, prospectors and pastoralists in cabbage-tree hats now propped up the bar and Howitt realised that the tiny outpost was already 'an explorer's township'.

While he gathered information from the bushmen, his men were plundering the stores Burke had left behind. As they sorted through boxes containing everything from harnesses to hog's lard, they were amazed to find that he had thrown out so many essentials including lime juice, medicines and fishing gear. Once Howitt was satisfied with his party, he spent the last evening, on 14 August, writing dispatches, telling his family:

> Do not frighten yourselves about me—I am certainly going into a part of the country which has a very bad name...but we are starting at a good time and...besides I have a very great objection to run myself into a place when I cannot see my way out again...My hair and beard are ragged and my face is the colour of a boiled lobster!!...tomorrow morning into the desert. I feel a sort of presentiment that I shall come back alright.

Howitt's journey from Menindee to the Cooper gave him every reason for confidence. He reached the creek with incredible ease in just twenty-five days, arriving on 8 September. Five days later, his men found camel tracks—the first signs of Burke's expedition. Soon he and Brahe were following the trail of discarded tins, scraps of oilskin and abandoned saddlebags that led them to Depot Camp 65 by the old coolibah tree. The word 'DIG' stared out at them from its trunk. Yet again the instruction was ignored.

Brahe and Howitt could see no signs of any recent disturbance to the cache so they assumed no one had been back to the tree. Howitt admitted that the mass of conflicting clues in the area 'puzzled me extremely, and led me into a hundred conjectures'. He left the depot, oblivious to the fact that all the answers lay just beneath his feet in an old camel trunk.

The rescue party continued downstream and set up camp at a place Howitt named Cullymurra, from the Aboriginal name Kaliumaru or 'wide lake'. It is a splendid waterhole, alive with birds and circled with rocks carved with sacred Aboriginal symbols. These showed that it was an important place of ceremony for the Yandruwandha and other tribes such as the Wangkamurra and Yawarrawarrka.

On 15 September, Edwin Welch was out on a reconnaissance mission downstream from the depot camp. His horse Piggy was jittery, and the surveyor soon realised that he was being watched by a group of local Aborigines. As they scattered into the bush, Piggy shied. Welch regained his seat and saw that a scarecrow-like figure had remained in the clearing. It was a man wearing the remains of a cabbage-tree hat. As Welch rode closer, the man dropped to his knees and raised his hands skywards as if in prayer. Welch stared in astonishment. Beneath the grime was a white man. 'Who in the name of wonder are you?' Welch asked. 'I am King, sir,' the man replied. The name meant nothing to Welch who only knew the officers on Burke's expedition. 'King?' he repeated. 'Yes sir,' croaked the figure, 'the last man of the Exploring Expedition.' And with that the scarecrow broke down and wept.

For the rest of his life, John King celebrated his birthday on

15 September. He believed it was the day that God had returned his life to him. It was a year and twenty-five days since he had ridden out of Royal Park.

Howitt's Aboriginal guides, Sandy and Frank, ran back to Howitt's camp with the amazing news: 'Find 'im whitefella; two fella dead boy and one fella live.' A few hours later the ragged figure was carried back to Cullymurra—'a miserable object and hardly to be distinguished as a civilised being'. The Yandruwandha followed their charge back to Howitt's camp. They were overjoyed he had been reunited with his companions and stood around the camp 'with a most gratified and delighted expression'.

King was almost too weak to stand. Sunburnt, emaciated and clothed in the greasy vestiges of a pair of flannel trousers and a shirt, he wore a leather pouch around his neck. It contained Burke and Wills' pocket watches and their last letters home. He had clung to them for two and a half months since their deaths.

Howitt's physician Dr Wheeler took charge and prescribed his patient small meals of sugar and fat. King began to improve almost immediately but he found it difficult to tell his story without breaking down in tears, and it was often hard to understand him. With a growing sense of horror, Howitt pieced together the jigsaw of coincidence and lost opportunity that had led to the deaths of Burke and Wills.

Somehow the terrible news had to be conveyed to Melbourne. Howitt turned to the carrier pigeons but found their tail feathers had been worn away by their wicker baskets. Undeterred, he shot some wild pigeons and spliced new feathers onto the stubs with cobblers' wax. After a successful trial flight within the main tent, the birds were released in the open. But it wasn't just Howitt's men who had been watching the experiment. Several hawks swooped and carried away the pigeons in their talons. Only one messenger survived the ordeal. It had wisely refused to take off at all.

On 18 September, King felt strong enough to return to Wills' gunyah at Tilka waterhole. Howitt found the surveyor's body in a sorry state. The sand was criss-crossed with dingo tracks and the corpse had been partially dismembered. Some grinding stones and a small supply of nardoo lay nearby, indicating that Wills had died before his food supply had run out. Howitt's men dug a proper grave nearby and laid Wills to rest with a short Bible reading. The grisly ritual was repeated the next day with the discovery of Burke's body lying intact under the coolibah tree at Yidniminckanie waterhole. He was clutching his rusting pistol in his right hand. It was loaded and cocked but had not been fired.

William Brahe dug Burke's grave, a grim task for a man who knew he would surely be blamed for his leader's death. The day was hot and oppressive. As sullen grey clouds piled up on the horizon, Burke's body was wrapped in a Union Jack and interred while Howitt read from St John, Chapter 11.

Several men wept as shovelsful of red earth were thrown onto the flag. An inscription was carved into the tree nearby and the men returned in silence to their camp. Even Howitt, who was not easily moved, said later: 'It is impossible to describe the feelings of sadness and awe that filled our minds as we gazed on the spectacle—the remains of brave Burke.'

Ernest Shackleton once declared, 'the line between death and success in exploration is a fine one'. Through a combination of bad luck and bad management Burke's expedition had collapsed. John McDouall Stuart's party was still intact—but only just. When the Scotsman turned back on 12 July 1861, his men were weak, short of food and still faced a trek of nearly 2000 kilometres to reach Adelaide. Stuart knew he had pushed his resources to the limit:

> The men are failing, and showing the effects of short rations.
> I only wish I had enough to carry me over until the rain will

fall next March…I had no idea that the hills would terminate so soon in such extensive level country without water…they completely deceived me.

Stuart's last comment was an acknowledgment that the Australian outback was inscrutable even for an experienced explorer like himself. It was an environment that could never be mastered.

The return journey was torture. Rations were low, winter had set in and the desert sparkled with frost. Stuart was suffering more than most of his men and, as the journey wore on, he became ever more reliant on his officers. The expedition staggered south, reaching Chambers' Moolooloo station on 7 September 1861. A week later, as Howitt was rescuing King on the banks of the Cooper, Stuart was on his way back to Adelaide.

He slipped back into the city to present his findings to the Chambers brothers and South Australia's governor, Sir Richard MacDonnell. He was surprised to find a gold medal waiting for him from the Royal Geographical Society. Stuart accepted it without ceremony. His mission to cross the continent was incomplete and, of course, he wanted to try again. Hiding the fact that his health was fragile and his eyesight wrecked, Stuart began to plan his next expedition. His backers were anxious that he should 'finish the job' as soon as possible. Money, men and horses were all procured with lightning speed.

Just over a month later, on 25 October 1861, Stuart left Adelaide with the beginnings of his third transcontinental party but, as the cavalcade stopped at an inn named The Heart and Hand, disaster struck. One of the horses panicked after catching its bridle in another harness. It reared high in the air and struck Stuart on the back of the head. He lay on the ground unconscious, the flailing hooves crushing his right hand and breaking several bones. Stuart returned to the city for six weeks of treatment but he never fully recovered the use of his hand.

On 24 September 1861, nine days after discovering King, Howitt was ready to leave Cooper Creek. A line of Aborigines waited patiently just outside the camp, summoned to receive their rewards for the compassion they had shown. One by one, they came forward. Each man collected a tomahawk, a knife or perhaps some rope or leather. The women received rations of sugar wrapped in Union Jack handkerchiefs and the children had pink ribbons tied in their hair. Carrawaw received an extra gift of twenty-five kilograms of flour. 'I think,' remarked Howitt, 'they understood that these [presents] were given to them for their kindness to the white men, and especially to King.'

As Howitt handed out trinkets, his surveyor Edwin Welch was busy letting out John King's trousers for the second time. The explorer continued to make good progress but his mind was still frail. The re-interment of Burke and Wills had disturbed him greatly. Often King stared into the distance, and when questioned he would burst into tears.

Having presented their gifts, the white men departed. Carrawaw and several other of the Yandruwandha sobbed as King was lifted onto his horse and led away. For now, life on the Cooper returned to normal but its secrets were exposed. The prospect of permanent water and large tracts of grazing land would soon bring the land speculators and the cattlemen in the explorers' wake.

On his way back to Menindee, Howitt passed through Burke's old depot camp once again. This time he took heed of the word carved into the trunk. The rescue party belatedly found the journals, letters and maps that would tell the Burke and Wills story. Over the next few days, Howitt read them with grim disbelief.

As the rescue party travelled south towards Menindee, King defended Brahe on several occasions. He also made numerous remarks about the 'neglect and mismanagement' of the expedition, which his companions interpreted as referring to the Exploration Committee.

Still apt to become hysterical, King suffered terribly on the journey home. Weak and self-absorbed, he was often strapped to his horse for hours on end. River crossings were especially traumatic. He refused to swim, so Howitt resorted to tying him to the tail of a quiet mare and towing him through the water. Afterwards the whole party halted while he was rubbed down with brandy inside and out. Progress was so slow that William Brahe rode on ahead. Someone had to break the news to the rest of the world.

Nineteen

The Continent Crossed

'The Australian comes in the end to the mysterious
half-desert country...And the life of this
mysterious country will affect the Australian
imagination much as the life of the
sea had affected that of the English.'
C. E. W. Bean

The coach from Swan Hill thundered into Bendigo late on
Saturday, 2 November 1861. People crowded around as passengers and luggage spilt out on to the main street, but one
man slipped away from the confusion, hurried to the local cable
office and demanded to send an urgent message. Minutes later, the
click of the telegraph machine sent his sensational story to
Melbourne.

The continent had been crossed. Burke and Wills were dead.
There was one survivor and he was on his way to the city. Within
a few hours, the whole colony was talking about the 'thrilling
news'. Melbourne was stunned. No one could believe that such a
well-equipped party could have met such a desolate end. The grief
and gossip penetrated every corner of the city—even managing to
dominate conversation at the running of the Melbourne Cup. In
Beechworth and Castlemaine, miners downed tools and gathered
in the streets to hear that their former police chief had died a
heroic death in the desert. By late evening the scandal had spread
to Sydney and Adelaide. It sparked international interest with
articles appearing in Britain, Ireland, Holland, Germany and
America. News of the tragedy shocked readers:

THE
VICTORIAN
EXPLORATION
EXPEDITION.

THE CONTINENT
CROSSED.

DEATH OF BURKE
AND WILLS.

THEIR REMAINS FOUND.

The Argus Office,
Sunday Morning.

The following despatch has been received from our Sandhurst correspondent :—

"SANDHURST, Nov. 2.

"Mr. Brahe, of the Exploration Contingent, arrived here this afternoon, from Cooper's Creek.

"The remains of Burke and Wills, who both died on the same day from starvation [supposed on or about the 28th of June,] near Cooper's Creek, have been found.

"Gray, another of the party, also perished.

"King is the only survivor.

"They had crossed the continent to the Gulf of Carpentaria.

"All Burke's books, &c., have been saved."

For several days Melbourne's newspapers printed special editions, and plans were under way for commemorative portraits, diaries and maps. In the midst of its collective grief, Victoria was strangely exultant. It was a society that had inherited so many peculiar British obsessions, and there was nothing the public celebrated more than a dead hero. Sensing the popular mood, the *Argus* realised that Burke's death had given the colony something it had been searching for since its inception a decade earlier: 'The name of Robert O'Hara Burke is henceforth of the people of Victoria. The glory of his deed, and the sorrow of his death, will each render that name memorable in the annals of our country. And well may Victoria be proud of this, her first hero.'

Victoria's champion had solved the mystery of the 'ghastly blank' and opened up territory of enormous potential:

> The sufferings and death of the first white men who crossed the Australian continent will be household words in Australia, when the iron horse has extended from the southernmost point of Australia to the shores of Carpentaria; a country large enough to absorb the surplus population of the world has been discovered. In years to come cities will arise where the explorers rested, and plenty will be found where the explorers perished. All honour then to the gallant four, of whom three died and one survives.

As more details emerged, the scale of the tragedy only increased. No one could believe that the expedition had fallen foul of so many coincidences and lost opportunities:

> Among all the chances which it was imagined might have overtaken the absent explorers, the dreadful reality never could have entered into the mind of anyone. That they should have reached Cooper's Creek upon the day on which BRAHE deserted it—that the track which the latter mistook for those of the natives should have been those of the missing men— that BRAHE and WRIGHT should have walked over the

ground where lay concealed the precious document which would have told of the whereabouts of BURKE and his companions—who in his wildest dreams could have supposed?

Burke's story, which at times had descended towards the ridiculous, was now elevated to the sublime. The Irishman was far more popular in death than he ever had been in life:

> The story of his great achievement, if it is the saddest, is also one of the highest in the history of manhood. No fiction was ever half so romantic—no hero more valiant, bold or loyal. The age of chivalry is restored in an achievement equal to all that war has shown us of hardihood, courage, and devotion. For this our hero was a soldier, in all the highest points of soldiership. No conqueror dying on the field of battle could earn a fame more pure or glorious.

Few dared suggest that the expedition was a failure. The original objectives, scientific endeavour and geographical discovery, were overshadowed by Burke's glorious death. He had conquered a continent—and Victoria had proved itself to the world. Sir William Stawell was anxious to harness the public enthusiasm. He lobbied Victoria's chief secretary John O'Shanassy, who announced his intention to apply to the British government for the annexation of the territory Burke had discovered. The press reacted eagerly, expressing the hope that this would be the start of a northern commercial empire and a base for the overland telegraph. For a time it seemed a real possibility that Australia might gain a new colony—a sort of 'Northern Victoria'—to be governed from Melbourne.

The news of Burke's demise was broken to Julia Matthews on 2 November just before she was due to appear at the Princess Theatre in the acclaimed comic drama *Handy Andy*. There are no reports of her reaction but she performed as usual that night, and later expressed her 'great regret' at Burke's death. The next day, she went for a walk in the botanical gardens and lost the miniature portrait Burke had given her before he left. An advertisement appeared in the Melbourne papers on Monday morning, offering £5 for its safe return. Some believed she was genuinely upset over the loss; others speculated that casting herself as the grief-stricken sweetheart of a dead explorer was a publicity masterstroke. No one knows whether she ever recovered her keepsake.

Preparations began for the reception of John King. Still fragile, he was now travelling by coach towards Melbourne. The further south he went, the more bewildered he became. By day, spectators lined the streets and cheered as his carriage went past; by night the local dignitaries plied him with sumptuous banquets and fine wine, but the excitement and the food suited neither his mood nor his digestion. Everyone wanted to hear his story but, each time he rose to speak, he broke down in tears and had to be led sobbing from the table. So many women offered to 'look after him' that he was locked inside his bedroom at night 'for his own safety'.

As the procession neared Melbourne, the celebrations became more exuberant. There were street parades, welcome banners and showers of rose petals. Everyone wanted to catch a glimpse of the returning hero. Some got closer than others. One onlooker reported that while 'one matron was kissing him, two were vigorously fanning him, and most of his hair had been cut off'. Burke might have relished the attention, but King retreated further into an unreachable silence. Edwin Welch tried to help his companion but confessed, 'I could not torture him out of his passive, dead-and-alive manner.'

Even before King reached Melbourne, the theatrical impresario George Coppin (who had supplied camels to the expedition from his circus) offered him £1000 to star in a panorama, which would tour Australia telling the story of the expedition. King later refused the offer on the grounds that:

I am totally unable to endure excitement, much less to appear before crowded audiences—to mentally travel over scenes so full of distressing reminiscences. I require absolute rest and if possible the diversion of my thoughts into other channels...my wonderful deliverance and ultimate preservation from death, is such that I am a wonder to myself. The Almighty has been so gracious to me, and I feel humble at His great mercy, that I cannot believe that it would be right for me to present myself under Mr Coppin's direction for any pecuniary advantage...I beg therefore, to leave myself in the hands of a paternal and just Government, to be rewarded by it as it may deem proper for my services as one of the members of the late ill-fated expedition.

It was obvious that King had not written the letter himself. The meticulous grammar and staged references to a 'paternal and just' government revealed he was already being manipulated by the Royal Society. The lone explorer was a vulnerable and dangerous commodity who must not be allowed to say anything that might prove damaging to the committee.

By the time King reached Melbourne on 25 November, the mood was at fever pitch. Anyone who has lived through the return of the Apollo 13 crew or the death of Princess Diana will have some idea of how one event can so consume the public imagination. And so it was in Victoria in 1861. People couldn't wait to see the man who had lived through such unimaginable hardships, who had trekked across a continent, witnessed the deaths of two heroes, lived among the 'savages' and then been snatched from the jaws of death.

The Exploration Committee had made detailed arrangements for King's return, but they underestimated both the public feeling and the determination of a grief-stricken Dr Wills. When the explorer arrived at North Melbourne station on his special train decked with garlands and bouquets, an overwrought William Wills senior barged into his compartment and demanded an interview. Total chaos ensued.

With King cowering in the corner, Edwin Welch intervened and insisted that everyone was to remain on the train to meet the Exploration Committee at the main Spencer Street station. Dr Wills delivered 'a volley of abuse' and then burst into tears. Unmoved, Welch thrust the doctor into the corridor and ordered the stationmaster to let the train continue towards the city.

Meanwhile, John Macadam had arrived at Spencer Street to escort King to an official reception at the Royal Society Hall. He soon found himself being crushed by several thousand well-wishers intent on seeing the famous explorer. The crowd surged forward, knocking over the police guards and surrounding the train. No one knew what King looked like, so people charged through the carriages, accosting strangers and demanding to know if they were with the expedition. King hid behind Welch, who locked all the windows and doors to their compartment and swore at anyone who approached. John Macadam was lost in the crush.

After several minutes of mayhem, police reinforcements cleared a path to the correct carriage. Welch slung King over his shoulder, marched through the station and shoved him inside a cab. As Dr Wills scrambled inside, the mob surrounded the vehicle. King sat white and shaking as Wills' father insisted they make for Government House instead of the Royal Society Hall. While he and Welch argued, the police managed to push the crowd to one side. The cab lurched forward and then sped away, pursued by more than thirty carriages and a hundred or so spectators.

And so the ordeal continued. The explorer was bundled inside Government House to be reunited with his sister, Mrs Anne Bunting. She was anxious to take her brother home but, before he could leave, King had to meet the governor. As the mob descended on Government House, Sir Henry Barkly was experiencing some difficulty getting into the building at all. By the time he arrived, King could barely stand to shake the governor's hand. He proved incapable of answering any questions.

Somehow the crowd had to be placated. The dazed explorer was led onto the balcony for a brief appearance, before slipping through a back entrance and away to his sister's house in the seaside suburb of St Kilda. 'John King,' the *Herald* observed, 'is regarded with feelings similar to those which made the people say of Dante, "There goes the man who has been in Hades."' He could be forgiven for wishing that he were back there.

These glimpses did little to satisfy the craving for answers. If anything, King's appearance inflamed public opinion. How could Victoria's favourite sons have been allowed to perish in the desert? Who was to blame? Burke was, for now, above criticism. The Royal Society wasn't. The *Argus* branded its members as:

> third-rate amateurs in science, of no special knowledge or experience in exploration, and having small natural capacity for the work...We have had meeting after meeting in Melbourne, involving much waste of words and many despatches to and from the explorers and the committee; but the plain, direct and obvious duty before the committee has been entirely and grossly neglected and to this cause mainly must be attributed the disaster.

Only the provincial newspapers dared to suggest that Burke might have been responsible for the expedition's high death toll. The *Bendigo Advertiser* had been most unimpressed with his behaviour when he was alive. Now he was dead, they published a series of letters criticising his leadership: 'Burke was not a fit man for such an expedition; and this was the general opinion of the squatters through whose runs he passed on his way...his want of judgement, or his obstinacy rather than submit to his junior led to his death.' The *Geelong Advertiser* added that Wills was the real hero of the expedition:

A distracted-looking and carefully coiffed John King poses for an official photograph in late 1861. A potentially explosive witness at the inquiry, he was kept under close watch by the Royal Society.

Australia's sons and daughters will speak in mournful pride, with subdued breath and beating hearts, of the fair-haired gallant youth who laid down his life in their country's cause; of him whose advice if followed might have proved the salvation of his intrepid leader and himself, but whose sense of obedient discipline impelled him to follow the orders, which in his last hour he could not approve.

Even Alfred Howitt pointed out: 'Without Wills, Burke would have been absolutely helpless.' These views infuriated Burke's supporters, who were even more outraged when Sir Henry Barkly announced that the expedition would henceforth be officially renamed 'The Burke and Wills Expedition'.

For months Melbourne was drunk on hero-worship and sentimentalism. At first the transformation of Burke into a valiant martyr was promoted in official circles to divert attention from other more embarrassing interpretations of the expedition's achievements. Memorial dinners were held, speeches were made lamenting Burke's loss and endless toasts were drunk. But the strategy backfired on the Royal Society. The more these 'affecting narratives' eulogised Burke, the more public fury mounted towards those responsible for 'sending him to his death'.

The newspapers began to ask if the explorers' remains were to be brought back to the city or left to rot in the desert. As usual the question provoked argument amongst Royal Society members. Should all the bodies be retrieved or just those of Burke and Wills? Would anyone care if 'lesser men' such as Ludwig Becker and Charley Gray were left in the wilderness 'so dogs may pick at their bones'?

Half the Exploration Committee thought it would be best to leave them all where they were. The other half was adamant that the bodies be reburied with full honours in the city. At one meeting, a member noted that he had taken the trouble to weigh a human skeleton that very morning, and since it was only nine pounds including the skull it would be no trouble to convey the entire remains back to the city. Resolutions were made, over-turned and redrafted until a decision was made on 11 November 1861. Alfred Howitt would be sent back up to the Cooper to recover the remains of Burke and Wills for a proper funeral back in Melbourne. The others would be left to lie in the desert for-ever. John King offered to go back and retrieve his fallen companions. Howitt was touched but it was clear that King was not strong enough to withstand the trip.

Every day the newspapers continued their attacks on the Exploration Committee. No one would be satisfied until an offi-cial inquiry was held. As usual it was politics that dictated the final outcome.

Public unrest over the expedition came at a time of instability in the Victorian government. The new chief secretary Richard Heales was entrenched in a long-running battle with John O'Shanassy, the previous incumbent who had supported the Victorian Exploring Expedition and provided it with government funds. Heales lost power in early November when two members crossed the floor to O'Shanassy's side. One of Heales' last acts before he resigned was to order an official inquiry into the deaths of Burke and Wills.

It was the political equivalent of throwing a hand grenade into Melbourne high society. O'Shanassy had no choice but to accept the inquiry. He had been involved with Stawell in plotting a more political aim for the expedition but he was less than keen for this aspect of the project to be explored in public. There was still a hope that part of northern Australia might be annexed to Victoria. If it was proved that Victoria had established a credible presence in the area and that the expedition's failings were due to the mistakes of junior officers, advantage might still be made of Burke's crossing. But if it emerged that the colony was incapable of organising an overland party to travel to the north coast and back, then not only would Victoria look foolish, it would also find it difficult to stamp its claim on the north coast.

O'Shanassy also had personal reasons for protecting the Royal Society and its organisation of the expedition. He held power with a slim majority and he was desperate to ensure vital allies such as Sir William Stawell remained unscathed by the inquiry's findings. In the small world of Melbourne politics, a finding against the Royal Society would have disastrous implications for many of its most powerful figures. On 12 November 1861, when governor Sir Henry Barkly announced a 'full and independent' royal commission of inquiry, there was general public approval—but most people had no idea just how much was at stake.

Twenty

From Absolute Necessity

'I envied them. They died having done something great.'
Tryggve Gran on finding the bodies of
Scott and his men in Antarctica.

The royal commission of inquiry into 'the sufferings and death of Robert O'Hara Burke and William John Wills' began on 22 November 1861. No mention was made of the other five men who had perished; it didn't occur to the politicians that anyone would care what had happened to them. From the outset it was evident that certain assumptions had already been made. The inquiry's terms of reference included the following clause: 'to investigate the circumstances under which the depot at Cooper's Creek was abandoned by William Brahe'.

In a typical conflict of interest, it was governor Sir Henry Barkly who appointed the board's five commissioners, despite the fact that he was also president of the Royal Society. The result could hardly be described as impartial. The chairman, Major-General Sir Thomas Pratt, was Barkly's father-in-law. Sir Francis Murphy was the speaker of the Legislative Assembly and a member of the Royal Society. James Sullivan and Matthew Hervey were also politicians with strong links to the Royal Society. The fifth member, Francis Sturt, was a police magistrate and the brother of Charles Sturt. He was the only man with any direct knowledge of exploration.

The inquiry sat for a total of twelve days in a hall next to the Legislative Council chamber. Of all the commissioners, only Sir Thomas Pratt attended all the sittings. The press and members of

the public with a specific interest in the proceedings were permitted to attend, but the commissioners sometimes held private
discussions before evidence was heard. The inquiry was as significant for what it omitted as for what it included. It did not ask
how such an inappropriate leader had been selected for such an
ambitious journey, nor did it stop to discover why an overloaded
expedition had been dispatched at the wrong time of the year.
Instead, the commission chose to concentrate on events after
Menindee.

Since Burke and the Royal Society were untouchable, it was
clear from the beginning that lesser players would have to take
the blame. The obvious candidates were William Brahe and
William Wright. Neither had influential connections; neither
was allowed legal representation.

The commissioners spent their first morning debating
whether Sir William Stawell should be asked to appear as a witness. After all, he was only the chairman of the Exploration
Committee! Reluctantly they agreed that he would have to be
disturbed, but only at his convenience, 'on as early a day as possible, to be named by himself'.

It fell to the secretary, John Macadam, to defend the actions
of the Royal Society. It was not a difficult task. He was asked 118
questions, most phrased in the most deferential of terms.
Macadam argued that Burke was given 'a wide discretion to do as
he pleased'. His only specific order was to form a supply depot
on Cooper Creek and establish a line of communication back to
Melbourne. Since this command had been disobeyed, the committee could take no further responsibility for subsequent events.
Macadam then insisted that Burke had been expected to take the
hired wagons as far as the Cooper, so the whole party could stay
together. He neglected to mention the repeated threats to Burke
over escalating transport costs, and he failed to explain how
the committee expected twenty-one tonnes of supplies to be

transported with just a handful of horses and camels.

The inquiry moved on: why had the committee not acted sooner to confirm William Wright's appointment and send up sufficient funds so that he could mobilise his back-up party at once? In the absence of any conflicting testimony, Macadam maintained that the committee had no idea any action was required until Hodgkinson galloped into town at the end of December with the 'startling news' that Wright was still in Menindee. But what about Burke's dispatch from Torowoto, which referred to Wright's appointment? It arrived in Melbourne on 3 December. Why did the committee do nothing then? Macadam argued that it assumed Wright would have considered himself third-in-command because Burke had appointed him to the position. Further confirmation was unnecessary. It also believed Wright would start for the Cooper at once, so any further instructions would have been unlikely to reach him in time. Again, the explanations stood unchallenged. Macadam stepped down.

William Brahe was next on the stand. He faced a total of 279 questions. Almost all of them were based on the assumption that he had recklessly abandoned his post and left his leader to die in the desert. Alfred Howitt had already defended Brahe in public, even stating that, in similar circumstances, 'I feel that I could have left Mr Brahe in charge during my absence with perfect confidence.' This support was ignored as the commissioners began their interrogation. They were looking for explanations to five critical issues:

What were Burke's intentions when he left Cooper Creek?

What instructions did Burke give to Brahe before he left the depot?

Why did Brahe choose to abandon his camp when he did?

Why did Brahe return to the Dig Tree with Wright?

Why did neither Brahe nor Wright notice that someone had

been back and disturbed the cache?

The first question was the hardest to answer because Burke had flirted with so many conflicting plans that none of his men ever knew what was to happen next. No one from the Royal Society was prepared to admit that, right from the beginning, there was a plan to split the expedition in two once it reached the Cooper. The secret plot to divide the party and release Burke to sprint for the north coast was never addressed during the commission hearings. With both its leaders dead, the Exploration Committee was content to blame Burke for breaking up the expedition.

Brahe found himself in an impossible situation. There were so many important issues that Burke had never made clear. Had he ever intended to send back horses and camels to help Wright bring up the supplies? Had he ever considered spending the summer on the Cooper to give Wright a chance to catch up?

On the stand, the young German did his best. He pointed out that since Burke failed to keep a diary or issue written instructions, he could not say for sure what his leader's exact intentions were—but his understanding was that Wright would be 'up directly' with more supplies. Brahe vehemently rejected the accusation that he had abandoned his post and his leader. He argued over and over that he had no choice but to retreat if he was to save the lives of his three men. He truly believed that, once the three months were up, there was no chance that Burke would return. Brahe thought his leader was almost certainly dead by that stage—if he was still alive, he was probably heading for Queensland.

But Brahe's arguments showed cracks under the pressure. If he was so sure Burke would not return to the depot, why did he bother to leave a cache of food, or such an absurdly positive note stating his men and animals were in 'good condition'? Brahe asserted that the note and the supplies were not for Burke at all.

They were for any rescue party that might come looking for them and the note was designed to prevent any unnecessary alarm. The explanation sounded hollow. Brahe stepped down, his credibility damaged.

The next morning, the commission produced its trump card—Wills' last letter. It stated that Brahe had promised not to leave the depot except 'from absolute necessity'. These were the words of a man dying alone in the desert and Brahe was no match for their emotional force:

Question: Would not it have struck yourself that you should not have moved from the depot except from absolute necessity?

Brahe: Certainly not.

Question: Did you conceive that an absolute necessity had arisen?

Brahe: Not exactly an absolute necessity. The time Mr Burke gave me was three months; he said after three months time I had no reason to expect him back, nor did I; I did not expect him back; but I might have stopped longer, and then used up those provisions I was able to bury.

Brahe had backed himself into a corner. If he was so convinced Burke had gone to Queensland, why did he go back to the cache with William Wright? 'Had you a lingering suspicion he might be there?' inquired the commission. 'Yes,' admitted Brahe, 'there was still a chance.'

The next witness was Thomas McDonough. Clearly bitter about the death of his friend Burke, he seemed determined to settle a couple of scores. Branding the relief party 'very disorganised', McDonough said Wright never had any intention of rescuing Burke because he believed the Irishman had 'rushed madly on depending only on surface water', and was either dead or lost in the desert. McDonough then turned on Hermann Beckler, suggesting that he had starved William Patten to death because he couldn't be bothered to prepare proper meals. Even the journalists were stunned. Having provided them with their headlines for the next day, McDonough retired.

Next on the stand was Menindee's postmaster, Edmund Wecker. His evidence was crucial to one important issue. Wright had always insisted that, as well as forwarding Burke's dispatches when he returned to Menindee on 8 November 1860, he also mailed a letter of his own asking the committee to confirm his appointment. Was this letter ever sent and was it subsequently ignored by the Exploration Committee?

Wecker stated he was 'pretty sure' that Wright had sent a letter addressed to the secretary of the Exploration Committee and that it was in a separate envelope to Burke's dispatches. He then proceeded to embarrass the Royal Society by describing the spate of bounced cheques that had resulted in credit being refused to the expedition. Warming to his subject, Wecker speculated that this might have been why Wright was so keen to receive his confirmation—otherwise he might never have been paid!

John Macadam stormed back to the witness stand. He was certain that no letter had ever been received from William Wright on 3 December and the only information the committee had to act upon was contained in Burke's Torowoto dispatch. The secretary defended the decision to send Trooper Lyons galloping after the main expedition. The commissioners did not ask him why reports of John McDouall Stuart's failure were reason enough to chase after Burke—yet the news that an unknown station manager was in charge of half the expedition was not worthy of any action. As Macadam completed his explanation, there was a mood of expectation in the hall. Everyone was anxious to move on to the next witness.

After several delays due to illness, John King took the stand on 5 December. His opinions on the expedition seem to have shifted now he was surrounded by the might and power of the Royal Society, and he began to insinuate that Brahe and Wright were to blame for the tragedy. Much of his evidence was so circumspect that it was suggested in the press that he had been thoroughly coached before the inquiry started.

One other factor dominated King's testimony—his complete loyalty to Burke. While Wills' diary hinted that the Irishman's frustration had sometimes boiled over into anger, especially in the expedition's final days, King was careful never to mention any discord or violence. But, as the questioning began, it became clear that not even King's blind allegiance was enough to disguise Burke's shortcomings in organisation and communication.

Asked if he knew anything about Wright's engagement, King replied that he had 'heard a rumour that Wright had been appointed an officer', but he was 'never told formally'. The explorer declared again and again that he had never been privy to any detailed plans regarding the forward or back-up parties, then contradicted himself by stating that he was sure Burke never intended to head for Queensland and had always planned to return to the Cooper. Was it just coincidence that King was certain on the one point that was most damaging to William Brahe?

For several hours, he picked his way painfully through the story of the journey to the Gulf and then described the terrible disappointment of arriving back at the deserted depot. When asked about Brahe's actions, an undercurrent of recrimination infiltrated King's testimony. It was as if he wanted to shout, 'You lost faith in us. You abandoned your post. You should have believed it was possible for us to return.' The commissioners had no hesitation in reinforcing the sentiment:

Question: Suppose he [Burke] had been away five months he would still have expected to find them there?

King: Yes, we should still have expected to find the party there. Mr Burke said they should have remained at any risk.

King completed his evidence by recounting a conversation he had with his leader just before he died. 'King,' Burke allegedly said, 'this is nice treatment after fulfilling our task, to arrive where we left our companions and where we had every right to expect them.' This testimony completed an indelible image of Burke as the brave adventurer, who had crossed the continent on his white horse and been abandoned in his hour of greatest need. Someone must be punished.

Ferdinand Mueller was determined not to be that person. Despite playing a major role in the early organisation of the expedition, the botanist said he doubted if he could help much, as he had been ill or travelling when most of the arrangements had been made. He faced just twenty-six questions and retired unscathed.

The day's final witness precipitated a rush for seats in the public gallery. After haggling with the Royal Society over his travelling expenses, William Wright had arrived from Adelaide. He faced a hostile and sometimes savage inquisition. The commissioners believed Wright was guilty. Now they set out to prove it. Their principal accusation was that his failure to rejoin the main party contributed directly to Burke's death. Wright defended himself with at least ten reasons why he hadn't left Menindee sooner:

> I did not have enough horses and camels to carry the stores.
> I did not have enough packsaddles.
> I was waiting for confirmation of my appointment and my orders.
> I did not have any financial means until my appointment was recognised.
> I had to wait for the return of Trooper Lyons.
> I was waiting for horses and camels to be sent down either with Brahe or Lyons.
> I was worried I would not get paid.
> I had to safeguard my family.
> Once I got authorisation I had to buy and train the horses, jerk the meat and get the expedition together.

I was waiting for another surveyor and a back-up party to
  come up from the city.

There was some validity to these explanations, and Wright
was justified in pointing out that he had neither the transport nor
the financial means to mount a proper relief expedition. He had
made a solid start to his defence so the commissioners changed
tack. What was Wright doing in Menindee while Burke was
dying in the desert? Was he 'merely looking after the stock'? they
inquired. 'Yes,' replied Wright, 'merely looking after the stock.'
Sensing a small victory the commissioners adjourned for the day.

When the inquiry reconvened two days later, Sir William
Stawell swept into the room and the tone of the proceedings
altered. 'Possibly Your Honour would be kind enough to make a
statement with regard to the general management of the expedition, the instructions that were issued, and the intentions of the
committee,' Sir Francis Murphy asked in deferential tones.
Stawell agreed that possibly he would.

The chief justice's statements were fluent and consistent.
Thoroughly at home in the courtroom, his strategy was to dismiss the commissioners' concerns as inconsequential. He backed
Macadam's view that Burke's only obligation was to form a depot
at the Cooper. From then on he was free to choose both his
route and his staff. 'The Exploration Committee,' said Stawell,
'considered that Mr Burke had full authority to engage Mr
Wright or anyone else who was necessary...this question of
confirmation always seemed a mere afterthought.'

What about Becker and Beckler's repeated pleas for help from
the Darling—why did the committee not respond to them?
Wasn't it obvious, replied Stawell, they were dispatches 'merely
enclosing some sketches', and since they were not from the expedition leader himself, they were not considered important
enough for the committee to discuss.

But what about the bouncing cheques—didn't the committee

take some responsibility for the expedition's financial troubles? Stawell conceded there were minor problems with 'some very trifling drafts' but he expressed surprise that anyone should be so petty as to worry about 'the veriest of trifles'. 'The commission is much obliged to you, Sir William,' announced the chairman, Sir Thomas Pratt, and the chief justice departed.

The proceedings livened up once more when George Landells appeared. Shunned by most of Melbourne as a deserter, Landells saw the inquiry as a way of setting the record straight. His character, he said, had been 'traduced'. He stalked into the hearing and demanded the right to call witnesses of his own. This was, of course, out of the question. Landells was furious: 'I am to understand that justice is not to be had. The doors of the Royal Society have been shut against me.' And with that he flounced out of the hearing.

As the inquiry drew to a close, the pressure mounted on William Wright. The commissioners decided to return to the question of his delay in leaving Menindee, and recalled him. If Wright thought his long list of justifications had strengthened his case, he was wrong. The commissioners insisted that he provide a single reason.

'The only answer I can give is the answer I have already given,' he faltered.

'You perfectly understand the question?' sneered Sir Francis Murphy.

'Yes,' he replied. 'I intended to stop at Menindee until my appointment was confirmed.'

'We have not the slightest evidence of that.'

'Another reason was my waiting for Lyons and MacPherson.'

'You strictly adhere to that statement that you would under any circumstances have stayed at Menindee until your appointment was confirmed?'

'Yes.'

'You state distinctly you would not have started?'

'Yes.'

'Therefore if you had had fifty horses and fifty camels you would not have started until your appointment was confirmed?'

'I should not—'

'Then it is to be presumed that the commission may consider that you have no answer to make to reconcile the statement in this dispatch with your garbled statement made to the committee?'

'I have no particular answer to make to that question.'

'It should be pointed out to you that unless you can answer that question satisfactorily, you stand in an awkward position before this commission.'

Wright was silent. The commissioners had won. He stepped down, his head bowed and his reputation in tatters.

The last word went to Ferdinand Mueller. After studying Wills' diaries and maps, he had reached a startling conclusion. Burke's party hadn't reached the Albert River as they and everyone else believed. In fact they were one hundred kilometres to the west on the Flinders River. The mistake may have been due to the surveyor's failure to factor in the six-degree magnetic variation of his compass, but there was another possibility. When one of the camels rolled over fully loaded on 7 January 1861, Wills mentioned that some of his instruments were damaged. If they included his chronometer, then all his subsequent calculations of longitude would have been inaccurate. One unruly camel could have caused the explorers to investigate an entirely different slice of the continent from the one they had imagined.

Before the inquiry broke up, there was one more embarrassing matter to deal with. It was revealed that despite repeated requests from John King, the Exploration Committee had failed to pay his wages. Victoria's returned hero was living on the charity of his sister. According to the assistant secretary Robert Dickson, the reason for 'this scandalous negligence' was King's failure to apply for the money. The commissioners ordered him to pay up at once. It was not the only humiliation Mr Dickson would have to deal with.

Later it was disclosed that Burke's pistol, which he intended to leave to his sister, had been pawned by Dickson. The matter came to light in October 1862 when Dickson's landlord found the pawn ticket and then told the newspapers that Burke's famous pistol was now 'in hock'. Dickson pleaded poverty, claiming he had not been able to extract even his own wages from the Exploration Committee. The next day he was arrested for theft.

While the commissioners retired to consider their verdict, another Burke-inspired pantomime had started at Melbourne's Theatre Royal. The performance featured 'The Apotheosis of the Victorian Explorers' and, as dancers twirled palm fronds above their heads, a huge image of Burke on horseback appeared and a winged angel descended to crown him with 'fame'. It was the first in a long series of melodramas, dioramas and waxworks that captivated Melbourne for many months.

The inquiry reconvened in February 1862 to deliver its findings. The commissioners were aware that too little censure of the committee would cause a public outcry and too much would embarrass some of the most powerful men in Melbourne. Their report was a balancing act. It blamed Burke on four counts: he 'most injudiciously divided' the expedition at Menindee; it was 'an error of judgement' to appoint Mr Wright without 'any previous personal knowledge of him'; he 'evinced a far greater amount of zeal than prudence in finally departing from Cooper's Creek…without having secured communication with the settled districts as he had been instructed to do'; and if he had bothered to keep a written journal or issue formal instructions to his officers then 'many of the calamities of the expedition might have been averted'.

William Brahe was also reprimanded but less severely than expected. His conduct 'in retiring from his position at the depot' was 'deserving of considerable censure' but the committee was of the opinion that 'a responsibility far beyond his expectations devolved upon him'. The Exploration Committee was criticised for 'overlooking the importance of the contents of Mr Burke's dispatch from Torowoto' and in 'not urging Mr Wright's departure from the Darling'. These were deemed 'errors of a serious nature'.

But it was Wright who bore the heaviest burden. His 'fatal inactivity and idling' was 'reprehensible in the highest degree'; he 'failed to give any satisfactory explanation of the cause of his delay', and this caused 'the whole of the disasters of the expedition, with the exception of the death of Gray'. This public scapegoating of William Wright and to a lesser extent William Brahe deflected most of the criticism away from the Exploration Committee. Many of its members were guilty of ignorance and arrogance. Others, the men who appointed Burke to fulfil their own ends and encouraged him to get to the north coast first, at any cost, were a good deal more culpable than that.

The commission branded Burke's division of the expedition at Menindee as his greatest crime and history has concurred with this opinion. Burke made many mistakes but, in the light of the evidence that there always was a secret official plan to split the expedition, this is one area where Burke can now be largely exonerated. Confident that he would be receiving the back-up of a second surveyor from Melbourne, Burke was merely following a pre-determined plan earlier rather than later.

Many mysteries still remain, the greatest of which is why Burke was so insistent that Wright would be 'up in a few days' when this was a practical and geographical impossibility. Perhaps, in the grip of his obsession to cross the continent first, he was deluding himself. Maybe he was so sure of his second surveyor and back-up from Melbourne, he assumed Wright would be able to mount his relief party without any problem. There is also, however, a more sinister theory.

Perhaps Burke knew he was deceiving his men. Unless they believed that support was on its way, Brahe and the rest of his men would never have agreed to stay behind, stranded indefinitely by the Cooper. It is quite conceivable that Burke was well aware it would take Wright several months to contact the committee and organise sufficient supplies and transport. Therefore he made a secret agreement with Wright to meet him back at the Cooper depot around the end of March, three and a half months after his departure. To prevent a mutiny amongst the men, this plan was never revealed.

There is even a clue that at least some members of the Exploration Committee were aware that this was Burke's intention. In the middle of the arguments about who was to blame for the expedition's failure, the *Argus* reported that 'the Committee knew that it was a necessary part of Burke's scheme that Wright should be at the depot by the end of March at the latest'. Without further documentary evidence, it is impossible to prove this theory. At best, Burke failed to think through the consequences of his actions and disregarded the safety of Brahe and his men. At worst he deceived them and left them to their fate, knowing that back-up would not arrive for several months.

Once the inquiry was over, William Wright retreated to Adelaide in disgrace. For many, he was the man who killed Burke.

The royal commission had managed to apportion blame relatively evenly between all the relevant parties, but if they thought this approach would satisfy public criticism, they were wrong. If anything, the anger towards the Royal Society intensified. Most people dismissed the whole inquiry as a cynical exercise in political expediency.

There was one other issue the commission failed to deal with—the death of Charley Gray.

Perhaps because Gray was an underdog, an ordinary man who died through the folly of others, sympathy for him had begun to grow. Newspapers began to wonder why Gray's remains were not being brought home from the desert. The discussion provoked a number of conspiracy theories. Rumours began to circulate that Gray's death was not accidental. King had admitted that Burke had struck the sailor in his hour of weakness. Had Burke hastened or even caused Gray's demise? Perhaps his body was being left in the desert in case it proved Burke's guilt? Was his death actually murder?

Twenty-One

An Unmanly Action

'We think of the unfortunate travellers whose
bones, bared by dingoes and polished by sand,
lie scattered on the central Australia wastes.'
J. W. Gregory

It was John McKinlay who made the grim discovery on 21 October 1861.

> We started at once for the grave, taking a canteen of water with us and all the arms. On arrival removed the ground carefully, and close to the top of the earth found the body of a European enveloped in a flannel shirt with short sleeves—the flesh, I may say completely cleared from the bones, and very little hair but what must have been decomposed...Description of body: Skull marked with slight sabre cuts, apparently two in number—one immediately over the left eye, the other on the right temple, inclining over right ear, more deep than the left; decayed teeth existed in both sides of the lower jaw and right of upper...body lies head south, feet north, lying on face, head severed from body.

McKinlay had left Adelaide on 16 August to search for Burke and Wills. He was on his way to Cooper Creek when a group of local Aborigines guided him towards a waterhole they called Kadhibaerri, in the Coongie Lakes region.

The next day he found a crudely scratched-out grave on the shores of the lake about 110 kilometres north-west of the Dig Tree. Of course he knew nothing about the discovery of King a month earlier, and assumed that Aboriginal tribesmen had slaughtered Burke's entire party. He christened the waterhole Lake Massacre.

As McKinlay investigated further, he was mystified to find a second grave, 'evidently dug with a spade or shovel'. There was no body but closer examination revealed 'a piece of light blue tweed and fragments of paper, and small pieces of a Nautical Almanac...and an exploded Eley's cartridge'. Nearby lay a 'pint pot' and a 'tin canteen similar to what is used for keeping naphtha in'.

When news of McKinlay's discoveries reached Melbourne, it provoked a furious debate. Had he discovered the body of Charley Gray? If he had, why did the skeleton bear scars around the head? Had Burke's thrashing been violent enough to cause Gray's death? The controversy was fuelled by Burke's detractors. William Lockhart-Morton suspected a cover-up:

> To strike a weak sick man, in any way and under any circum-
> stances must ever be regarded...as an unmanly action...there
> has been much concealment of the facts so that the whole
> truth cannot be known.

According to Lockhart-Morton, King told Howitt's party that, after Gray was caught stealing, he had been 'knocked down, kicked, and so ill-used, that he [King] would have shot the leader, if he had had a pistol' and that 'poor Gray was never again allowed to eat his meals with the others'. An anonymous letter to the *Register* claimed King had also stated that 'Gray was thrashed unmercifully by Burke when near to death's door', and that he had died soon afterwards. King denied the reports. He main-tained that Burke had never been cruel to his men:

> The fact is that poor Gray died on the 17th of April 1861,
> which was twenty-two days after he was chastised by Mr.
> Burke for pilfering from the little store on which we all
> depended. There is a discrepancy I admit between the record
> in Mr. Wills and my statement before the Royal
> Commissioners, but I may say in explanation, that I was
> present and Mr. Wills was not...it is possible that Mr. Burke

told him [Wills] that he had given Gray 'a good thrashing' to satisfy him that conduct so dishonourable and cruel had been duly noticed and corrected…During the period that intervened between the chastising that Mr. Burke gave Gray and his death, nothing could surpass the kind attentions of both Mr. Burke and Mr. Wills to him, *after* it was found that he really was ill; and on the last evening of his life Mr. Burke assisted Wills and I to make the poor fellow as comfortable as we could by covering him with our blankets, such as we had, to keep him warm, in the hope he might rally a little by morning. But he died in the night—died from sheer exhaustion. I wish that those who are now so cruelly attempting to blacken the name and the memory of Mr. Burke saw him on the morning of the next day weeping over the corpse, as only a brave and generous man could; declaring that if he had thought he should have lost even one of his party, he would never have entered on so perilous an exercise. [italics added]

King's response went some way to exonerating Burke, but there was general suspicion that he was now just a mouthpiece for the Royal Society. Since the inquiry he had changed his views on many things. Previously King had declared that Burke's journey north was too disorganised and too hurried for the men to supplement their provisions with bush foods. Now he asserted that Burke had planned the journey 'with judgement', constantly adding to their supplies by fishing and hunting. He also maintained that his leader trusted and respected the Aborigines at all times and made strenuous efforts to foster relations with them. No one was convinced.

In the years since the Burke and Wills expedition, there has been much speculation about whether McKinlay really did discover Gray or whether the corpse was a member of a different expedition (possibly even Leichhardt's party) or even just an unfortunate settler lost in the desert. The most important opinion available was that of John King. Given the body's scars, he had every reason to deny it was Gray's, in order to protect Burke from accusations of murder. Yet King was convinced that the corpse was Charley Gray from McKinlay's description. He described how he and Wills, 'tied the body up in a flannel shirt, trousers and a large piece of oilcloth' just as McKinlay found it and he even remembered the pint pot and the tin canteen discovered nearby.

Today, with the passage of time and the shifting of the landscape, the evidence is harder to assess. The matter is complicated by the fact that more than one area has been called Lake Massacre over the years. Descriptions given by King, and by Wills in his diary, show that it is geographically possible that Gray was buried on the shores of McKinlay's Lake Massacre. Given King's certainty, it is fair to conclude that the body was Charley Gray. But, if it was him, several intriguing questions remain.

Why were two graves discovered adjacent to one another? Why was Gray discovered in the shallow scratched-out hole and not in the other deeper grave, which had been dug with a shovel? Why was he laying face down, when the Christian burial position is face up? Why was his head severed and his flesh completely decomposed after only six months buried in a hot dry climate?

Five main factors influence the decomposition of a corpse: its depth underground; environmental temperatures; type of soil; accessibility by necrophagic organisms; and the extent of injuries allowing points of entry for bacteria and carrion insects. Although it is not possible to be exact about the rate of decomposition of Gray's body, expert opinion points to the fact that, after six months buried in desert conditions, the body should still have had some flesh attached to it.

A body needs to be buried at least a metre deep to prevent animals from digging it up. This would have been a difficult task for John King to achieve in his exhausted state, so the most likely explanation for the lack of flesh and the severed head is that animal scavengers attacked the corpse, hastening the rate of decay. It is also possible that Burke, Wills and King removed flesh from the body before burial to supplement their failing rations—not something they would have admitted in their diaries.

So how did the body get back into the second grave? Did local Aboriginal people rebury the disturbed corpse out of respect for the dead man? There is another possibility. Gray was originally buried near an important waterhole. This would have been unpleasant for the local people, as it meant that an unknown spirit inhabited the area. It is important in Aboriginal culture that the proper burial practices are carried out in order to release the spirit. Since these would have been neglected in Gray's case, his body may have been dug up by the Aboriginal people so that the appropriate rituals could be observed. It is also possible that during this process, flesh was removed from the bones and eaten for ceremonial purposes, before the body was reburied in a shallow grave.

As for the scars on Gray's skull, Burke's critics suggested these were evidence that he had been beaten far more severely than anyone admitted. In rejecting these accusations, King pointed out that the marks were described as 'sabre cuts' when the party had not so much as a knife left between them, let alone a sword. Yet we know that Burke had access to a shovel because King used it to dig Gray's grave, and he could have used it as a weapon to beat his subordinate. The mystery is only increased by the fact that several pages of both Wills' diary and Burke's pocketbook were removed before the official diaries were printed. We will never know if those pages contained more information about Gray's death.

As it is, there is not enough conclusive evidence to charge Burke with murder, but he had a history of losing his temper and, if he did strike Gray, who was already a sick man, then a blow or blows to the head may have hastened his death. Several expeditions have been mounted in recent years to find the remains of Charley Gray. While the location of the camp where he died has almost certainly been established, the body has never been found.

There is one final mystery. McKinlay noted that the Aboriginal man who led him to the corpse also had a recent wound on his knee:

> He showed how he had been shot, by pointing to my gun, and carried from the spot on another native's back. Besides the wound on his knee, there was another bullet-mark on his chest, reissuing between his shoulders, and four buckshot still protruding from the centre of his neck.

The man was wounded before McKinlay's party arrived, but who shot him? Had a skirmish taken place at the lake to which Burke, Wills and King never admitted?

John McDouall Stuart was convalescing from his hand injury in Adelaide when he heard of Burke's success in reaching the north coast and of his tragic death on the way home. The news did not dampen the Scotsman's enthusiasm to cross the continent himself. If anything, it made him more determined—like most South Australians, he believed that Adelaide could still grab the overland telegraph. Besides, Burke's route did not technically allow the Victorians to claim the £2000 prize for crossing the continent, since Burke's track was too far east of 'Stuart's country'.

Without waiting for his hand to heal, Stuart rejoined his men at Chambers' Moolooloo station. On 1 January 1862, flanked by his trusted lieutenants, Francis Thring and William Kekwick, he rode north once more, his right arm dangling by his side. Stuart cursed his disability but in secret joked that it wasn't his greatest impediment—the politicians had insisted that he take a scientist with him on his latest journey.

Stuart crossed through the MacDonnell Ranges and headed into the dreaded scrub country further north. The heat took its toll on Stuart's weakened constitution and on several occasions he was forced to send Thring and Kekwick ahead, because he was not well enough to leave camp himself. 'No rain seems to have fallen here for a length of time,' wrote Stuart as his hopes of success faded, 'we have not seen a bird, nor heard a chirrup of any to disturb the gloomy silence of the dark and dismal forest.' North of Newcastle Waters, the discovery of another chain of ponds, christened Daly Waters, lifted their spirits but the explorer admitted in his diary, 'I feel this heavy work much more than I did the journey of last year, and feel my capability of endurance giving way.'

Yet Stuart refused to turn back. As his party entered the lush tropical forests of the Australian north, the mulga scrub gave way to stringybarks, woollybutts and pandanus. The men reached the Roper River on 25 June 1862. Calculating that he had reached Augustus Gregory's east–west track, he knew the coast couldn't be too far away. But his health was failing fast. 'I have scarcely been able,' he wrote, 'to endure the motion of horseback for four hours at a time.'

Suddenly there was water everywhere, but Stuart's party soon found the rivers and swamps brought new tortures. Pat Auld recalled:

I have not said a word about our minor troubles, the ants, the sandflies, the common flies, and the mosquitoes...From the time we struck the Roper until we left it, the mosquitoes and flies were terrible. Our hands, wrists, necks and feet were all blistered with their bites, and many earnest inquiries were made as to who could explain their use in this world. One of the party thought they were sent to teach a man how to swear fluently.

The Roper led Stuart and his men into what is now Kakadu National Park. The region, which takes its name from the Gagudju people, is rich in Aboriginal culture. Intersected by an extensive network of rivers, swamps and wetlands, it is packed with 1000 species of plants, fifty native mammals and more than 270 species of birds. Now designated a world heritage area, it is an ancient landscape with the power to entrance even the most hardened explorer. In 1910, the pioneer Stuart Love wrote:

> Quite suddenly we came to a steep ravine, and riding down this found ourselves on the bank of a lovely river. All around stretched acres of long, green grass; the river banks, steep and sandy, were covered with iron-bark and many another shady tree and with great clumps of bamboo; the stream itself, blocked just below by granite boulders formed a magnificent pool. Beyond this bar the cool, sweet fresh water flowed away over the stones with a soothing murmur.

But this new paradise was more difficult to cross than Stuart had anticipated. There was so much water that the rivers and wetlands barred their way. Day after day, Stuart forced himself back into the saddle. He even ate on his horse for fear that he might not be able to remount after his meal. Could he reach the north coast before his health collapsed completely?

In Melbourne, the royal commission was over, but throughout the latter half of 1862, Burke and Wills fever still gripped Victorian society. After all there was still the funeral to look forward to.

Ignoring the summer heat, Alfred Howitt was already on his way north to retrieve the bodies of the fallen explorers. For him, the journey was almost routine and on the way he even found time to correspond with his British relatives. About halfway between Menindee and Cooper Creek he left a packet of letters

buried in a pickle jar with a sign asking that they be posted by
whoever next passed by. One of them duly arrived in England a
few months later:

> I am slowly progressing towards Cooper's Creek which I hope
> to reach in 10 days...I am quite well only when I knock a
> piece of skin off, the millions of flies make a sore and keep it
> so—imagine me in a pair of buckskin gloves—an explorer in
> gloves!

Yet again, Howitt achieved his goals with breathtaking ease.
During one reconnaissance mission towards Mount Hopeless he
confided, 'At Cooper's Creek I have left the main party building
a fort, catching the finest fish in this part of the world and gar-
dening.' His men nicknamed one campsite 'the Fish Pond' after
they pulled out more than a hundredweight of fish in a single
afternoon. Howitt returned a few weeks later to find pumpkins,
melons and radishes thriving along the side of the creek. He settled down to a meal of horse steak and fresh vegetables—just a
few kilometres away from where Burke and Wills had expired
from exhaustion and malnutrition.

After several weeks exploring the Cooper area, Howitt
decided it was time to commence the grisly task of exhuming the
bodies. Burke and Wills were now little more than skeletons, and
even these had been extensively mauled by dingoes. Wills' skull
was missing (except for his lower jaw) and Burke had lost his
hands and feet. Howitt collected all the bones he could find,
wrapped each set in a Union Jack, and put them in boxes to be
taken back to the city. He decided to travel back to Melbourne
via Mount Hopeless and Adelaide, as Burke had tried to do eighteen months earlier. Yet again Howitt showed how easy the
journey could be with the right supplies and preparation.

When he arrived on 8 December 1862, the mood in the South
Australian capital was sombre. Burke may have been a rival but
the sight of the tiny black box containing his bones was enough

to silence even the most critical commentators. John McDouall Stuart was still out in the desert somewhere far to the north. Nothing had been heard from him for nearly a year.

Thousands lined the streets to watch the remains being carried through the centre of the city. 'For a time all business was suspended and the streets were silent,' observed the *Register*, 'making most audible the slow tread of the crowd who followed the hearse and the solemn sounds of the military band playing "Dead March in Saul".'

During his stay in Adelaide, Howitt was forced to undergo a gruelling round of memorial dinners and formal receptions and it was with some relief that he set sail for Melbourne with his macabre cargo. On Sunday, 20 December 1862, with her flag trailing at half-mast, the *Havilah* sailed into Port Melbourne. She cut through the glassy waters of Port Phillip Bay, bathed in early morning sunshine, and pulled alongside Sandridge Pier. 'It was,' decided the *Leader*, 'as if the elements were hushed into mournful stillness by the presence of the dead.'

Standing on the docks waiting for the ship's arrival was a delegation from the Exploration Committee and a small elderly woman who addressed the men in a strong Galway accent. Ellen Dogherty had been Burke's nurse, his nanny and life-long friend. Now in her seventies, she had decided to travel around the world to see 'Master Robert' one more time before she died. But instead of being reunited with her favourite son in the prime of his life, she found herself surrounded by strangers watching his bones being unloaded in a tin box. Four of Howitt's men carried the remains ashore, placed them in a hearse and watched as they were conveyed to the Royal Society Hall. Once inside, Nurse Dogherty asked to be left alone. She stayed for several hours, leaving members of the Exploration Committee shuffling uncomfortably outside as they listened to the harrowing sound of an old woman weeping.

Eleven days later, on New Year's Eve 1862, the Royal Society gathered for the formal ceremony of 'coffining' the bones of the two dead explorers. There was just one problem. The metal boxes were locked. John Macadam had the only key. It was late afternoon and he was nowhere to be found.

Embarrassment, impatience and anger rippled through the invited audience. Several other keys were tried without success. The members were about to embark upon the undignified process of forcing open the boxes with a small crowbar when Macadam made an unsteady entrance into the hall. The rather dishevelled secretary explained that he had been so upset, he was 'overcome with a sudden indisposition', which prevented him attending earlier. The newspaper reporters had a less delicate explanation. Macadam was drunk.

As the *Age* put it, 'It was New Year's Eve, and Scotchmen on that night of all others are apt to grow "sympathetic".' Others were outraged at the sight of 'the weeping Doctor, overcome by emotions which he had imbibed, staggering over the bones of poor BURKE, and slobbering drunken kisses upon those sacred remains'.

Amongst much ostentatious sniffing and dabbing of eyes, the gruesome ceremony continued:

The remains of Burke were the first opened, and Dr Murray cut the bags and revealed the bones, wrapped in a piece of black alpaca. The nurse of Burke, who was present, now came forward, and it was remarkably affecting to see the care with which she had provided for the melancholy occasion. A clean sheet was spread by her over the iron shell, and a small frilled pillow was then placed for the accommodation of the skull.

The skull was now placed by Messrs Murray and Gillbee, and after it the collar bones, shoulder bones, vertebrae and the remainder of the skeleton was laid out in the shell in conformity with their proper positions. These bones were remarkably perfect, a few of the smaller ones only being missing. Having been properly laid out, poor Mrs Dogherty again pressed forward, and folding over the left side of the sheet, devoutly kissed the skull, sobbing bitterly all the while.

But not everyone was as upset as the nurse. Amongst much 'crying and kissing' of Burke's skull, several members of the Royal Society slipped a couple of his teeth and a few locks of hair into their pockets as souvenirs. (It later became quite common in certain circles to pass around Burke and Wills body parts as a conversation piece at dinner parties.)

To everyone's relief, Dr Wills senior felt unable to attend the 'coffining' of his son. But in the absence of any other relatives no one had thought to provide a winding sheet to wrap up poor Wills. An assistant was dispatched and the explorer was eventually swathed in a piece of old calico. As the *Age* recognised, it was a sad end for a young man who had died by himself in the desert:

> The contrast between this and the preceding ceremony was remarkable and affecting. No pitying female hand waited to perform the last sad offices towards the remains of him to whom Australasia and the world alike are indebted for one of the most interesting and touching narratives ever penned, and all that remained of the head which dictated it was the lower jaw. The remains of Wills were somewhat imperfect; several of the other bones were gone. The vertebrae and skeleton were kept together by the remains of the shirt in which the poor fellow died, and in this condition, it was coffined. Among these bones was a small portion of sandy-coloured beard, sufficient in itself to prove the identity of the remains.

Once this 'indescribably disgusting' ceremony was over, the full force of Melbourne's communal grief could be unleashed. For a period of fifteen days the public was invited to view the explorers' remains through special glass-topped coffins laid against a spectacular backdrop. As the *Melbourne Post* recorded:

> Long veils of black cloth relieved with white, are draped around the upper part of the walls and windows...the panels

in the lower walls are draped with Maltese crosses and on the
pillars between the panels are sixteen white shields, bearing
the names of the principal explorers of the Australian continent...In the centre of the hall stands the catafalque upon
which the coffins containing the bones rest...The catafalque is
raised on a dais two feet from the ground, and is reached by
four steps covered with black cloth and crimson bands. Above
the catafalque is a canopy, surmounted with a heavy plume of
white ostrich feathers...and on each side are three large silver
candelabras, which will be lighted with gas...

Nurse Dogherty completed the lavish display. Inseparable
from Master Robert, she sat next to the coffin entertaining the
crowds with bouts of loud and persistent wailing.

Veiled and escorted through in a private viewing, Julia
Matthews was one of the first to pay her respects. John King also
visited the hall, but on seeing the remains of his dead companions he broke down and had to be removed. Such was the public
obsession with Victoria's dead heroes that up to 7000 mourners a
day queued to see the remains. Those with enough influence
were actually allowed to climb up beside the coffins and handle
the bones. Pickpockets ran through the crowds and stalls sprang
up outside the hall selling food, drink and commemorative handkerchiefs. More than 100,000 people filed past the bodies.

This ostentatious display confounded some commentators
who found the death pageant vulgar in the extreme. 'The spectacle which Victoria presents at this moment,' complained the
Examiner, 'is anything but an edifying one. The bones of its
heroic explorers have been brought with infinite trouble and
expense from the silent spot where the rude natives vouchsafed
the remains a truer sympathy than we, in our boasted civilisation,
seem capable of expressing.'

There was a strong feeling that the public displays of sorrow
from various members of the Royal Society were designed for 'a
maximum of show and a minimum of feeling'. In the same way

that many people follow the exploits of royalty or the antics of movie stars, the residents of Victoria had become obsessed with the Burke and Wills saga. It had been talked about, gossiped about, argued about, criticised, complimented, glorified and speculated upon at every public bar, every private club and on every street corner around Victoria. The public and the press had followed the expedition as it degenerated into a petty but compelling human drama and then watched in amazement as it rose again to attain tragic status. Now the whole of the colony prepared itself for the magnificent final act: Burke and Wills would be buried on 21 January 1863. It would be Victoria's first state funeral.

Twenty-Two

A Bloodless Triumph

'Lives of great men all remind us
We can make our lives sublime,
And, departing, leave behind us
Footprints on the sands of time.'
'A Psalm of Life', Henry Wadsworth Longfellow—
Wills' favourite poem

The thrilling prospect of a state funeral established Burke and Wills as the nearest thing Victoria had to heroes such as Nelson and Wellington. Burke had been wise to choose Sir William Stawell as custodian of his personal papers. The chief justice declared all the documents 'private' and embarked on a strenuous campaign to ensure Burke's image survived untarnished. The explorer's intentions towards Julia Matthews and his outrageous will, leaving her everything, were all covered up. The bequest was largely irrelevant anyway. Burke had few possessions, his bank account contained just 7s 8d and the largest thing he left behind was his debt of £18 5s 3d to the Melbourne Club.

In order to protect his son's reputation, Dr Wills senior suppressed the last words of his son's final letter, which stated that his religious views 'were not in the least bit changed'. Atheism was incompatible with the image of a heroic explorer. In some circles, it had already been suggested that Stuart survived his expeditions because he observed the Sabbath and that Burke died because he did not. (There might have been an element of truth in this, because Stuart rested his horses and men one day a week and Burke did not.)

The funeral also prompted renewed discussion about whether the expedition had been a success. It was a difficult question to answer. Burke had crossed the continent first, but at a cost of seven European lives and one Aboriginal life. The official interpretation was that the explorers had achieved everything they set out to do. Sir Henry Barkly informed the British Colonial Office that the outcome was of 'the very highest importance, both to geographical science, and to the progress of civilisation in Australia' and Georg Neumayer declared that the expedition was 'the most brilliant achievement as yet on record in the annals of Australian exploration'.

But the question endured and was thrown into sharp perspective by the exploits of the four expeditions sent to rescue Burke and Wills. With embarrassing ease, 'big John McKinlay' and his party of ten continued from Lake Massacre to Cooper Creek, and up as far as the Gulf. Here, he had hoped to meet up with the *Victoria*, but he arrived at the mouth of the Albert River to find the ship had departed. McKinlay was forced to continue overland. He travelled south-east, crossing several crocodile-infested rivers to reach the Queensland coast, where he caught another ship back to Adelaide. The mammoth march through many stretches of difficult territory took him more than a year. McKinlay didn't lose a man.

William Landsborough had an eventful start to his journey. On 24 August 1861, he left Brisbane with eight men on the brig *Firefly*, only to be shipwrecked on the east coast of Cape York eleven days later. Everyone including the horses had to be swum ashore while the *Victoria* pulled the vessel free. Once it had been refloated, the stricken ship was towed as far as the Albert River. Landsborough struck south-west and discovered the Gregory River near the present-day town of Camooweal, before backtracking and heading south across 'a finely undulating, park-like plateau...richly clothed with the best grasses'. He named it the

Barkly Tableland after the governor of Victoria. Landsborough didn't lose a man.

Accompanied by eleven men, Frederick Walker set out on horseback from Rockhampton on 7 September 1861, and rode north-west to the Flinders River, where he found Burke's dismal final camp. He followed the old camel tracks south for a while, before running short of food, and turning south-east back to Rockhampton. Walker didn't lose a man.

The eight deaths on the Burke and Wills expedition now looked more unnecessary than ever. Including Howitt's journeys, the five rescue missions collectively covered more than 11,000 kilometres through harsh terrain, without a single loss of life. They opened up millions of hectares for pastoralists and miners and lifted the final folds of the 'shimmering veil' that had hidden Australia's central and north-eastern regions for so long.

It is ironic that the failure of Burke's expedition led to far greater geographical discoveries than its success ever would have done. The achievements of the rescue parties were outstanding but they worked against Victoria's interests. Throughout 1862, the colony petitioned the British government to annexe a new territory on the Gulf of Carpentaria. It was to be called Burke's Land. To strengthen the claim, Melbourne's Department of Lands ignored the evidence of Wills' diaries and produced several duplicitous 'official' expedition maps. These showed the explorers' return route well to the east of their outward journey. It was a deliberate attempt to make it seem as if they had covered more territory than they actually had. But the British had more important things to think about than the allocation of obscure corners of northern Australia, and in government circles the matter was ignored. Once again, it was private enterprise that dictated events in Australia's north.

Queensland's squatters soon realised that the country around the Gulf was not as hostile as they had feared. Hundreds took

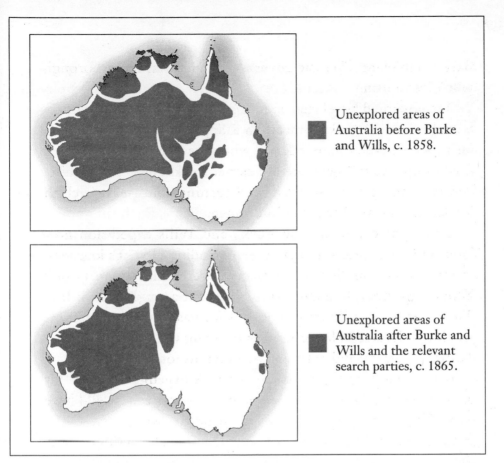

Unexplored areas of Australia before Burke and Wills, c. 1858.

Unexplored areas of Australia after Burke and Wills and the relevant search parties, c. 1865.

matters into their own hands and poured in from the east coast to colonise the area. Thousands of kilometres away, the Victorians could only sit helpless as 'those wretched sheep farmers' overran one of the most promising agricultural areas in Australia. All thoughts of telegraph lines, railways and northern ports vanished in the desert haze. 'Like the monkey in the fable,' commented the *Argus*, Queensland has 'made off with the whole of the roasted chestnuts' while taking 'care not to burn her paws in the operation'.

Today the expedition stands in a very different light. The venture was a product of a wealthy and complacent colony. It belonged to a peculiarly British tradition—one that valued breeding, and the courage to have a go, above ability and experience. With its unshakeable faith in military training, the empire had been dispatching legions of improbable explorers to unsuitable destinations for decades. It was a practice that saw soldiers delivered to the Arctic without learning to ski and naval officers consigned to the Sahara in full dress uniform. Armed with only a commanding gaze and an inflated sense of their own importance, they blundered around and died miserable deaths from nothing more glamorous than a dose of scurvy, a bout of tropical fever or a well-placed spear. Given the history of British and early Australian exploration, it was not surprising that the Victorian Exploring Expedition was, at times, a fiasco. Once Burke had been chosen as leader, the die was cast. The enterprise was doomed before the first camel was ever saddled.

Burke was proof that, in exploration, bravery is rarely an alternative for experience. As Ernest Shackleton's biographer H. R. Mill pointed out, there is no substitute for an innovative and capable leader in the field:

> The best explorer is the man who can both 'conceive and dare', who carries his organizing committee with him on his own feet, and knows that there is no one to blame for his failings but himself. To such an explorer is due on his return the undivided praise for plan and execution.

Burdened with ill-chosen staff and cumbersome supplies, Burke did not have the knowledge or the skills to reorganise the expedition. An explorer such as Stuart would never have set out with such an unsuitable outfit in the first place. As Alfred Howitt noted:

> It is evident to me that at no time was there the necessary means of conveying the 21 tonnes of equipment and stores from Menindie to Cooper's Creek. This could only have been done if an organised train of packhorses or camels, or both, had been arranged, and the most important parts of the

loading conveyed there first, leaving such as spare supplies, duplicates, &c. to the last. But such an organised service neither Burke nor anyone else in the party was, so far as I know, competent to arrange.

Once on the road, Burke's inexperience was aggravated by his impulsiveness. With good organisation his divisions of the expedition may have proved successful, but his flimsy management skills only produced a morass of confusion from which his subordinates never managed to extricate themselves. To a great extent Burke's mistakes were due to his inability to think through the consequences of his actions. He compounded his errors by leaving his safety in the hands of men who had neither the authority nor the resources to ensure his instructions (whatever they happened to be that day) were carried out.

Burke's all-or-nothing attitude and his fascination with dying a heroic death made him a dangerous leader. His failure to establish any kind of foundation to his life gave him something in common with Stuart. Both men were lonely bachelors who had never found their place in society, and felt the need to escape in order to prove themselves. The critical difference was that, while Stuart risked all based on his extensive knowledge of the Australian landscape, Burke had no such experience to fall back on.

There is a perception in Australia that Burke and Wills were victims of a vast waterless desert. In reality it was too much water that contributed to their deaths not too little. The constant rain on the way to Menindee delayed the expedition and the heavy monsoon weather up in the Gulf country took a heavy toll on the men and their animals. The explorers died next to one of the greatest permanent watercourses in central Australia. Thirst was never a serious problem.

As a feat of endurance, Burke and Wills' trek to the north coast and back was an amazing achievement. When in 1977 Tom Bergin and Paddy McHugh re-created the journey from the

Dig Tree to the Gulf using camels, their theory was that if Burke had undertaken the trip in the cool season, he could have completed the task with relative ease, perhaps even inside the ninety days he had originally predicted. But even though they travelled in the winter months, with the benefit of tracks, wells and advance knowledge of the terrain, their outward journey took about the same time as Burke's had done. By the time they arrived at the Gulf, their camels were in poor condition and needed several weeks to recover. They abandoned their expedition because they did not have the time or the resources to get back to the Dig Tree.

The experiment proved that trying to complete the journey as fast as possible was a major factor in Burke's downfall. He pushed his animals beyond their limits and reduced his party's ability to supplement its rations with bush foods. Why did he set himself such impossible targets? The pressure on him to win the race with Stuart brought out the worst aspects of his character. In the end Burke became a victim of 'an excess of bravery'. Once in the desert he seemed to lose touch with reality, until he was oblivious to the disasters that loomed before him. Blinkered by the conventions of his era, Burke found it impossible to embrace the expressions of generosity shown by the Aboriginal people he encountered. His innate sense of superiority made it difficult for him to understand his new environment and so he starved to death in an area where indigenous people had thrived for thousands of years.

Despite all his failings, there is still something romantic about Burke. He was a flamboyant, charismatic man who had never really lived up to his own self-image. He was a man motivated by emotion, and his passions had found their object in Julia Matthews. As William Howitt (Alfred's father) commented later, Burke was 'suffering under the irritation of disappointed love, which made him moody, fitful…restless at nights, hasty in the day and apparently undecided what course to pursue'.

Burke's fatal flaw was his talent for mistiming events. He missed the height of the gold rush in Victoria, the war in the Crimea and the riots in Buckland. His arrival at the Dig Tree just a few hours after Brahe had left seemed almost predestined. The twentieth-century Arctic explorer Vilhjalmur Stefansson believed that any adventures that happen during an expedition prove only that something has gone wrong; that adventure is interesting enough in retrospect (especially to someone who wasn't there), but that it constitutes a very disagreeable experience derived from poor planning. But what makes exploration of any sort so fascinating are the factors that cannot be controlled even by people like Stefansson. Good expeditions also fail.

Burke's errors of judgment were exposed by a run of misfortune. Good planning would have overcome some of his mistakes, but equally, just a tiny piece of good luck could also have saved him. Once events began to spiral out of control, the Burke and Wills saga became the expeditionary equivalent of the *Titanic*. No one believed that such a magnificent enterprise could end in such tragedy. Complacency was the final mistake. Overwhelmed by mismanagement and ineptitude on all sides, perhaps the most striking thing of the Burke and Wills expedition is not that it failed, but how close it came to success.

On 21 January 1863, the day dawned bright and filled with sunshine. As the morning of the funeral wore on, the air grew warmer and the atmosphere heavy. Ladies ordered their maids to lay out their black dresses, their largest hats, their fans and their parasols. All over Melbourne people prepared for the largest public event the city had ever seen. Visitors poured in from around the colony. The trains were packed and the pubs were full.

From early in the morning, people jostled for the best position along the procession route. Some scrambled up trees,
shinned up lampposts or climbed onto rooftops. The pavements
'looked like a forest of umbrellas' as onlookers sought to shade
themselves from the sun. By midday, government offices, busi-
nesses and shops were closed. Estimates put the crowd
somewhere between seventy and one hundred thousand. Several
hotels draped their facades with swathes of black crepe, cherubs
decorated balustrades and banners were festooned across the
roadways. Stalls were set up selling Burke and Wills souvenirs,
including commemorative pamphlets, medals, portraits, poems,
even 'Burke Exploring Hats'.

As with any event overseen by the Exploration Committee,
the funeral had already created controversy. After some initial
confusion about whether Burke was Catholic or Protestant (he
was Protestant), it emerged that organisations with even the
remotest connection to the explorer were desperate to bask in his
reflected glory. More than 200 public bodies applied to take part
in the procession. Only a few were chosen. Since Burke had
served as a soldier and a policeman, a row broke out over
whether the police force or the army should play the most
prominent role in the ceremony. A sub-committee was
appointed. Perhaps, it was suggested, the Castlemaine Volunteer
Corps could supply a military band while the police could perform the gun salute over the coffin?

But who was to stand for Wills? The Ballarat Cavalry saw
their opportunity and volunteered to take part, but when the
government offered them single railway passes to Melbourne
(the Castlemaine contingent was offered returns), they not only
pulled out but threatened to disband permanently. The same
generous offer of return railway passes was extended to the coun-
cillors of Beechworth but they declined, owing they said 'to the
absence of the railway itself'. Georg Neumayer boycotted the

ceremony when it was announced that no one from the Melbourne Observatory was included in the official cortege.

Given the public hostility towards the Royal Society, it was feared that some members of the Exploration Committee would be too embarrassed to attend the funeral at all. A proposal was put forward that all members should walk together as a sign of solidarity. Dr Richard Eades responded enthusiastically. He was not ashamed, he said, of belonging to the 'much maligned' committee. In fact he was so proud that he decided to 'carry a pole erect, indicating he was a member of it'.

At 1 p.m. on 21 January 1863, a hush fell over the crowd around the Royal Society Hall. People removed their hats, as the undertakers carried the explorers' coffins outside to the funeral carriages and the police began to clear a way forward. Led by the Castlemaine Rifle Volunteer Regiment and the Castlemaine Light Dragoons, the procession would make its way towards Parliament House before turning down Bourke Street, then into Elizabeth Street and out towards the Melbourne Cemetery.

The centrepiece of the cavalcade was the funeral car, a magnificent vehicle modelled on the carriage used for the Duke of Wellington, who had started quite a fashion in elaborate state funerals. It was five metres long, seven metres high, and pulled by a team of six horses sporting elaborately decorated harnesses and black plumes. The *Argus* noted that:

> The wheels, four in number, are bronzed, and in the space between them the panelling of the car descends in graceful curves and pillars nearly to the ground. The front panel bears the royal arms and on the back the inscription 'Carpentaria'. On the top of this framework, about eight feet from the ground, rested the two coffins, surmounted by a canopy bearing plumes of feathers, and supported by four silver columns springing from the body.

Not everyone was so impressed. One observer branded the

vehicle 'that hideous affair', and closer inspection revealed that the carriage was only a poor imitation of Wellington's. His funeral car cost £11,000. Burke's was knocked up for less than a thousand. As the coffins were slid into place, the police contingent came forward, raised their rifles to the sky and fired a volley of shots. The crowd fell silent once again. The funeral procession was about to start.

On the very same day in Adelaide, crowds were also gathering around the city. Since dawn, workmen had been hammering decorations in place until the streets 'presented a truly gay appearance'. Pavements were cleared of rubbish and water carts were towed up and down the main avenues to dampen down the dust. Giant drapes of tartan adorned many buildings, flags flew from every lamppost and in front of the Treasury building was a 'splendid arch of palms, laurels and evergreen shrubs' leading to a specially constructed platform. Nearby, variegated lamps spelt out a message: 'Welcome'. By noon, the streets were full and the balconies and rooftops 'well sprinkled with ambitious spectators anxious to get a bird's-eye view of the whole demonstration'.

The clattering of hooves silenced the crowd and a procession appeared. At its head, a horseman carried a flag embroidered with the initials JMDS. Behind him was a small, wizened, hairy figure mounted precariously on a packhorse. John McDouall Stuart was coming home.

Stuart's successful journey across the continent was a triumph of determination and stamina. It had taken him more than a month to complete the last 300 kilometres through the Kakadu area to the north coast. Slowed by a maze of mangroves, mud and marshland, he had finally approached the ocean on 24 July 1862. Even then, he kept his suspicions of success to himself:

> At eight and a half miles coming on a plain I could hear the
> wash of the waters and seeing a dense heavy bushy scrub on

the other side of the plain, I knew it at once to be the bounding of the sea...Thring and I rode forward a yard or two and were on the beach delighted to see the broad expanse of salt water. I immediately dismounted, walked into the water, or rather dipped my feet into the Indian Ocean as I promised Sir Richard MacDonnell I would do if I got the chance, and not only did I do this but I washed my hands and face in it as well.

Thring got so excited at first sight of it that he could not restrain himself but called out, the sea, the sea, the sea, which so took the rest of the party by surprise that they seemed quite bewildered, and he had to repeat the words two or three times before they could understand him.

PLANTING THE FLAG ON THE SHORES OF THE INDIAN OCEAN.

Stuart celebrated his crossing by raising a Union Jack lovingly embroidered with his name by James Chambers' daughter Mary. Stuart named the area Chambers Bay.

At length, understanding what was meant they commenced cheering at a terrible rate which lasted some time.

Stuart had emerged on a headland now named Point Stuart. It flanks a small bay nestling behind glorious forests of palms and cycads. The ocean is turquoise, the sand fine and white and the beach is dotted with turtle nests.

Stuart's men were elated and tumbled into the waves. After a ceremony to raise the Union Jack and toast the British empire, they approached their leader to ask for an extra cup of tea by means of celebration. Stuart refused.

One of his men said later that although their leader was 'in their black books for a few days', they realised that Stuart denied the request because he thought it unlikely he would survive the return journey. He wanted to be sure there would be enough rations for the rest of his party to get home. From now on speed was essential. For the first few days Stuart was strong enough to lead the march south but scurvy was beginning to take its toll once more and his eyesight was now so afflicted that he could not see at all after dark.

In early October 1862, as the party retraced their steps past Attack Creek, Stuart was finding it hard to sustain the necessary twelve-hour days in the saddle:

> What a miserable life mine is now. I get no rest night or day from this terrible gnawing pain, the nights are too long and the days are too long, and I am so weak that I am hardly able to move about the camp…I am afraid soon I shall not be able to sit in the saddle and then what must I do?

Stuart now had to be lifted on and off his horse. He could barely walk and strips of rotting flesh inside his mouth made it difficult for him to eat. By 18 October, the situation became critical:

> While taking a drink of water, I was seized with a violent fit of vomiting blood and mucus, which lasted about five minutes

and has nearly killed me...I have kept King and Nash with me in case of my dying during the night, as it would be lonely for one young man to be there by himself. Wind south-east.

The next morning Stuart was unable to stand. His men constructed a stretcher, which they tied between the two quietest horses, and it was in this giant sling that the explorer was carried south. For the last few days of the journey home, Stuart's men were convinced their leader was dying. He lay semiconscious in his stretcher and was only just lucid when the emaciated party arrived back at the outpost of Mount Margaret Station on 27 November 1862. It had taken three attempts but John McDouall Stuart had at last achieved his dream. He had crossed Australia from coast to coast.

News of Stuart's success did not reach Adelaide until the end of December 1862. When he heard of the triumph, Sir Roderick Murchison, president of the Royal Geographical Society, hailed the explorer as a hero:

> In no time or country has any geographical pioneer more directly advanced the material interests of a colony than Mr McDouall Stuart has done those of South Australia; whilst as a geographer we especially recognise the value of the numerous astronomical observations he made under the severest of privations, by which the true features of large portions both of the interior and the north coast have been for the first time determined.

The successful party recuperated for several weeks in the Flinders Ranges before setting off for their reception in Adelaide. The men were told to wear their 'bush attire', so they salvaged what was left of their moleskin pants, red shirts and cabbage-tree hats. One man counted thirty-nine patches on his trousers. 'The explorers in this guise were like victorious soldiers,' wrote the *Register*, 'returning from a well fought field, carrying the tattered flags and dented weapons which bear witness to their valour.'

Stuart himself was still weak, prone to violent stomach pains and choking fits, but he managed to ride unaided through the streets of Adelaide. As he passed the crowd cheered and waved their flags. Their hero had returned. 'The poor horses,' wrote one observer, 'they look so tired.'

In Melbourne, the Castlemaine band struck up 'a most satisfactory' rendition of 'Dead March in Saul' and the cortege moved forward. Around the funeral car marched the pallbearers: John King (still pale and prone to fits of sobbing), Sir William Stawell, Ambrose Kyte, Frederick Standish (Burke's old boss), Alfred Howitt, Ferdinand Mueller and Dr Richard Eades (minus the promised 'erect pole').

Six mourning carriages followed, carrying, amongst others, Nurse Dogherty (still wailing) and Sir Henry Barkly (eyes lowered). Towards the rear, there was an assortment of marchers including consular officials from nine nations and representatives from organisations as diverse as the Municipal Council to the Society of Oddfellows. The entire cavalcade was so long it occupied several streets at once and it took more than two and a half hours to march the five kilometres to the cemetery. This was the most glorious spectacle Victoria had ever seen, even more glorious than the party which had marched out of Royal Park nearly two and a half years earlier.

A hush fell over the crowd as the funeral carriages passed by and people strained for a glimpse of all that was left of the most famous men in the colony. As the procession reached the cemetery, spectators thronged around the newly constructed vault 'in a rather unseemly manner', forcing the pallbearers to push their way towards the grave. When police had cleared the audience

Shops and offices closed as around three-quarters of Melbourne's population turned out to mourn their heroes.

back to a respectable distance, the bodies of Robert O'Hara Burke and William John Wills were lowered into the grave and laid side by side. A police guard fired three volleys of shots as a mark of respect.

In Adelaide, John McDouall Stuart dismounted and stepped awkwardly onto the stage. As he accepted the keys to the city of Adelaide, it seemed as if the whole of South Australia was cheering his name. A few streets away in the city surveyor's office, his maps were already being scrutinised by engineers as they plotted the route for the new overland telegraph line.

In both cities, as the crowds dispersed, the ladies fanned themselves and the men loosened their ties. The sultry northerly breeze was blowing down from the desert once more.

Today, the same hot wind still rustles through the branches of the old coolibah at Depot Camp 65 on the banks of Cooper Creek. Floods have washed away the remains of the stockade but some engravings on the tree are still just visible locked away inside deep round scars on the trunk. The creek still murmurs as it sweeps past the cracked red earth, and the air is filled with the chattering of the parrots and the raucous shrieks of the cocka-toos. The Cooper was never a silent place.

Epilogue

If Victoria had capitalised on Burke's journey and annexed a new colony in the Gulf country, the map of Australia could have been changed forever. As it was, the Victorians gained nothing, politically or territorially, from the Burke and Wills expedition. The unclaimed land between the 138° and 141° meridians was officially incorporated into Queensland in 1862, and after Stuart's journeys South Australia extended its northern boundary to take in what is now the Northern Territory. For many years Adelaide controlled central Australia from coast to coast.

South Australia won the fight for the overland telegraph line and the British–Australia Telegraph Company began construction in 1870. An underwater cable was taken from Java and landed on the northern Australian coast near present-day Darwin. The irrepressible Charles Todd took charge of the venture, and 36,000 poles carried the wire down through the centre of the continent, following Stuart's original route almost all the way. Once it was finished, the chief engineer Robert Patterson cut the cable so he could ceremonially rejoin it and send a message to the South Australian governor. But Patterson's celebration did not go to plan:

> Half the party seized hold of me and of the wire, and the other half the other end, and stretched with might and main to bring the two ends together.
>
> All our force could not do this. I then attached some binding wire to one end. The moment I brought it to the other end the current passed through my body from all the batteries on the line. I had to yell and let go. Next time I proceeded more cautiously, and used my handkerchief to seize the wire

with. In about five minutes I had the joint made complete, and Adelaide was in communication with Port Darwin.

The first telegram from London to Adelaide was sent on 22 August 1872. Later, a road from Adelaide to Darwin via Alice Springs was built alongside the telegraph line. It is now known as the Stuart Highway.

John McDouall Stuart never recovered from his last expedition. As he convalesced at the Seaside Family Hotel in the Melbourne suburb of Brighton, he at last received the £2000 reward for crossing the continent. It yielded an annual pension of £162 a year, barely enough to sustain him. His only other rewards were a gold watch and a Patrons Medal from the Royal Geographical Society. After several unsuccessful attempts to resume his surveying career, he gave up and sailed to London in 1865. Described soon afterwards as a 'half-foolish...hairy, purblind, silent man', Stuart was crippled, bad-tempered and sustained only by a continuous intake of whisky. He lived in relative poverty, cared for by his widowed sister until his death on 5 June 1866, aged fifty-one. Without losing a man, he had travelled more than 20,000 kilometres through some of the harshest territory on earth, much of it on the same grey mare, Polly. Former members of his expeditions never forgot their leader. Nicknaming themselves 'Stuart's companions', they gathered once a year, until their deaths, to drink his health with a bottle of the finest malt whisky.

In Melbourne, the Exploration Committee continued to meet for several years after the funeral, tying up various loose ends and even suggesting another search for Ludwig Leichhardt. A final set of accounts for the Burke and Wills expedition put the cost at £57,840, more than five times the original budget. The Royal Society exists today and meets in the same building in La Trobe Street.

Tributes to Burke and Wills continued for many years. Burke

was awarded a gold medal from the Royal Geographical Society in London but since only one could be made to any expedition, Wills missed out and King was sent a gold watch instead. Dick the Aboriginal tracker was awarded a brass medal and £5 for saving Trooper Lyons and Alexander MacPherson.

A thirty-four-tonne monolith was placed over Burke and Wills' Melbourne graves in 1864 and a giant bronze statue of the explorers was erected on the corner of Collins and Russell streets in 1865. It has now been moved to Swanston Street, where to this day you will find Burke gazing into the distance with Wills sitting by his side writing in his diary. Major memorials were erected in Castlemaine and Beechworth and the expedition is remembered with countless plaques and memorial cairns throughout Victoria and Queensland. There is even a commemorative obelisk to William Wills in Totnes, the town of his birth.

The Victorian government awarded pensions of £60 a year to Nurse Dogherty, £120 a year to Wills' mother and payments of £500 to each of his sisters. When Dr Wills senior decided to return to England, the committee couldn't wait to hand over the £125 to cover his fare. Dost Mohomet, disabled by a rogue camel in Menindee, was given £200 and lived in the tiny outpost for the rest of his life. Charley Gray's family received nothing.

Hermann Beckler's career as a doctor and explorer in Australia ended in failure. He returned to Germany in 1862 in a fit of pique, when the Exploration Committee declined to give him a reference on the grounds that the royal commission was still investigating the expedition. He settled in Bavaria and continued to practise medicine until he died in 1914.

Ludwig Becker was remembered with affection by sections of the German community in Melbourne, but his contribution to the art and literature of Australian exploration has never been fully recognised. The beautiful sketches he made during his time with the expedition are now stored in the State Library of Victoria.

Soon after Burke and Wills' funeral, the controversial secretary of the Royal Society, John Macadam, sued the *Argus* over claims that he was drunk during the coffining of Burke's bones, but he received the sort of derisory damages that indicated the judge was not entirely convinced of his innocence. He continued in his numerous public positions until his death from pleurisy in 1865. He was thirty-eight. Macadam is now famous for giving his name to the macadamia nut, which was discovered by Ferdinand Mueller.

After Alfred Howitt's successful journeys to the Cooper, he was appointed a police magistrate and goldfields warden for the Gippsland area, positions he held for the next twenty-five years. He became interested in geology and anthropology, leading many prospecting parties through eastern Victoria and writing several books on Australia's Aboriginal people. William Brahe continued to defend his reputation for many years after he was pilloried at the royal commission. Backed up by Howitt and the German community in Melbourne, his character underwent a significant public rehabilitation. He worked for a time in Fiji and as a pastoralist in Queensland. Brahe died in Melbourne in 1912. Wills' patron Georg Neumayer continued his eccentric scientific career. He focused his efforts on establishing the earth's magnetic fields, but many of his experiments at the Melbourne Observatory were irrevocably damaged when the city ran iron tram tracks alongside the building.

William Wright faded into relative obscurity as a farmer on the Darling River. In 1863, he was one of the first to mount a search party for a missing lands commissioner, but he never recovered his good name. History has judged him harshly with many books and newspaper articles branding him the principal villain in the Burke and Wills disaster.

After Burke's funeral, Julia Matthews gave several memorial performances for the dead explorers. In 1864 she married her manager William Mumford, a drunk who beat his wife and used her income to support his debauched lifestyle. The couple had three children. Julia sailed to England in 1867 and became the first Australian-trained singer to perform at Covent Garden. She filed for separation from her husband in 1870 and went on to tour Europe and America. Later she became a devout Catholic. She died in St Louis, Missouri, of 'malarial disease'. She was thirty-four.

There were calls after the expedition for more appreciation to be shown to the Aboriginal people who had cared for the stricken explorers and saved King's life. In what they supposed to be a generous gesture, the South Australian government 'gave' the Aborigines 670 square kilometres of land around Cooper Creek in 1863. Of course, this generosity was meaningless to a group of people who had been living in the area for many thousands of years. The gift was soon exposed as a ruse to start a Lutheran Mission and promote the gospel amongst the indigenous population. The project collapsed and native rights to the land were revoked in 1869. By that time the cattlemen had arrived and the dismantling of the traditional cultures was under way. Many indigenous people were moved away to Christian missions and their descendants are now scattered throughout New South Wales and Queensland. Several Aboriginal groups are currently seeking to reclaim their native title rights to the land.

As European settlement spread, camels became instrumental in opening up central Australia. They were imported from India and the Middle East and were used to carry materials for the construction of telegraph lines, railways and roads. Over the years, many escaped into the wild and there are now up to half a million roaming Australia's interior. They make up the largest wild disease-free population in the world and are exported back to the Middle East for racing and breeding.

Today there is little physical evidence to mark Burke and

Wills' transcontinental crossing. The exact route to the Gulf of Carpentaria has been much discussed over the years and confused by inaccuracies in Wills' maps, misreadings of his diaries, fake 'Burke and Wills trees' and numerous local myths. Burketown in northern Australia is in fact far to the west of the explorers' track and Julia Creek, commonly assumed to have been christened by Burke, is also well away from their route and was named much later. Placenames and spellings have also changed over the years. Menindie is now usually spelt 'Menindee' and, to conform to Australian mapping conventions, Cooper's Creek is known as Cooper Creek.

Some sections of the Burke and Wills route run through private land or terrain that is inaccessible, even by four-wheel-drive, but it is possible to follow considerable portions of the journey on public roads and tracks, and to see some of the genuine campsites and carved trees. Burke and Wills' original graves on the Cooper are marked with cairns, as is the waterhole where King was found. They can be reached from the small outpost of Innamincka in South Australia. Howitt's depot at Cullymurra waterhole remains one of the prettiest places to camp on Cooper Creek.

Some of the desert country that the explorers encountered is still much as they would have seen it, but the introduction of cattle into more fertile regions has caused extensive soil erosion and a subsequent loss of woodland habitat. Rabbits have destroyed large tracts of land. Areas such as the Simpson Desert and the far north-western corner of New South Wales have been designated as national parks, while other parts are used for farming. Oil and gas have been discovered in the Cooper basin and sections of the desert now echo with the thump of seismic exploration.

The Dig Tree stands on the Nappa Merrie cattle station, just inside the Queensland border. The old coolibah has survived droughts, floods and termite infestations for an estimated 350 years. Since William Brahe carved his famous inscription, it has been the subject of much speculation and argument. So many versions of the message have been included in historical accounts of the expedition that there is considerable confusion about exactly what was engraved into the tree. But, by examining early photographs and studying the testimonies of William Brahe, John King and Alfred Howitt, it is possible to decipher the original message.

There are three separate blazes on the tree. The first faces the creek and consists of the letter B for Burke and the camp number LXV (65) underneath it. This is now the most visible of the carvings. On a lower bough, there is another engraving. This was made by Brahe just before he abandoned the depot camp and consists of the date of the expedition's arrival: 'DEC 6-60' and the date of Brahe's departure: 'APR 21-61'. The inscription is evident in early photographs of the tree but because of extensive bark regrowth only a small deep scar remains.

The main 'DIG' message is on the trunk facing away from the creek. The most common interpretation of the original inscription is that it read 'DIG 3FT NW', with an arrow underneath pointing from left to right. But examination of photographs taken in the 1920s and 1930s clearly shows the word 'under' carved into the trunk. Early settlers to the area suggested that the message read '40FT NW' not '3FT NW'. They believed the coolibah's root system could have made it difficult to bury the camel trunk any closer. Evidence given during the royal commission contradicts this interpretation. John King stated that 'Mr Wills saw marked on the tree, Dig three feet north-west or north-east, I am not sure which...' William Brahe described the camel trunk as 'buried near the stockade at the foot of a large tree, and marked with the word "DIG" on the tree.' Brahe also mentioned that, when he buried the cache, it was 'within six or seven yards' of the stockade. Since the stockade itself was near the tree, it could not possibly have been forty feet away.

Matters are further confused by the fact that Alfred Howitt also mentioned that he marked the Dig Tree as well, and there is an old photograph (on display near the tree) that shows the initials 'AH' inscribed above the word 'DIG'. Howitt was also in the habit of using large arrows to show where he was going next. It makes sense that he added the arrow to the tree, since it points in the wrong direction to mark the cache, but correctly indicates his direction of travel. It is quite possible that he inscribed the figures '3ft NW' as well to show where he had re-buried the trunk, not to point to its original position. In the light of this evidence, the original message would have read:

DIG
UNDER

The Dig Tree is still in remarkably good condition but the Cooper itself is creeping ever closer and soil erosion is an increasing problem. A conservation plan has now been established to preserve the site, and a boardwalk has been placed around the trunk to protect the roots. With care, the tree should survive for many decades to come.

John King, the only survivor of Burke's final party, returned to live with his sister in St Kilda. He was 'disabled for life—thoroughly shattered in body and weakened in mind, by his great sufferings' and never recovered 'a semblance of health or spirits'. He married his cousin Mary in 1872, but died a year later aged thirty-four from 'pulmonary consumption', a disease he had probably carried with him throughout the expedition. In 1863, the government granted him a pension of just £180 a year. It was not extended to his wife after his death.

Descendants of the Yandruwandha still remember the stories of their ancestors caring for a solitary white man stranded on the Cooper. While most members of the tribe wanted to look after him until he was reunited with his countrymen, a few of the younger warriors distrusted their guest and suggested he should be killed.

John King's descendants, now based in Ireland and New Zealand, have long known of an enduring connection between the explorer and his saviours. Their beliefs coincide with a story now acknowledged by senior members of the Yandruwandha. In 1867 a drover named James Arnold, also known as 'Narran Jim', was riding through the Cooper area. He came across a little half-caste girl around five or six years old who was living with the Aboriginal people. She was nicknamed 'Yellow Alice' and 'Miss King'. The Yandruwandha alive today believe she was John King's daughter.

The only visible carving on the Dig Tree shows Burke's initial B with the camp number LXV underneath.

Acknowledgments

This book, more than most, has been the result of the generosity and expertise of many people. I would like to thank Tom Bergin, who has spent many years investigating this expedition, retraced the explorers' route using camels in 1972 and went on to write *In the Steps of Burke and Wills*. He gave me access to his extensive research, especially his work on the nutritional problems faced by the expedition, the management of the camels and the role of Robert Bowman. Dr Ross Mackenzie, Professor A. S. Truswell and Jo Duflou provided valuable insights into the scientific side of things. Paddy McHugh taught me about camels. Gerard Hayes and all the staff of the State Library of Victoria, the Mitchell Library in Sydney, the National Library in Canberra and the Mortlock Library in Adelaide responded patiently and efficiently to my many requests for information.

Thanks also to Tim Flannery, for his support in the first place, and for reading the manuscript; to Helen Tolcher for her assistance on matters Aboriginal; and to the wonderful people I met in towns such as Menindee, Innamincka, Birdsville, Boulia, Cloncurry and Normanton, while retracing the Burke and Wills route through outback Australia. Their local knowledge and enthusiasm has added so much to the story.

Arran Patterson and his family are direct descendents of the Yandruwandha tribe from the Cooper Creek area. Arran has painstakingly researched his family history and the role of the indigenous people in the Burke and Wills story. He and his relatives believe that better understanding between black and white will only come with the sharing of knowledge. *The Dig Tree* stands enriched by their generosity.

I am indebted to many people for support and sustenance: the Melbourne Support Crew—David, Melissa, Callum, Sonia, Paul, Dale and Annie; the Brisbane Support Crew of Heidi, Andy, Angie and Benson; and the Sydney Support Crew—Eleanor, Edward, Dominic, Sophie, Peig, Rod, Andrew, Kerry, Jamie, Kristen, Stuart, the Keadys and Debs. I want to thank Nick and Geraldine, for helping to provide me with a writer's paradise; Monty, the man who is not my husband, for saying what he thinks, enduring my attempts at baking damper and taking the photographs. Marie Adams got me out to Australia in the first place and kept me here. My family have not only forgiven me for living in Australia but have supported me unflinchingly in everything I have ever attempted, with the possible exception of buying a motorbike. My husband Kevin suggested I write the book, then let me loose in a four-wheel-drive and rescued me when necessary.

Michael Heyward, my editor, believed in me in the first place, and I am grateful for his skill and sensitivity ever since. Melanie Ostell and everyone at Text guided me through the process.

And I want to express my heartfelt gratitude to Professor Michael Friedlander and all the staff at the Prince of Wales in Sydney. No statement of appreciation can fully reflect the magnitude of the contribution they have made to my life and to the lives of so many others. Without them none of this would have been possible.

All errors and omissions that remain are my own.

Select Bibliography

THE BURKE AND WILLS EXPEDITION

Bergin, Tom, *In the Steps of Burke and Wills*, ABC/Griffin Press Ltd, Sydney, 1981.

Bonyhady, Tim, *Burke and Wills: From Melbourne to Myth*, David Ell Press, Sydney, 1991.

Clune, Frank, *Dig: The Burke and Wills Saga*, Angus & Robertson, Sydney, 1991 (first pub. 1937).

Colwell, Max, *The Journey of Burke and Wills*, Paul Hamlyn, Sydney, 1971.

Corke, David, *Partners in Disaster: The Story of Burke and Wills*, Nelson, Sydney, 1985.

Jackson, Andrew, *Robert O'Hara Burke and the Australian Exploring Expedition of 1860*, Smith Elder, London, 1862.

Moorehead, Alan, *Cooper's Creek*, Hamish Hamilton, London, 1963.

White, John, *The Stockade and the Tree*, Footprint Press, Melbourne, 1992.

EXPEDITION DIARIES

Beckler, Hermann, *A Journey to Cooper's Creek*, Stephen Jeffries and Michael Kertesz (trans. and eds), Melbourne University Press and State Library of Victoria, Melbourne, 1993.

Davis, John, *Tracks of McKinlay and Party across Australia*, Sampson, Low, London, 1863.

The Explorers, Tim Flannery (ed.), Text Publishing, Melbourne, 1998.

Flinders, Matthew, *Terra Australis*, Tim Flannery (ed.), Text Publishing, Melbourne, 2000.

Gregory, Augustus C., and Gregory, Francis T., *Journals of Australian Explorations*, J. C. Beal, Brisbane, 1884.

Landsborough, William, *Journal of Landsborough's Expedition from Carpentaria in Search of Burke and Wills*, Libraries Board of South Australia, Adelaide, 1963.

Leichhardt, Ludwig, *Journal of an Overland Expedition in Australia from Moreton Bay to Port Essington*, T & W Boone, London, 1847.

McKinlay, John, *Journal of Exploration in the Interior of Australia*, Libraries Board of South Australia, Adelaide, 1962.

Mitchell, Thomas Livingstone, *Three Expeditions into the Interior of Eastern Australia, with Descriptions of the Recently Explored Region of Australia Felix, and the Present Colony of New South Wales*, vols I & II, T & W Boone, London, 1838.

Stuart, John McDouall, *Explorations in Australia: The Journals of John McDouall Stuart, during the Years 1858, 1859, 1860, 1861 and 1862; When He Fixed the Centre of the Continent and Successfully Crossed It from Sea to Sea*, William Hardman (ed.), 2nd edn, Saunders, Otley & Co., London, 1865.

Stuart, John McDouall, *Exploration of the Interior: Diary of J. M. Stuart from March 2 to September 3, 1860*, S. A. Government Printer, Adelaide, 1860.

Sturt, Charles, *Journal of the Central Australian Expedition*, J. Waterhouse (ed.), Caliban Books, London, 1984.

Sturt, Charles, *Narrative of an Expedition into Central Australia: Performed under the Authority of Her Majesty's Government during the Years 1844, 5 and 6; Together with a Notice of the Province of South Australia in 1847*, vols I & II, T & W Boone, London, 1849.

Sturt, Charles, *Two Expeditions into the Interior of Southern Australia, during the Years 1828, 1829, 1830 and 1831*, vols I & II, Smith Elder & Co., London, 1833.

Wills, Dr William, *A Successful Exploration through the Interior of Australia*, Friends of the State Library of South Australia, Adelaide, 1996 (first pub. 1863).

GENERAL AUSTRALIAN EXPLORATION

Cannon, Michael, *The Exploration of Australia*, Reader's Digest, Sydney, 1987.

Cumpston, J. H. L., *Augustus Gregory and the Inland Sea*, Angus & Robertson, Sydney, 1965.

Favenc, Ernest, *Explorers of Australia*, Tiger Books International (Senate), London, 1998.

Haynes, Roslynn D., *Seeking the Centre*, Cambridge University Press, Cambridge, 1998.

Howitt, Mary, *Come Wind or Weather*, Melbourne University Press, Melbourne, 1971.

McIver, George, *The Drover's Odyssey*, Angus & Robertson, Sydney, 1935.

Madigan, Cecil T., *Central Australia*, Oxford University Press, London, 1936.

Madigan, Cecil T., *Crossing the Dead Heart*, Georgian House, Melbourne, 1948.

BIOGRAPHIES AND AUTOBIOGRAPHIES

Beale, Edgar, *Sturt, the Chipped Idol: A Study of Charles Sturt, Explorer*, Angus & Robertson, Sydney, 1979.

Ferguson, Charles, *Experiences of a Forty-Niner during Thirty-Four Years Residence in California and Australia*, Frederick T. Wallace (ed.), The Williams Publishing Company, Cleveland, 1888.

Lockwood, Kim, *Big John: The Extraordinary Adventures of John McKinlay*, State Library of Victoria, Melbourne, 1995.

Mudie, Ian, *The Heroic Journey of John McDouall Stuart*, Angus & Robertson, Sydney, 1968.

Tipping, Marjorie, *Ludwig Becker: Artist and Naturalist with the Burke and Wills Expedition*, Melbourne University Press, Melbourne, 1979.

Webster, Mona S., *John McDouall Stuart*, Melbourne University Press, Melbourne, 1958.

Young, Rose, *G. F. Von Tempsky, Artist and Adventurer*, Alister Taylor, Martinborough, 1981.

ABORIGINAL HISTORY

Howitt, Alfred, *The Native Tribes of South-East Australia*, Aboriginal Studies Press, Canberra, 1966 (first pub. 1904).

Mulvaney, D. J., *The Prehistory of Australia: Ancient People and Places*, Thames & Hudson, London, 1969.

Tolcher, Helen, *Drought or Deluge*, Melbourne University Press, Melbourne, 1986.

MONOGRAPHS, PAMPHLETS AND MAGAZINE ARTICLES

Bergin, Tom, *Courage and Corruption: An Analysis of the Burke and Wills Expedition and of the Subsequent Royal Commission of Enquiry*, unpublished thesis, University of New England, Armidale, 1982.

Blanchen, B. J., 'From Melbourne to Menindie: A Tourist's Guide Based on the Diaries of Ludwig Becker', *La Trobe Library Journal*, October 1978, pp. 34–36.

Fitzpatrick, Kathleen, 'The Burke and Wills Expedition and the Royal Society of Victoria', *Historical Studies of Australia and New Zealand*, 10 April 1963, pp. 470–78.

Kerwin, Bennie, and Breen, J. G., 'The Land of the Stone Chips', *Oceania*, vol. 51, pp. 286–311.

McKellar, John, 'John King: Sole Survivor of the Burke and Wills Expedition to the Gulf of Carpentaria', *Victorian Historical Magazine*, December 1944, pp. 106–9.

McKellar, John, 'William John Wills', *Victorian Historical Magazine*, 2 February 1962, pp. 337–50.

McLaren, Ian, 'The Victorian Exploring Expedition and Relieving Expeditions, 1860–61: The Burke and Wills Tragedy', *Victorian Historical Magazine*, 29 April 1959, pp. 211–53.

Threadgill, Bessie, *South Australian Land Exploration, 1856 to 1880*, vols I & II, Board of Governors of the Public Library, Museum, and Art Gallery of South Australia, Adelaide, 1922.

OTHER SOURCES

McKnight, Tom L., *The Camel in Australia*, Melbourne University Press, Melbourne, 1969.

McNicoll, Ronald, *Number 36 Collins St: The Melbourne Club*, Allen & Unwin, Sydney, 1988.

Rajkowski, Pamela, *In the Tracks of the Camelmen: Australia's Most Exotic Pioneers*, Angus & Robertson, Sydney, 1987.

Riffenburgh, Beau, *The Myth of the Explorer*, Oxford University Press, Oxford, 1994.

Sadleir, John, *Recollections of a Victorian Police Officer*, George Robertson, Melbourne, 1913.

Serle, Geoffrey, *The Golden Age: A History of the Colony of Victoria*, Melbourne University Press, Melbourne, 1968.

Stawell, Mary, *My Recollections*, Richard Clay & Sons, London, 1911.

Stroud, Mike, *Survival of the Fittest*, Vintage, London, 1999.

NEWSPAPERS

Argus, Age, Ballarat Star, Bendigo Advertiser, Castlemaine Advertiser, Examiner and Melbourne Weekly News, Galway Advertiser, Geelong Advertiser, Herald, Illustrated London News, Illustrated Sydney News, Loughrea Journal, Melbourne Leader, Melbourne Post, Melbourne Punch, Mount Alexander Mail, Ovens and Murray Advertiser, South Australian Register, Southern Courier, The Times, Yeoman and Australian Acclimatiser.

ORIGINAL MATERIAL AND MANUSCRIPTS

The La Trobe Library at the State Library of Victoria houses the largest collection of material relating to the Burke and Wills expedition, including many original letters, diaries, records of the Royal Society and a transcript of the royal commission of inquiry. Other documents including Burke's pocketbook and Wills' diaries and field books are held at the National Library of Australia in Canberra. The Mitchell and Dixson libraries at the State Library of New South Wales also hold manuscripts relevant to Burke and Wills and the subsequent rescue expeditions. Much of the material pertaining to John McDouall Stuart is housed in the Mortlock Library, Adelaide.

Index

Aborigines 104, 132, 135–36, 145–54, 186–88, 203, 211–12, 215, 239, 242–43, 246–49, 293, 322, 327, 357; help ailing explorers 178, 194, 250, 252–53, 255, 258–60, 285–88; attack 249

Aitken, Alexander 278

Arnold, James 361

Auld, Pat 200, 328

Babbage, Benjamin Herschel 49

Banks, Joseph 88

Barkly, Henry 91, 301, 306–7, 337

Becker, Ludwig 49–51, 88–91, 97, 101, 104, 107, 109–11, 116, 123, 155, 355; injured 116; illness 240–42, 248; death 251

Beckler, Hermann 3, 89–91, 95, 97, 99–101, 105, 108–10, 120, 175–78, 242–44, 257, 355; resigns 118; stays on at Menindee 124; sets out with Wright 236–37; illness 244

Belooch 83, 107, 115, 175, 178, 244, 257, 265

Bergin, Tom 202, 341–42

Birnie, Richard 81

Blandowski, William 20–21, 48–49

Bleasedale, John 49

Bowen, George 128

Bowman, Robert 70, 106, 118–19

Brahe, William 70, 107, 136, 164–67, 175, 214–16, 356; stays at the Dig Tree 166; leaves Dig Tree 232, 235; meets Wright party 251; returns to Dig Tree 254; sets out for Melbourne 265; meets Howitt 280; at royal commission 308–11

Brooks 94, 105

Bruce, John 65, 68

Bruce, Robert 44

Bunting, Anne 301

Burke, Hessie 272

Burke, James 61

Burke, Robert O'Hara 3, 6, 52, 70–71, 82–83, 95, 181, 340–43; early life and career 56–69; bathing habits 60; appointed to lead expedition 55; lack of navigation skills 65–66; exploring ambition 85, 204; leadership style 98–99, 106–7, 341; debts 102, 336; attitude to Aborigines 153–54, 260, 287, 342; diary 173–74, 188–89; decides to head for Mt Hopeless 244; illness 261, 271; death 274; burial in Melbourne 351

Burke and Wills Expedition see Victorian Exploring Expedition

Cadell, Francis 95, 121

camels 2–3, 31–33, 54–55, 81–83, 88, 93, 98–99, 111–17, 158–59, 178–81, 194–95, 207, 226, 357

Carnegie, David 188

Castieau, John 65

Catherwood, Dr 78

Chambers, James 38–39, 44, 46, 198

Chambers, John 38–39, 44, 198

Cook, Frederick 162

Cook, James 1, 88

Coongie Lakes 186
Cooper Creek 13, 141–45, 160–64
Coppin, George 299
Coulthard (explorer) 9–10
Cowan, Owen 4, 70, 85
Creber, Henry 70, 85

Dampier, William 16
Denison, Lady 90
Depot Camp 65 *see* Dig Tree
Diamantina River 193–94
Dick 157, 175, 237, 355
Dickson, Robert 132, 317–18
Dig Tree 161, 214–26, 231, 234–35,
   246, 254, 258–59, 352; original
   inscription on 359–60
Dogherty, Ellen 56, 331–34, 350, 355
Dost Mohomet 83, 115, 166, 215, 355
Drakeford, John 83

Eades, Richard 20–21, 49, 131
Embling, Thomas 31–32, 129, 132
Esau Khan 83, 105
Exploration Committee *see*
   Philosophical Institute; Royal
   Society of Victoria
Eyre, Edward John 15

Favenc, Ernest 36
Ferguson, Charles 83–85, 93, 102,
   106–7, 134
Finke, William 38–39, 46
Fletcher, Robert 70, 85
Flinders, Matthew 17
Foster, George 39
Franklin, John 220

Gisbourne, Francis 28–29
Gray, Charley 105, 178, 184–85; illness
   221–28; steals food 224; death 228,
   321–27

Gregory, Augustus 14–16, 20, 48, 70,
   88, 94, 106

Heales, Richard 305
Hervey, Matthew 307
Hill, Ernestine 144
Hodgkinson, William 105, 115, 159,
   282; rides to Melbourne 196; illness
   244
Holloway, John 101
Horrocks, John Ainsworth 31
Howitt, Alfred 277, 290–91, 309, 356;
   leaves Melbourne 278; resumes
   relief expedition 281; reaches
   Cooper Creek 288; retrieves Burke's
   and Wills' bodies 330–31
Howitt, William 342
hunger and malnutrition 220–21,
   226–28, 240, 262–64
Huxley, Thomas 17

Kekwick, William 200
King, John 83, 115, 178–79, 182–84,
   218, 271–74, 285–94, 324, 334;
   diary 173; marks trees 182; finds
   Wills' body 285; with
   Yandruwandha 285–87; found 289;
   mental state 293, 299–302; at royal
   commission 313; death 360; possible
   daughter 361
King, Phillip Parker 17
Knuckey, R. R. 284
Kyte, Ambrose 26

La Trobe, Charles Joseph 22
Landells, George 6–7, 32, 54, 71,
   81–83, 85, 98–99, 111–17, 132–33,
   184, 277, 281; fired 117; at royal
   commission 316
Landsborough, William 282, 337–38
Lane 94, 105

Langan, Patrick 70, 105
Larkworthy, Falconer 66
Leese, Arnold 195
Leichhardt, Ludwig 13–14, 19, 256
Ligar, Charles 48
Lockhart-Morton, William 276, 323
Love, Stuart 329
Lyons, Trooper 156–57, 175, 177

Macadam, John 21, 48, 50, 69–70, 86, 131, 196, 332, 356; at royal commission 308–9, 312
MacDonnell, Richard 28–29, 46
McDonough, Thomas 70, 115, 158–59, 166, 257; at royal commission 311
McHugh, Paddy 202, 341–42
McIlwaine 94, 107
McIver, George 150
McKinlay, John 282, 322–23, 337
MacMillan, Angus 48
MacPherson, Alexander 105, 157, 175, 177
Madigan, Cecil 40
Matthews, Julia 62–64, 85–86, 272, 276, 278, 298–99, 334, 357
Menindee 118–22
Michie, Archibald 23
Mill, H. R. 340
Mitchell, Thomas Livingstone 10, 13, 14, 48, 102
Moorhouse, Geoffrey 226
Mueller, Ferdinand von 20–21, 30, 48–49, 88, 90–91, 94, 281; at royal commission 314, 317
Mumford, William 357
Murchison, Roderick 349
Murphy, Francis 307, 315

nardoo 151, 253, 255, 257, 261–63
Nash, Richard 86–87, 102

Neumayer, Georg 69–70, 80, 103, 109, 130–31, 134, 276, 281, 337, 344, 356
Newcastle, Duke of 128
Nicholson, William 48–49, 134

Oates, Lawrence 227–28
O'Shanassy, John 32, 129, 298, 305–6
overland telegraph 27–30, 46, 284, 351, 353–54

Parry, Samuel 214
Patten, William 70, 166, 169, 216, 235, 256; death 265
Patterson, Arran 151, 287
Patterson, Robert 353
Peter 175, 177
Philosophical Institute (later Royal Society of Victoria) 19–21, 24–25, 30, 33, 47
Polongeaux, John 105
Poole, James 36
Pratt, Thomas 307
Purcell 241–42, 244; death 246

Richardson, John 220
royal commission 307–21; findings 318–19
Royal Society of Victoria (previously Philosophical Institute) 48–55, 275–77, 280–81, 300, 304–6, 345; seeks expedition leader 48–55; appoints Burke 55; secret plans 129–31; appoints Howitt 277
Russell, William 34–35

Saint, Charles 85
Samla 83, 93
Scott, Robert 227–28
Selwyn, Alfred 48, 130
Selwyn Ranges 202–4, 223
Shackleton, Ernest 214, 250, 291

Sherer, John 9
'Shirt' 247, 249
Smithe, P. H. 52
Stawell, Mary 67
Stawell, William Foster 26, 30, 33, 48,
    67, 69, 71, 86, 102, 127, 129, 134,
    280–81, 298, 306, 308, 336; at royal
    commission 315–16
Stefansson, Vilhjalmur 343
Stokes, John 17
Stone 240, 244; death 246
Stuart, John McDouall 34–46, 336,
    341; drinking 38, 44; first expedition
    39–42; second expedition 51, 53,
    126, 132; third expedition 197–201,
    282–85, 291–92; ill-health 198, 292,
    328–29, 348–50; expedition rules
    199; fourth expedition 292; fifth
    expedition 328–29, 346–50; crosses
    the continent 347; death 354
Sturt, Charles 10–13, 36, 48, 162–63,
    212
Sturt, Francis 307
Sturt's Stony Desert 12
Sullivan, James 307

Tempsky, Gustav von 51–52, 55, 67–68
Thring, Francis 200, 347
Todd, Charles 28–29, 353
Tolcher, Helen 149

Victorian Exploring Expedition:
    selection of men 69–70; equipment
    2–4, 94–95, 103, 106, 110, 168, 340;
    instructions 71–72; leaves Melbourne
    1–7, 73; scientific aspects 88–92,
    110; reaches Swan Hill 101; money
    problems 100, 102–3, 134; reaches
    Menindee 117; reaches Cooper
    Creek 141; leaves Cooper Creek
    169; reaches Gulf of Carpentaria
    212; returns to Cooper Creek 231;
    renamed 'Burke and Wills
    Expedition' 304
Vinning, William 278

Walker, Frederick 281, 338
Warburton, Peter Egerton 49–52, 55
Wecker, Edmund 312
Weddell, William 70
Welch, Edwin 278, 299, 301; discovers
    King 289
Wickham, John 17
Wilkie, David 19
Wills, Tom 75–78
Wills, Dr William 73–75, 77, 276, 333,
    336, 355
Wills, William John 5–6, 81, 91–93,
    133, 135–37, 157–59, 167–68,
    181–82, 220, 255–65; early life and
    career 73–80; beliefs 78–80, 269,
    336; takes on greater responsibilities
    115, 117; becomes Burke's deputy
    118; attitude to Aborigines 153–54,
    255, 258–61; diary 171, 201–2, 269;
    surveying methods 172–73; returns
    to Dig Tree alone 258; illness 261–64;
    unable to continue 266; last letter
    267–69; death 271; burial in
    Melbourne 351
Wilpie 149
Wooldridge, Edward 70
Wright, William 124, 135, 137–39,
    155–57, 196, 309–312, 319, 356;
    becomes third in command 137;
    returns to Menindee 155; sets out
    for Dig Tree 214, 235–36; meets
    Brahe party 251; reaches Dig Tree
    254; at royal commission 314–17

Younghusband, William 46